This Miraculous Life

a memoir

This Miraculous Life

a memoir

Robert Maoz Kržišnik

First Printing: 2019

Print on demand

Cover design: Orianne Shavit, based on the sketch by Lucija Kržišnik

Editor: Graham Timmins

ISBN 978-961-94753-0-0

Publisher:
Robert Maoz Kržišnik, s.p.
Ob dolenjski železnici 12
1000 Ljubljana, Slovenia, EU

www.thatfield.eu

to Filip, Lucija, Dorian – with love and hope

to Noa, with eternal gratitude

Contents

Foreword

Sometime around my 52nd birthday I set out to collect stories from my life. Those that I thought had marked and shaped me, or had played an important role in my ever-present quest: "What is this, that we call life? What is this, that we call existence? How come anything exists at all?" The list of stories became quite extensive and I decided to put them together into a book.

With that decision, my stories took on a second life and began passionately writing themselves through my fingers, evolving in their own direction, not necessarily aligned with my ideas. Quite a few of them I deleted after they were written, as their life seemed to have somehow died out in the writing. Still, this ended up a much longer book than I initially anticipated. And a much, much more personal one.

In each episode I firstly tried to re-experience a key moment and then to write from that place, with the understanding and the feelings I had at that time. Along the way, I was trying to be as fair as I could towards others as well as towards myself. Yet, of course, despite my best intentions, this is still a selection of my memories and a presentation of a certain self-image I hold of myself. My words can never be fully objective, as I don't believe it's at all possible to stand outside my inner, subjective world. As I wish to protect people from possibly being judged by readers because of my subjective bias, I have changed some names.

I'm fortunate in having a keen memory of individual conversations that carry emotional charge for me. Of course I don't remember every word, but I can recall enough to capture the essence of many dialogues that are stored in my memory. What's more, I've kept comprehensive diaries over the years, both conventional accounts of my daily thoughts and also dedicated dream diaries, and I never threw any of them away, which proved to be enormously helpful. Without these, the book would have been less alive and also less reliable.

Writing the first two chapters was downright self-therapy; I had to prepare myself for writing sessions in an almost ritualistic

11

way. I struggled through many of the childhood stories really slowly, step by step, as memories surfaced and flooded over me, accompanied by pain, sadness and loneliness and often leaving me feeling totally exhausted. With the third chapter, the writing started to flow more easily and joyfully, and then it slowed down again radically with the last three chapters, as the processes I was writing about were still so fresh and alive, and many of them were not yet integrated and complete in my inner system. Writing these chapters demanded a lot of honest self-exploration.

I decided to include many of my dreams (aligned right and italicised) and also some of my transpersonal experiences (centre aligned): by which I mean instances when the sense of self melts away into oneness, when linear time is transformed into an eternal moment, and, well, when there are no words that can do justice to the immensity of the experience.

A part of me that wants to be accepted by everybody would prefer to just delete all these out-of-this-world experiences, fearing I could get labelled as a weirdo. Yet another part of me is stronger, the one that doesn't want to merely adjust to contemporary social norms, but rather to meet life fully, in sheer authenticity, and see where this gets me. So here I stand, rather naked, exposed and vulnerable.

I feel loads of gratitude to my first readers, Jaka and Iztok, for their encouragement and trust. Eternal gratitude to my beloved Noa, for her support, patience and faith in me, which has helped me through many difficult moments. And Graham, my dear editor, you totally saved me, as you know, and because of your incredible focus, dedication, support and appreciative approach, I am now able to present this book with joy and inner peace.

As I was reading the text of this book for one last time before publishing it, it hit me: I have experienced a lot, an incredible amount in this one lifetime. And for all these experiences I am deeply grateful, whether they were beautiful or painful.

What a miraculous life I have been gifted with!

Robert Maoz Kržišnik, June 2019

Prologue: Did I Get Out at the Wrong Station?

Just as my later life would run outside of established paths, so too did my name Robert come to me in a rather strange way, in a way that never became entirely clear. When my mother got pregnant, my father was still a student, and the two of them stayed as lodgers with his parents, who were rather eccentric. My grandmother had a bit of the inventor flowing through her veins. For me, her most fascinating invention was a one-of-a-kind bicycle light comprised of a burning candle in a glass jar fixed to the handlebars. The police rolled their eyes, but the bike actually did have a working light, so they couldn't do anything.

Granny liked to bring all sorts of junk home to their apartment in Ljubljana, whether it was broken stoves and television sets, or a slightly despondent old hen, who made her home in the bathroom, where she gently clucked at anyone who unsuspectingly sat on the toilet, hoping for a little quiet and relaxation. My grandfather was a manual labourer working in a warehouse. He was hard-of-hearing, an alcoholic and a chain smoker and he got louder and more difficult the later the hour. Because of this, my parents decided it would be better if my mother were to give birth in Prekmurje, in the eastern part of Slovenia, where her own parents and two sisters lived. At least there, she would have peace and calm, not to mention the help and support she needed.

Before her departure, my parents had already decided that they would give me the Hungarian name Zsuzsa if I was a girl, and the very traditional Slovenian name Gorazd (meaning mountain-like) if I was a boy. No one in the family had a phone and in those days people kept in touch through letters and postcards. Anyway, I was born in hospital in Prekmurje on February 9th, 1966, at about three a.m., and after the birth, my mother and I slept for a few hours. In the morning, the nurse who was responsible for such things came to collect certain necessary information: the mother's name, the father's name, the baby's weight and the baby's name. The nurse asked my mother for my name and it just shot out of her mouth as if from a cannon:

"Robert."

The nurse wrote it down and left. Everything was fine until a telegram from my father arrived in the evening. He had already learned from an aunt that he had a son. In the telegram, he had written, in addition to the usual expressions of joy and love, the following words:

"Give a kiss to our little Gorazd."

Oops! Only at that moment did my mother realize that she had said the wrong name to the nurse. But by now it would be written in the register and no doubt a time-consuming bureaucratic process would have to be initiated in order to change it. And so, I ended up with the name Robert. It was never clear to my mother how the name came to her, because she'd never known anyone by that name, and indeed it hardly existed at that time in Slovenia. It was more like the name of a Hollywood actor that she'd once heard in passing.

When I was older, my mother told me that I stopped breathing immediately after I was born. There was great panic in the delivery room and it took some effort to revive me. Whenever she told this story, I always got an intuitive flash that maybe I had reconsidered when I saw where I had landed, that maybe I realized at that moment that I'd got off the train at the wrong station and wanted to quickly get back on board, but it was already too late.

Be that as it may, throughout my whole life I have to some degree or another felt like a stranger in a strange land, never fully integrated into the human life around me, like a lone wolf observing this bizarre world from a distance.

One: First Years, First Cracks

I'm four years old. It's a sunny afternoon. I wake bleary-eyed from my afternoon nap. I'm still in bed, and Mummy and Auntie Marta are talking. I'm happy. I feel good.

I rapturously observe my mother as she undresses. She looks so beautiful to me. She unbuttons her blouse, takes it off and reaches for another one. I look at her breasts, enchanted. Something awakens in me, something special, mysterious. My mother notices me staring at her and smiles:

"What is it? Do you want a little suck?"

I nod enthusiastically, eyes wide. She turns her breasts toward me, smiles again: "Come…"

Thrilled, I rush across the room, happy, ecstatic. But just before I reach her, she buttons her blouse again, turns away, and laughs loudly:

"Yeah, sure, don't be silly… What were you thinking?!"

Mummy and Auntie Marta laugh and I just stand there, confused, ashamed, lost. I don't know what to do. Who should I go to for warmth, for closeness? I'm alone, confused. Slowly, my head hanging, I leave the room. If only I knew how to embrace my own sadness and powerlessness. If only I knew what to do with it. But I don't, and so I just sit and stare at the floor.

∞

I'm outside with my father, in front of the apartment building in Ljubljana, where we live together with my grandparents. It's afternoon. I hold his hand while he chats cheerfully with some neighbours. Another neighbour joins us. He's carrying a cardboard box in his arms and he calls out to me:

"Robi, look what I have for you…"

Excited, I watch as he approaches me and places the box on the ground. He slowly opens the lid and says:

15

"Look, it's a bunny rabbit, Robi."

A grey rabbit, with long ears, sits in the box, his head pressed into the corner.

"Do you want to hold it?"

I nod happily. The neighbour sits me down on a bench in front of the apartment building, puts the rabbit in my lap, and instructs me to hold it firmly by its hind legs. Everything around me disappears. I hear nothing, I see nothing but the rabbit. How warm it is. I'm wildly excited, even more so than when I feed the geese at my grandmother's farm. Much more. I would happily sit like this forever, this warm rabbit in my lap, feeling its trembling body, loving it. If I knew that it had been brought from the farm to the city for the purpose of killing it, skinning it, and eating it, I would have run off with it somewhere and let it go in the bushes. Maybe I would have cried or begged for its life.

But as it is, I just sit there, ecstatic, hoping that this minute will last forever.

∞

Today my father's friend comes to visit. They sit on two armchairs, one facing the other, silently staring at the table between them. It seems very strange to me, and so I look closer. I see that the table is filled with black and white objects. They are so interesting. I enthusiastically pick one up:

"What's this?"

My father grabs the object from me and puts it back on the table.

"We're playing chess! Leave us alone!"

They're playing a game! That's even more interesting. I want to play with them. I reach out my hand again to touch the chess piece but my father's voice stops me.

"No! Didn't you hear what I said? Leave us alone!"

I'm upset. I'm also a little afraid, and frustrated that I'm not allowed to play. The whole thing still interests me enormously, especially because I don't understand what they are doing. I thrust out my hand and flick the piece that he won't let me hold. I try to laugh. I wish my father would also laugh so that we could all be happy and have fun together. But my father raises his voice:

"No! Don't touch the pieces! Leave us alone! This is the last time I'm going to tell you!"

Now I'm even more upset and confused. My hand, as if of its own volition, jumps toward the chess pieces and sweeps them all off the table. I'm still trying to laugh. Surely this is a game and soon we will all be laughing together.

My father stands up and pulls his belt from his pants. I stare at him in confusion. He grabs me, roughly throwing me over his knees, and starts to beat me with his belt. In shock, I begin to scream. I don't understand what is happening. Why is my father holding me down and hurting me? My bottom hurts, my heart even more, pure terror exploding within it. Finally my father puts me on my feet again and says:

"That's so you'll know better next time. Now leave us alone!"

I leave the room sobbing. Everything hurts: my bottom, my heart, my head. I don't know anything, not for now and not for 'next time'.

I feel so alone and helpless, and I just cry and cry.

∞

We've moved to a new apartment, just the three of us. It's very bright and airy. I like it. And I have my own little room now.

I've been going to school for a couple of months: I'm in the first grade. I have a few friends. I'm madly in love with one of my schoolmates. She's called Maya. I'm doing fine. The other kids are all nice. We learn interesting things about nature and that sort of thing, but it slowly becomes a bit too much for me, too much

17

sitting, too little movement and playing. It was more fun in kindergarten. At break time I ask my schoolmate Damjan if he happens to know how long we will go to school for, because no one has actually told me that. Damjan thinks about it, and then says that, as far as he knows, we'll be going for quite a few more years. Horrified, I reject the idea. It's impossible, because surely I would have been told something so important and dramatic. Somebody would have mentioned it when they were telling me how wonderful school was supposed to be. But Damjan is sure he's right. We decide to ask the teacher standing in the hallway talking to her colleagues. I tug at her sleeve and bravely speak:

"Comrade teacher, for how many years will we go to this school?"

Her eyes widen. She smiles nicely. She leans toward us as if to tell us the most marvellous news.

"Eight years, boys, eight whole years. Isn't that wonderful?"

I nod and give her a bitter smile. I turn and slowly slip away. I feel the world inside me crumbling. I feel powerless, desperate. In that instant, school becomes a prison. I'm only six years old. I'll be going to this same school for eight whole years, more years than I've been alive. A darkness enters my life at that moment, a hollow blackness in my head. I'm trapped and have no power.

∞

My grandfather is an important man. He owns the village pub, and I feel wonderful when I run in from the courtyard, all dirty and thirsty, and get a soft drink or a juice. Sometimes I hear my grandmother nagging him, saying how lazy he is, but I can tell how much everyone respects him, and so I respect him too. I like to listen when he tells me stories, for example the ones about him encountering packs of wolves or even bears in the forest, always ending with him heroically chasing them away. Sometimes I wonder if he really had so many dramatic encounters with bears and wolves, but I dismiss my doubts because I want to believe it. I love him. I feel proud when I hear that he used a horse-whip to throw people out of the pub just because they got too loud, even though it resulted in him losing customers. I admire him when I hear relatives say that even though he could earn a lot more money, he doesn't want to have weddings or other parties in the pub because drunk and loud people get on his nerves.

He teaches me how to play cards and we play rummy together, usually in the evenings in the warm kitchen. The fire flickers in the stove. Granny and Auntie Marta wash the dishes and clean the kitchen. Grandad and I drink tea, eat home-made cake, and play cards. He often lets me win, and that makes me really happy.

The holidays I spend in Prekmurje with my grandparents are always wonderful. I run around the farm, ride my bike, help to carry water from the well in the courtyard. I come up with 'inventions' that never work. I go on walks with Auntie Marta. My cousin Miki, who is two years older than me, and an excellent companion, lives in a nearby town and often comes to visit the farm too. Everyone loves me, and I love everyone, and also all the hens, the geese, the baby chicks, the cats…

∞

I'm sitting in the back of an ambulance. My mother is next to me. Two men in white uniforms are in front. I'm so excited my mouth is hanging open. I ask the drivers if they can turn on the siren, just for a bit. They just smile. I don't care. It's enough that I'm in an ambulance, and what's more, it's a Mercedes ambulance.

That morning I'd complained of a pain in my belly. The doctor soon visited us at home, examined me and concluded that I had appendicitis. Whatever that means. They called the ambulance and now we're on our way to the hospital. My mother says they're just going to have a quick look at me. That makes me feel better.

In the waiting room, my mother reassures me that I will go into a room where the doctor will examine me, she will wait outside and then we'll go home. When I go in, the nurse writes my name in a notebook and then takes me to a bathroom, where she baths me and dresses me in pyjamas. I tell her that I'm not going to sleep at the hospital because my mother is waiting for me outside and we're going home. The nurse tells me that my mother left long ago, and I am going to sleep here, but first I will have an operation.

I go mute. Everything stops. All of a sudden, the hospital looks grim, cold, unfriendly. Numb and powerless, wearing pyjamas, a bathrobe, and plastic slippers, I walk behind the nurse. I'm afraid, confused. Tears slide down my cheeks. I wipe them away with the sleeve of my pyjamas.

Soon I find myself lying on a bed in a very brightly-lit room. There are many large instruments in the room. People in white robes smile pleasantly, wink at me, pat me on the shoulder, and tell me that everything will be alright. My good mood and curiosity return. I look around with interest. A young man smiles at me and hands me a plastic mask. He tells me to put it over my mouth and breathe and that I will have beautiful dreams.

I take it enthusiastically, I breathe in, and I'm gone…

…

I wake up in the morning. There are lots of other children and a nice nurse who plays with us and says that I must be careful and move slowly because I had an operation.

Later, I'm resting on my bed in the children's ward. We're relaxing after lunch. I hear my mother at the door calling out to me. She's standing there with the nurse. I turn away, pretending I don't recognize her. It hurts that she lied to me, that she abandoned me. It hurts very much and I'm angry. I don't like her anymore. She calls out to me again. I clench my teeth and look away. She calls me a third time. I persist. I clench my teeth and look away.

Then I hear her say: "Alright then, if that's the way he wants it, I'll go."

Tears pour down my face. My voice is trembling: "Mummy…"

I turn toward her. She approaches me smiling. I fall into her arms.

Don't leave me. I'm afraid.

∞

I'm seven years old. I'm sitting in my room. I've just finished my homework when my father comes in. He asks me, pleasantly but also somehow strangely, to come to the living room because he and my mother want to tell me something.

I stand in the living room. My mother and father sit on the couch. Everything is quiet, serious.

Then my father speaks: "You know, Robi, Miki has died."

Miki, my cousin, my companion, my friend from Prekmurje is dead. I stand still, silent. I look at my father, my mother, the floor. I feel empty, confused. My father says he will go with my mother to Prekmurje for the funeral, and I will stay a few days with Aunt Majda, my mother's cousin, who lives very close to us here in Ljubljana.

I finally speak: "May I go now?"

My father nods and I slink away to my room. I sit on the floor in front of the French window and look at the building site where an apartment building is going up. I like watching the brave man who climbs up an endless ladder up to the top of the crane where he works all day. Everything is silent in the room. I can hear only my own breathing.

I spend the next couple of days with Aunt Majda. I love her. She often takes care of me. My father bought me a little red remote-controlled racing car. It's sunny outside. Majda and I are in the playground between the apartment buildings. She's very gentle and patient with me.

Several years later I learn from my mother how Miki died. His mother, my Auntie Olga, was always worried about his safety and never let him go out to play on his own in the communal area in front of the apartment building where they lived. My mother

21

had often tried to convince her that she didn't need to be so afraid. Nothing would happen to him so close to home. One day Olga finally allowed him to go out and play with the other children. They ran outside. Their game drew them to the edge of the communal area, where a number of large concrete pipes for the construction of a new sewage system were lying on the ground. The children figured out that if they pushed hard enough, they could roll the pipes back and forth, and that's what they started to do. The laces on one of Miki's shoes were untied, and he sat inside one of the pipes to retie them. At that very same moment, the other children rolled one of the other pipes as fast as they could and it crashed into the pipe in which Miki was sitting. The pipe shattered and collapsed onto him. A large piece of concrete broke his skull. And Olga's heart broke when the neighbours came to fetch her, and a piece of my mother's heart also broke because she never stopped blaming herself for Miki's death.

Majda patiently watches and waits as I play. The sun slowly goes down. I stare with disappointment at my new little car which lies motionless by my feet. It too is already broken.

∞

Today is a sunny day and I go outside with my father to the front of the apartment building. We're going to clean the rugs. There's a metal frame there, provided for that purpose. We hang our rugs on it and beat them with a carpet beater. I'm having a good time. We laugh as we take turns to thrash the rugs. I admire my father as he talks casually with the neighbours, throwing out a funny remark now and again, laughing. When we're finished, we roll up the rugs, carry them up to the apartment, and unfurl them on the living room floor.

I'm still on all fours, straightening out the corners, when my father suddenly raises his voice and speaks angrily:

"Stay like that and don't move! You're going to get a spanking!"

22

He grabs the carpet beater. I freeze. The whole world is reduced to my held breath, my wildly beating heart. My father lifts the carpet beater and swings it down toward my bottom.

I scream and start to cry. I don't notice that the carpet beater doesn't even touch me because my father stops it right in time. I cry. I sob. I tremble in terror. I'm gasping for breath and can hardly hear my father laughing at me and saying he was only joking. But I cannot stop the attack of tears and desperation. My whole body shakes. My father says with irritation:

"Why are you crying? I was only kidding. Tell me why you are crying!"

I'm overwhelmed with fear and powerlessness. My body won't stop shaking. I sob convulsively. I try to answer his question but can only cry. Anyway I wouldn't know what to say. My father impatiently raises his voice and repeats the question, this time with a threat in his voice.

"Why are you crying? I didn't do anything to you! So why are you crying?"

I sob and shake. I can't say anything. My father raises his arm again and brings the carpet beater down hard on my bottom, twice.

"There, now you have a reason to cry."

Trembling and sobbing, I drag myself to my little room where I cry for a long time, holding on to my bottom. I feel so alone. I have no one, no connection with anyone, least of all with my father who I love so much. I'm confused, bewildered, shaken. I don't know what is happening. I'm scared. And I'm very, very lonely.

∞

I lie on the rug in my room. My head rests in the crook of my left arm. My right hand slowly propels a miniature car across the floor in front of my eyes. Back and forth, back and forth. The car is perfect, an off-road type, for safaris in Africa. And I'm in Africa too, driving across the savannah. I watch the animals: the giraffes and lions and leopards, the wildebeest and rhinoceroses. I know all the animals because I read about them in my books, and I also watch wildlife shows on television. For hours and hours I drive across the savannah. I'm an explorer who tries to understand and help the animals. I'm like Dr. Tracy in the TV series Daktari, which I never miss.

I spend more and more time with my little car in the savannah. I'm calm there, happy, relaxed, and safe. The outside world, which is becoming more and more incomprehensible and unpleasant, disappears.

∞

Everything is the same size,
everything is equally far away.
Everything is now.
I am endlessly large,
and endlessly small at the same time.
The whole world is inside me,
and I am inside the whole world

...

...

Gradually this experience vanishes and I am back, lying on the carpet in the middle of my little room. I stare at the ceiling, thinking about what just happened.

Lately it's started happening, perhaps twice a week, when I'm alone in my room, resting, my eyes closed, lying on the floor or on the bed, that I spontaneously slide into this special experience. Something opens somewhere inside me, and a great space enters me. Or I enter it. Each time it happens, I want to stay like this forever because I feel so peaceful and free. I have no one to tell this to, but maybe that doesn't matter.

∞

In the bedroom in Prekmurje, my grandparents have a very large and thick book which they keep almost hidden on top of the wardrobe. The title on the front is 'The Illustrated Bible'. Nobody in our family is openly religious. My father often mocks religion because in Yugoslavia it's viewed as obsolete and naïve village thinking. Still it happens once that I take the book down and open it. I'm 9 years old now and I'm a good reader. I start turning the pages and, before I know it, I can't stop reading the words and studying the illustrations. I plunge enthusiastically into the stories. I become obsessed with the image of Jesus. Reading the words and gazing at the illustrations of this peaceful and inspiring man awakens something deep inside me. This is how I want to live: I want to approach people with sincerity and openness, to fearlessly and serenely enter the world and go through life, and to be prepared to die for my truth. Yes, to live for some higher ideals, for some higher purpose...

∞

I spend a lot of time with my father. We go on walks together in the mountains. We make drawings together, and play with Lego blocks. I enjoy being with him. My heart dances from the joy of our connection, the love and the light. Sometimes it bothers me that I always have to listen to his stories and can hardly get in a sentence or two of my own. Or the times when he's doing some amazing drawing, and I just have to watch. Or when he uses the drill to do some work in our apartment, and he only lets me watch him and then clean up afterwards. But still we're together. We're enjoying ourselves. I respect and admire him: he knows a lot, he likes to laugh, he does important things at his work. It seems to me that he has mastered life, and I want to be like him one day.

∞

I'm sitting in the classroom, getting more and more nervous. I'm going to put into action the plan that my mother suggested yesterday, when I told her about a girl in my class called Saša who I like. I told my mother I didn't know what to do about it. Today is March 8th, International Women's Day, when we always make cards for our mothers at school, and my mother has suggested that I make a card for Saša as well. I make the card for my mother in record time, and then one for Saša. I decorate it beautifully, colour it, and write a simple message of love inside. Now I just have to find the right moment to give it to her.

I notice that Saša has left the classroom, probably to go to the toilet, and I quickly go to her place and put the card on the edge of her desk. Her neighbour immediately notices this, and reaches out her hand to look in the card. I go back to my own desk, starting to get a bad feeling about the whole thing. Saša comes back into the classroom and sits down at her desk where three girls are now already giggling. Two more come to see and start giggling as well. Saša reads the card with a nervous expression on her face.

Suddenly she stands up. She walks decisively towards me, grabs me by my sweater, and starts pulling it back and forth:

"Why did you do that? Why did you do that?"

I look at her numbly. I don't know what to say. All the giggling girls are watching us. Saša keeps shaking me and asking:

"Why did you do that? Why did you do that? Tell me!"

I stare at the floor. My head sinks between my shoulders. I want to disappear. Finally Saša lets go of me, throws the card on my desk, and says:

"Don't do anything like that ever again!"

I stare at the card and sense the mocking looks of my classmates. I hear only my own breathing. If I had been older, I might have known that I didn't do anything wrong. That on the contrary, I had enough courage to express my affection for another person. I would have known that it's beautiful when love is offered with an open heart. If I were older, I might also have understood that Saša was just embarrassed by all the laughing and teasing of her friends, that perhaps the card might have affected her in a different way if she had read it alone, if I had perhaps tucked the card in her bag and she had found it when she got home. But the way it happened I can only stare at the card in my hand, slowly crumple it up, and pretend that I don't care. It doesn't seem to be such a good thing to be sincere and honest.

∞

I come home from school and announce that I want to learn to play the piano. On my way home, I had spoken to a classmate who was going to music school and I realized right then and there that that's what I wanted to do too. I wanted to learn to play the piano, which of all instruments was by far my favourite. I'd always admired the people who played the piano at school celebrations.

My parents look at each other and say that a piano is too large an instrument for our apartment, that it's not a good instrument for an apartment building in any case, that it's too loud. I insist that I really want to play the piano. They suggest that I learn another instrument, perhaps the violin. I roll my eyes and repeat that I want to play the piano and nothing else. They say it won't work because a piano is not suitable for an apartment building, and that's that. I stand for a while longer in the living room and then slink back to my room, head down.

If I had had the power and the persistence, I would have explained to them how much I wanted to play the piano, how I would practise every day. I would have talked to each of them separately, as well as when they were together. It would probably have taken a week or two for them to realize how important it was to me, but then they would have enrolled me in music school and bought me a piano, maybe just an electric keyboard to start with. But I'm powerless. I'm not persistent enough. I don't have confidence in myself. So I just stand at the window and watch the large crane in the building site across the street.

A couple of weeks later my father brings me an accordion that he got from his stepfather, as if to say, "You wanted to study music and now I've brought you an instrument". He is satisfied with himself, convinced that this will make me happy. I stare at

27

the accordion. Of all the instruments in the world, it is probably the least interesting to me. But I smile politely and pretend to be grateful, and for the next couple of weeks, I drum now and again on the case until my father realizes that there will be no bread from this flour and takes it away again.

∞

I'm in Prekmurje spending the holidays with my grandparents. I wake in my room from an afternoon nap. The sun is shining outside. Everything is silent and calm in the courtyard. My eyes are open. I stare at the ceiling for a while, thinking. All of a sudden, an opening, a sort of window into another space, appears above me, directly beneath the ceiling. I stop breathing. I lie motionless and stare up at the small mysterious opening. A rope is released through it and slides down toward me until the tip of the rope hangs a few inches above my breastbone. The rope is yellowish, the thickness of a thumb, but it looks unreal somehow, as if it's transparent and glowing with an internal light. My heart pounds, my thoughts stand still, and before I know what's happening, I spot a pair of tiny legs. It's a little man lowering himself down the rope. The little man is also a pale yellowish colour, slightly transparent and glowing, and about as big as a cat. I stare at him as he gets closer to me, and when he has descended to the middle of the rope, another pair of legs appears in the aperture, and another little man begins to lower himself into the room.

All of this takes place quite quickly. I have no time to think or react. I lie motionless, my heart beating loudly, hardly daring to breathe. The first little man is already quite close to the end of the rope. He looks down and stares straight into my eyes. Suddenly he stops, because he realizes that I can see him too. We look at each other for a second or two, and then he looks up and with his elbow pokes the other little man, who has just caught up with him, in his foot. He points at me with his hand and, for a second, both of them stare into my eyes. Then they look at each other, nod, quickly scramble up the rope and disappear into the aperture.

A second after that, the rope disappears and then the aperture as well.

For a long while, I lie motionless on the bed and stare at the celling. What just happened? What did I see? Was it real or did it just look that way to me? Can I speak to anyone about this? Everyone would laugh at me, make fun of me to others. Who can I trust? Nobody. I can't trust anybody. I will keep it all to myself. Anyway there is no one who really gets me, who really understands me…

After a while, I get up and go out to the courtyard to play.

Two: The Twilight of Childhood

I'm ten years old. The twilight of my childhood begins today. I come home from school in the early afternoon, shut the door, lock it behind me, take off my shoes, and hang up my jacket. Suddenly I hear strange sounds from the bathroom: moaning, spitting, panting. I slowly approach the open door. My father is sitting on the floor, holding the toilet bowl, throwing up and spitting into it. I greet him cautiously. He doesn't answer, just takes a deep breath and spits again. I ask him if he's sick. He doesn't answer. After a while, he stands up, slowly and with great difficulty, and staggers into the living room. His eyes frighten me. They're empty, absent, dazed. They don't see me. It's as if I don't exist. He lies down on the couch and falls asleep.

I flush the toilet, turn off the light, close the door, and go to my room.

Shaken, I sit on the floor by the window and look at the construction site across the street. It's a good thing that they're working so slowly on the new apartment building, so there's always something going on for me to watch.

∞

Life suddenly becomes complicated and foggy. More and more often, I feel on the edge of something incomprehensible and intense happening, something that I don't understand, and which scares me. My father is frequently drunk. I feel tense, frightened, uncertain when I'm at home. More and more often he orders me around for no apparent reason. He gets irritated and snaps at me:

"Go to your room!"

His tone reminds of the way I've heard dog-owners talking to their animals.

"Sit down!" "Lie down!"

"Go to your room!"

Whenever he talks to me like that, I realize that I'm not important. I don't exist for him anymore. That he wants to change the channel, just like with a TV, that my channel no longer interests him. He tells me to remove myself, so I will no longer intrude into his world, so I will no longer bother him.

I slowly begin to retreat into the solitude of my own room, my shelter, where I have the most peace and safety. I spend a lot of time reading, mostly Jules Verne and Karl May's novels about Winnetou, the brave Apache chief. His calmness, his nobility, his solitude inspire me. I experience him as a sort of kindred spirit, an older brother. And I continue as always to be fascinated by the crane towering above the building site across the way.

∞

As usual I'm standing at the back of the bus and staring out of the rear window. I'm coming back from ice-skating at the indoor ice-rink, where I like to go on Saturdays and Sundays. I hold my skates in my right hand. In my left hand, I'm holding the bar because it's a 'bendy' bus and it sways from side to side a lot. I notice a man standing very close to me. We're almost touching. It seems strange, because the bus is almost empty. Strange.

I suddenly notice his hand, how his extended little finger is approaching the area between my legs. I lift my head and glance at him. He's staring out of the window as if nothing is happening. I wonder if anything is actually happening, but at that instant I feel a slight pressure on my penis.

I look down and see that his hand is gently touching me. I've never experienced anything like this, and it's strange to me, and very, very unpleasant. The man is old, serious-looking, and I feel a certain awe of him. Holding my breath, I take a step away. I nervously wonder what will happen now. I hope he will stop.

The man also takes a step to be next to me again and reaches his hand towards me. Before he can touch me, I step away again, this time two steps. My heart is racing with fear. The man steps towards me again, but this time I move quickly and walk to the middle of the bus. I sit down in a seat facing the back so I can keep my eye on him.

We look at each other for a moment. He looks sad somehow. I redirect my gaze out of the window, but I can still see him out of the corner of my eye scanning the bus around him. Then he slowly approaches a young man about eighteen years old, who's grimly looking out from beneath a black cap pulled down over his eyebrows. The man goes up close to him and whispers something. The young man looks at him for a couple of seconds without lifting his head, and then he roughly pushes him back.

"Piss off!"

He strides towards the exit.

The doors open at the next stop and the young man steps off the bus, angrily muttering into his parka. I have two more stops until home but I make a sudden decision and jump off just before the doors close. I'd like to go with that young man, but I have to go in the other direction. I'd like to have a brother like that, or at least a friend. To learn from him. To perhaps be safe with him.

∞

It's early evening and I'm reading a book in my room. My parents are talking in the living room. All of a sudden, I hear a scream:

"Robi!"

I put down my book, my heart pounding, and slowly make my way to the living room. My parents are sitting on the couch. A terrible weight hangs in the air.

My mother says: "Just so you know, your father just hit me."

I look at my mother. I look at my father. I look at the floor. My heart is pounding. I don't know what to say. My father is clearly irritated but nevertheless tries to speak in a calming manner:

"Robi, your mother drank too much today. Everything is alright. Don't worry."

My mother looks at him and mutters: "Oh yes, sure, yeah, yeah, I drank too much, yeah right…"

I look at them numbly. If I knew how to, if I was able, I'd say to them that they should work this out between themselves, because it's scary and confusing when they try to involve me. I would ask them to please not drink any more, either of them. I'd ask them if we could be a family again, a family in which there was calm and peace, happiness and laughter. I would cry. I would scream out all my powerlessness and fear.

But I can't do any of that. I don't know how. None of it is possible. I whisper to them that I would like to go back to my room. My father says fine. My mother silently looks at the floor. I close the door behind me and return to Winnetou.

∞

I get the idea for my favourite fantasy from the film The Omega Man, in which all of humanity dies out from an epidemic and only one man remains. The idea of being alone in the world is incredibly appealing to me, and I begin to design the details of my fantasy.

In the morning, I wake up and notice that bodies are lying on the streets and everything is silent. Humanity has died out. When the bodies begin to decay, they'll attract dogs, wolves, and other animals, so I must equip myself and leave the city and get away from any human settlements as soon as possible. First I go to the showroom for Mercedes-Puch off-road vehicles, because they are certainly the best. My father and my uncle have taught me the basics of driving and I'll be able to figure out the rest. I choose a 4x4, and load it with tools and spare tanks of fuel.

My next stop is the hunting shop in the centre of the city. I choose a gun and lots of ammunition, as well as various other necessities: a compass, ropes, knives. Then to the department store where I select clothing and shoes, always the best and most durable I can find. And lastly to the supermarket where I load the 4x4 up with canned food, juice, milk and pasta. Then I slowly drive in the direction of the Croatian coast. The qualities of this top-of-the-range 4x4 come in handy now as I'm able to avoid all the crashed and overturned vehicles on the road. Somewhere on the Croatian coast – in Pula or Rijeka – I load everything onto a motor boat and slowly and carefully make my way to the nearest island where there will be a manageable number of dogs and no wolves, and above all not so many human corpses. I'll be able to drag the few there are into the sea and to barricade myself into a small house with a good view of my surroundings. Then I'll come up with a strategy as to whether I want to look for any other survivors, and how I can protect myself from the violent ones who might try to find me.

I have plenty to think about. But above all, I enjoy myself immensely in this imaginary world where I'm free, where I can decide everything on my own, and where there is no abuse to be afraid of. It's up to me, and me alone, to manage my life.

∞

There are two grocery shops not far from our apartment building. My parents send me to one of them nearly every day with a basket and a list of items to buy. Sometimes I buy the wrong thing and have to take it back. Sometimes that even happens several times in a row. But in general I like going to the store. I'm only afraid that the cashier will ask me something when I'm at the checkout counter, and I won't know what to say. So I always look down at that point and hold my breath.

Today I go to the grocery shop with my mother because there's a shoe shop in the basement. They're having a sale and I need winter boots. We look through the whole stock with the salesman. It turns out that they have no boys' winter boots left in my size. But my mother insists we have to buy something here because she doesn't have time to go into the city centre to shop for shoes. She spots a pair of black girls' winter boots and tells me to try them on. The salesman says they're girls' boots, not boys', but my mother says:

"Well, it doesn't really matter. They're all the same."

"They're not the same: these have a high heel, they're for girls," I say.

"No, the heel isn't high at all. Try them on, just for fun," says my mother with slight irritation.

I stare at the salesman in confusion, hoping for his help. This is definitely not my idea of fun. But he just stares back at us, then shrugs, and disappears into the back room. I stand in silence with my mother and wait for him to come back. If I would have had the strength and courage to stand up to her, I would have said that I would not wear boots with high heels. I would tell her that and persist. I would ask her why it would be a waste of her time to look for shoes that I would like and would wear with pleasure, when it wasn't a waste of time when she shopped for her own shoes and clothes. I would say quite a lot if only I dared to stand up for myself, if only I had any hope of success, if only I had any confidence in my abilities, or if at least I had the support of the salesman. But I have nothing. I have only my uncertainty, my fear.

The salesman returns with the girls' high-heeled boots in my size. I know where this is going. I try them on, and sure enough they fit.

"They have high heels and I don't like them."

"Listen Robi, they're fine to wear to school. No one will even be able to see the heels in the snow."

"Everyone will see it."

"Stop making such a fuss, you'll forget all about the heels in a couple of days."

My mother buys the boots, and I return home with my head hanging.

The next day outside school everyone immediately notices that I'm wearing high-heeled boots. Everyone makes fun of me. There's nowhere for me to hide. One girl even has exactly the same boots as me and confirms that, yes, they are definitely girls' boots.

When I get back home I report what happened. To my great relief, my father enters the conversation to say that the boy doesn't need to wear girls' shoes if he doesn't want to. He takes me in the car to buy a new pair of winter boots, and the girls' boots go to a neighbour.

∞

School is becoming an unpleasant and unkind place. I'm so deeply absorbed in my own thoughts and emotions that I can't concentrate, can't listen, can't learn. I always have scenes from home in my head, a constant feeling of anxiety, fear, being lost. Until this year I easily got top grades but now everything is falling apart. My teacher, a very kind woman, asks me completely out of the blue if something is wrong, if something is going on at home. I look at the floor and shrug. I wish she would invite me into her office on my own and sit me down and ask me the same questions again. It would take me a while but I would eventually be able to speak openly. I might even start to cry. Maybe she would listen. Maybe she would speak to the school psychologist, who would find a way to help. But she never asks again. She just shrugs and says that she can't give me good grades if I'm not performing well.

I always feel nervous opening the door when I come home from school. I never know what will await me on the other side. Things are somehow more predictable, more known, at school and in the community park in front of our building. But when I come home I step into a world of tension, anxiety, and danger. I'm more relaxed when I'm on my own at home, but not completely even then. I always keep my ears pricked for the sound of the key turning in the lock.

∞

Today is Saturday, a calm and lazy day which I really enjoy. In the morning I watch skiing on TV. Then we have lunch. Mother washes the dishes in the kitchen. Father and I laze around on the couch in the living room. Sometimes I love him so much, and I'm excited by the love and joy I feel. My father lies motionless on his back, dozing, but I can't completely relax because of all the love and pleasure I feel being close to him. I slowly take his hand in mine and study it. It's so big and strong. I slowly and lovingly caress his palm, immersed in my own thoughts.

Suddenly he pulls his hand away from mine, turns towards me and says:

"Don't do that. Only homosexuals do that. That's not okay."

Then he dozes off again.

I don't understand what just happened. I don't even know what a homosexual is. I think it's a man who likes other men, but I'm not completely sure. Why isn't tenderness okay? Why isn't touch okay? I don't understand. If I were brave enough, I'd wake him up and ask about all of this, try to understand what he's saying. But as it is, I just stare at the ceiling and don't dare to touch him again. If my father says that touch between men is not okay, then he must know what he's talking about.

∞

I'm eleven years old. Mother is at work. Tonight she has the night shift. My Aunt Marta is staying with us this week because she has some medical tests at the hospital in Ljubljana. In the evening, my father's cousin, Edo, comes to visit. The two men start to drink in the living room, and soon Marta and I each go off to bed.

In the middle of the night, I'm awoken by loud and angry sounds from the entry hall of our apartment. My heart pounds in my chest as I go to my bedroom door, kneel down, and look through the keyhole. I can see the hallway. Edo is standing in front of the front door to the apartment.

"Come on, Jože, calm down, what the hell…"

My father is standing facing him. He looks so tense, so aggressive and enraged, that the blood runs cold in my veins. He's holding a big stick in his right hand, one that we once brought home from a walk in the hills. He's hissing at Edo:

"What did you say? What did you just say? Get out! Out!"

My heart pounds like crazy.

Edo tries again:

"Calm down, Jože, just calm down…"

My father suddenly raises the stick and brings it down twice on Edo's head. Edo collapses on the floor. My father opens the door, grabs him by the collar, and drags him into the hallway outside.

Everything in my body and head is going wild. I jump back into bed, cover my head, roll into a little ball. I'm shaking with fear. What should I do? Where's my father taking Edo? What now? What now? What should I do?

I hear my father return to the apartment after a few minutes, shut the door, and go into the bathroom. Then he lurches into my room, pulls me out of my bed without speaking, lies down on my bed, and falls asleep with a smile on his face. I guess that was easier for him than making up his bed on the living room couch, as Aunt Marta is sleeping in the bedroom tonight. I leave my room and shut the door behind me. I stand in the corridor and stare at the puddle of Edo's blood in front of the door. Marta slowly and cautiously comes out of the bedroom, and we stand there in the silence looking at each other. She seems even more shocked and frightened than me, just standing there, passive and helpless. Suddenly we hear Edo in the hallway outside. We can hear his shallow gasps and indistinct words as he slowly staggers to the front door. Then he starts banging on the door:

"Jože, open the door, Jože…"

My heart begins to race wildly again. Edo's banging is loud, his cries even louder. I'm afraid he'll wake up the whole apartment building. Marta and I look at each other in silence. Then she unlocks and opens the door. Edo stumbles into the apartment and collapses on the floor mumbling something we can't understand. Marta closes the door. She tells me to phone my mother at work. I phone my mother and tell her what happened. She tells me she will call an ambulance. It's not long before the ambulance comes and takes the now unconscious Edo away. Mother had somehow convinced them not to call the police, and when I speak to her again on the phone, she tells me that Marta and I need to clean up the blood. We each take a bucket of soapy water and some rags, and go out into the hallway. A streak of blood as wide as a fist runs along the wall of the hallway. It seems that Edo's head slid along the wall as he was dragging himself back to our apartment. We follow the bloody trail as it continues down the staircase from our apartment on the second floor, down to the first floor, and then makes a circle around the lobby until it finally stops at the main entrance to the building. We start cleaning there and slowly make our way back up.

By three thirty in the morning, the staircase and the hallways are spotless. We wash our hands and go to sleep in Marta's room. I wake up and go to school in the morning, very tired. Father is still sleeping.

∞

I started to stutter last year. I simply can't speak normally, can't get the words out of my mouth, can't end a sentence. I'm constantly overwhelmed by tension and fear. Now the fear is worse because I never know if I'll be capable of actually saying something. I don't dare to raise my hand in school even though I know the answer to the teacher's questions. I don't dare tell a good joke among friends because I fear it will be torture for everyone. I'm afraid to speak to anyone at all. It's safest just to be quiet.

I'm not the only one in the classroom with a stutter. Three boys besides me have the same problem. Who knows what is happening to them at home? The teacher is astonished that there are so many of us. She says we should all go to speech therapy. I don't think any of us will actually go. I certainly won't mention the idea at home. Everything is so complicated, so difficult. It's best just to be silent and only respond when I have to. The four of us feel connected in a special way. Something unites us. We know something, have experienced something that the others have not.

∞

I'm running as fast as I can, my heart beating in wild terror. I'd like to scream with fear but I don't have time. I can hear barking at my heels, growling, the panting of two dogs. At least I think there are two. I glance back into the darkness and yes, right behind me I see the flash of teeth and two pairs of eyes. I'm even more terrified now. I run even faster. The bag containing my judo uniform swings against my shoulders. I slip a bit on the snow. Just don't let me fall. Don't let me fall.

Twice a week I go to judo class and have to walk home in the dark. My route takes me from the modern estate on the edge of the city where we live through a run-down semi-rural area with unlit, muddy streets and spooky old abandoned farm buildings. It seems to be empty of living souls, but there are always a few half-wild dogs waiting for me somewhere in the darkness. I run there and back in complete terror. I've told my father that I'm afraid to go to the judo club because of the dogs. In response he told me a story from his own childhood, how a dog attacked and bit him, and he had to get stitches in his hand. And that it was essential not to fear the dogs or they would sense it. I mustn't be afraid of them.

Nothing he told me helps me in anyway, not the slightest bit.

A glimmer from the first street light washes over me. I feel a tiny bit of hope after the long stretch of darkness. I run on. I slow down and look back when I no longer hear the barking right behind me. Two dogs are sitting under the street light and staring threateningly at me.

I decide never go to judo again, even though it's the same club where my father trained and he's going to be even more disappointed in me than he already is.

∞

When I'm on holiday in Prekmurje, Marta and I share a room with two beds that gives directly onto the courtyard. We're partially separated from the main house and from my grandparents. I love them but it suits me that there's a little distance between us now that I'm 11 years old already. Marta and I are close in many ways. She's my mother's twin, though not identical, and was born mildly handicapped because of difficulties during the birth. She suffered from various illnesses later in life, and never married as a result, staying at home with her parents. Her life is mostly housework, watching TV, and talking with her neighbour. She took care of me when I was a baby, and I like spending time with her. I feel accepted and unconditionally loved by her. I can talk to her about anything in my life and what I'm experiencing. She always listens and tries to understand to the best of her ability. She always accepts me as I am. And always, absolutely always, she takes my side, supports me. We are allies. We're both different from other people, and lonely because of it. That's why we stick together.

But things get complicated.

Sometimes late in the evening when Marta and I are each lying in our own beds, talking in the darkness, a shadow appears in the courtyard and knocks on the window. Marta and I go silent, but the knocking continues, louder and somehow impatient. Marta gets up, opens the window, and whispers to the person outside. It's always a man who has come in to the courtyard after the local pub has closed. There are two or three men who come on different nights. They try to convince her of something with their whispering. At first she firmly refuses and then she starts to relent. In the end she gives in and either goes outside for fifteen minutes or lets the man into our room. It seems disgusting to me in both cases. I know that they're all married men, that they're drunk, and that they don't care the slightest about Marta. I know that Marta doesn't want to have anything to do with them, but she doesn't know how to stand her ground. And I also think that a part of her likes that someone wants to be with her, to be intimate. I decide that I'm going to help her, that I will take her side and defend her, but I don't know how.

Tonight it's the farmer Franc knocking at the window. He's a huge man with a fat head, his face flushed from meat and alcohol, a cold expression in his eyes. While they're whispering at the door to the room, enormous Franc groping Marta, I gather my courage, get up from my bed and say, with a trembling voice:

"Leave us alone and go away!"

The whispering stops. Franc's huge silhouette slowly turns. His leather jacket creaks ominously, and all of sudden he is moving towards me. Although he only takes two steps, those steps strike me as the most dangerous thing in the world. Marta screams for him to leave me alone and tugs on his sleeve, small and helpless. My legs turn to jelly, and I collapse back down on the bed. Franc stands above me. He stinks of manure and alcohol. He's enormous. His voice booms threateningly:

"Shut up!"

I cover my head, my heart pounds wildly, and I can hardly breathe as Marta's bed squeaks, and her pleading whispers are drowned out by Franc's loud grunting.

∞

My mother has been talking for an hour without pause, upset, frenzied, but also powerless, desperate. We're sitting in the kitchen at home on our own, and it just bursts out of her. What my father is like and how dares he and who in the world does he think he is! She tells me about his lovers, how he's ruined her life, how she works all day, every day, and gets nothing from it. And on and on and on.

This scene is repeated more and more often. I sit and listen to her, although I would rather be reading a book in my room, or playing football or basketball in the playground with my friends. Or riding my bike. But I end up sitting with her and listening to all these things I don't want to hear. She tells me the same story each time but with more and more details, again and again, and it becomes more and more unpleasant to me.

If I dared, I would ask her to not tell me any more about it, that I'm not her friend, but her son, that she should talk about her problems with her friends, that I want to go out and play, that it would be better for her to ask me how it is for me, how I feel after all the terrible scenes that have happened at home. She should ask me how I deal with what I'm feeling, with what I've been exposed to. She should provide me with support. But I don't know how to say that to her. I just sit, stare at her, listen to her, and wait for it to end.

It's also true that it feels good in a way. I feel like a grown-up supporting my mother. Still, I also wish I could just be a child.

∞

It's a warm summer's night. My father and I are walking fast along the local street that runs from my grandparents' house on the outskirts of the village to its centre. My father is drunk and very aggressive. We're heading towards the village party, because Marta has gone missing and was last seen there with Franc. I know what Franc looks like, and I'm supposed to point him out to my father so we can find out where Marta has gone. I'm beside myself with fear and anxiety as I walk alongside my father. In his drunken rage, he's grinding his teeth, and alternating between extending his fingers and making a fist, as if he's warming himself up for a fight. His speech is slurred as he explains to me that some men like to touch women, that maybe I don't understand that yet. We even stop for a few seconds so he can show me the type of touching he's talking about. If I wasn't scared to death, the whole situation would be comical and bizarre.

We finally come to the village party where a lot of people are standing around with drinks in their hands, laughing loudly. I pray that Franc won't be among them. We stand on the edge of the group. My father tells me to point him out. Unfortunately I spot him right away. He's talking and smoking with a group of half-drunk men not far from us. Stiff with fear, I raise a finger towards him and briefly describe him. My father walks over in a rage, stands right in front of Franc's nose, and demands answers from him. He pushes his body against the other man's. He is still

43

alternating between stretching his fingers and making a fist. Franc is a head taller than my father, and answers him calmly, with a faint smile on his face even. I observe the scene. One part of me would like the other men to quickly knock my father to the ground so the whole thing would be over. Another part of me wants to escape, somewhere faraway, forever. A third part of me is numb inside and out, only my heart beating wildly.

After a few seconds, my father comes back to me. Franc and his companions mockingly watch him go. My father hisses at me:

"Come on. Let's go."

We walk back along the street to the edge of the village. He tells me that Franc said that Marta had left a while ago, and he has no idea where she is. We enter the courtyard and hear women's voices from the house, the sound of shouting and crying. Everything begins to unravel so fast when we step into the living room that I can only stand there with my mouth open.

Marta is crying in the corner, loudly demanding that everyone leave her alone. My mother, my grandmother, and Aunt Olga are standing in front of her, pouring out their disgust and anger at her. My father pushes them away, steps in front of Marta, and slaps her hard across the face, twice. Everything is quiet for an instant. Marta is bleeding from her mouth. The other three women pull my father away, begging him to stop. My father says he only wants to 'calm Marta down'. Marta wipes the blood from her mouth, weeps, and says bitterly:

"Thanks, thank you for this, thank you all for everything."

I just stare at them, my heart still pounding. My grandmother tells me to go outside so I don't see any more of this. She's right. I have seen enough. But sadly, I don't know where to go.

∞

I'm standing in line at the shop, looking at the tips of my shoes. I shift the shopping basket full of groceries from one hand to the other. A boy named Matjaž from the neighbouring apartment building is in front of me in the queue. He's four years older than me and we know each other by sight. He probably doesn't even know my name though, as I'm so much younger and thus not very interesting to him. I admire him a lot: his long hair, his serious face, his cool and slightly torn blue jeans, his relaxed manner. Suddenly something completely inconceivable to me starts happening. A middle-aged woman, with a superior attitude, wearing a fur coat, her head held high, slowly walks to the head of the queue, in front of me and in front of Matjaž who is next in line at the cash desk. Matjaž speaks loudly and clearly:

"Madam, where are you going?"

The lady throws a contemptuous glance his way and pushes past him with slow dignity. Matjaž continues even more decisively:

"Madam, please stop pushing in. I'm asking you nicely."

My heart is beating hard as I take in the situation. The shop assistant lifts her gaze, but continues tapping on the keys of the cash register.

The lady finally speaks, her voice ice cold:

"Boy, stop being so impertinent! Behave yourself!"

But Matjaž's voice grows even louder, his words more clipped:

"Madam, you have no right to push in front of me. Go to the end of the queue, and wait your turn like we all had to."

The lady stiffens, stares at Matjaž for a moment, then slowly moves back to the end of the queue, muttering:

"What an impertinent young man! You should learn to behave yourself!"

Matjaž responds loudly, a faint smile on his face:

"Who do you think you are? So what if you're a few years older than me! Go to the back of the line and wait like the rest of us."

The lady, red in the face and almost panting from rage, stands stiffly at the end of the queue, still muttering under her breath about young people today. I can only stare at Matjaž with my mouth open. Wow, I think, it's actually possible to stand up for yourself, to express yourself, to persevere. I look at him as I if were looking at a paragon. I realize that it might be possible to stop these arrogant, superior, rude adults who want to shove me around, act like they're so smart, and humiliate young people.

Matjaž immediately becomes my idol, my role model. If I would only be able to stand up to these domineering adults: the teachers, the neighbours, the driver on the school bus. Maybe one day even to my father.

∞

I slowly scuff my shoes along the ground, dragging my feet behind me. Once again I find myself doing this unpleasant and frustrating task. It's Sunday and all the stores are closed. Mother is working today. I'm on my own at home with my father. He gets irritated in the afternoon and orders me to go to the bar and buy him twelve bottles of beer. He gives me the basket of empties, some money, and sends me off.

It's absurd that my father won't come to this bar to buy his own beer, simply because he's embarrassed. I feel powerless because I can't say no, can't stand up for myself, can't say to him that this is also my Sunday and that I would like to sit and read a book in my room. Or play football outside with my friends. But I'm always too afraid to take such risks.

The whole thing makes me sick, walking along the street the five hundred metres to the drinkers' den in the basement of a boarding house. I know that, like always, there will be a bunch of strange drunk men there. I know that the laconic barman will give me an irritated look and tell me that he's not supposed to sell alcohol to minors. Why doesn't my father come and get his own beer? I know that my hands will hurt, too, as I carry the heavy basket back home. I'm also disgusted because I know exactly how our evening will go. He will get drunk and nasty, and I will stay in my room hoping that he'll fall asleep in the bedroom and not on the couch in the living room, so that I can watch a movie in the evening.

I know that my father loves me. I know that he had a difficult childhood, that his own father was violent and drank a lot. I know that my father is under pressure, that something is eating away at him, and he's trying with all his strength to solve his problems. I know he doesn't want anything bad for me. I know all of this. But it doesn't help. If only he would look me in the eyes once in a while after these miserable scenes and apologize. Tell me he's sorry that he's so hard on me, that he regrets all of it. Why can't he even ask what effect all of this has on me? In my fantasy, he says:

"My dear son, I love you, and I'm very sorry that I do this. Tell me: how did you feel yesterday when I was drunk, how do you feel now…?"

And he would listen to me and he would see me. Yes, if he would at least see me. But no one sees me. He's in his own world, my mother is in her own world, and I'm forgotten somewhere in the void.

I walk slower and slower. I drag my feet behind me. That's the most resistance I can muster. About halfway there, I happen to glance behind me and in sheer horror, I spot my father walking very fast towards me. He's probably seen me from the balcony, dragging my feet, and that has angered him so much that he's coming down after me. My heart beats wildly as I watch his rapid approach, and I feel, more than see, the aggressive expression on his face. I speed up as much as I can at this point and walk in a panic towards the bar. I look back and calm down a little when it seems that I have succeeded in maintaining the distance between us. As I step through the doors of the bar, I look back one more time and see him: he's stopped and is standing with his legs apart, his hands on his hips, looking towards me.

Out of breath, I stand in front of the bar. I put the bottles in the basket, I pay, and then I don't know if I should hurry as fast as I can or linger. I don't know which is better. Or which is less bad. When I finally step out onto the street with the full basket, I see with relief that my father is no longer where I last saw him. He's probably satisfied with how thoroughly he's frightened me, and has gone home, and is now waiting calmly for his beer, knowing I will walk fast on my way back. I feel defeated, trapped, powerless in my prison.

∞

I'm more and more numb at home, always making sure no signal comes from me, no emotion, no thought, nothing at all. Anything I might express can be dangerous and bounce back against me.

One day my father proudly waves a family contract that he's just written, in which he's sworn he won't touch another drop of alcohol, and he demands that both my mother and I sign it too. I stare into the distance because I know that he's made such a promise countless times before and has always started drinking again after a couple of weeks.

When he tells visitors that he hasn't touched alcohol for the last six months, I know that only a few days ago he was on the floor, shaking in delirium, foamy saliva coming out of his mouth, and so I just stare blankly into the distance. It's safest just to be quiet and not to give off any signs of how I feel. Not to give him any excuse, any provocation, and just to retreat into my own space at the first opportunity.

∞

I gaze out of the window at yet another construction site.

A few months ago, my father decided to leave us and moved from Ljubljana to Kranj, half an hour away, because this is where his job is. Probably he was the first to move in, because I can see that they're still finishing the apartment building, that the electricians are still fitting the place out, and we never meet any other people living there. Today, as always, we went to his favourite restaurant, and then to see a movie starring Clint Eastwood, and now after a couple of beers he's fallen asleep on the couch. I don't know what to do with myself. The apartment has only one room and I have to be completely quiet so I don't wake him up. There's no TV, no books, not even a newspaper. There's no park nearby, no playground, nothing…

My mother begs me to take the bus and go and visit him every weekend so that he won't forget me, so I'll maintain contact with him, so when he gets sick of his new girlfriend and comes to his senses, he'll come back and we'll live a normal family life again. I beg her just to divorce him, so it will all finally be over, and she and I can live our lives without any more dramas. I'm through with him. I just want peace and quiet. But my mother is, unfortunately, way more persistent and agile in our conversations and I always end up feeling the weight of responsibility, as if everything depends on me: the survival of our family, her happiness, everything. And so I get on the bus to Kranj again.

I would much rather be riding my bike around, reading books in my room, relaxing, going to the movies or the ice-skating rink with my schoolmates. But it's always the same. The bus ride, lunch at the restaurant, the cinema, and then a big fat nothing in my father's tiny flat.

Outside it's just got dark and only the faint sound of my father's snoring breaks the total silence. I stand in the middle of the room, powerless, trapped. I quietly drink a glass of juice, go into the bathroom to brush my teeth, and then carefully lie down on the sofa bed next to my father. I hope I will fall asleep right away and then I can go back to Ljubljana tomorrow.

∞

"Robi, what are you doing?"

I hear a soft voice. I don't know where I am. It's dark.

"Robi, can you hear me? What are you doing?"

Slowly my consciousness starts to put itself together. I'm sitting at home in Ljubljana on the couch in the living room in front of the television. It's dark. It's my mother's voice. She is sleeping on the couch.

"Robi, Robi, what are you doing?"

I answer her irritably:

"I'm watching TV, can't you see what I'm doing?"

Mother doesn't answer, and only then do I realize that the television isn't even turned on, and who knows how long I've been sitting in the dark in the middle of the night staring at a blank screen.

My mother speaks to me in a soft whisper: "Go to bed, Robi, go to bed…"

I get up and slowly make my way along the hallway to my bedroom. I think about how strange it is that my mother has been sleeping on the couch in the living room since my father moved out.

When I lie down in my bed, I realize that I must have been sleepwalking again. Like the time a noise from the hallway woke my mother up. It was me banging with my forehead against the closed bathroom door, again and again, until she finally came to open it and I went in to pee. Or the time years before when I was awoken one morning by the sound of my mother's loud coughing and rushing through the apartment. She had gone into the bathroom and discovered my shit in the bathtub. As she cleaned it up, I remembered that the night before I'd sat on the edge of the bathtub and relieved myself, then looked in confusion for the toilet paper, which was nowhere to be found.

I slowly fall asleep, wondering whether I should be worried about any of this.

∞

I'm twelve years old. I'm lying in bed and feeling happier than I've ever felt before. I've just experienced the first orgasm of my life.

I've been trying to masturbate on and off for several weeks. I heard about it from some older schoolmates. But I didn't learn the details about how to do it or how long it took. I didn't dare ask

anyone and simply started to experiment at home. And today I
have finally succeeded. I worked on pleasuring myself decisively,
persistently, and it kept getting better and better, until suddenly an
unbelievably wonderful feeling overwhelmed me. At that
moment, I suddenly feel felt like I urgently had to pee. I knew I
wasn't going to be able to hold it in and I just let go. Surprised
and relieved, I realized it wasn't pee coming out of my penis, but
semen. Total ecstasy.

Now I'm lying on my back, the little puddle of milky white
fluid slowly drying on my belly. It feels so good. Not only the
feeling overwhelming my whole body with infinite pleasure but
something even more wonderful, something even more important:
the realization that finally something great has happened.
Something that nobody can ever take away from me. I can create
complete satisfaction and happiness for myself, independent of
anyone or anything else. I've done it. I've succeeded. And I have
the power to repeat the magic.

...

For a time, masturbation becomes my main hobby. I even
record each of my achievements in my diary. I break the record
one Saturday when I'm on my own at home: seven times in one
day.

∞

Today my childhood od ends for good, here, in the orchard
behind my grandparents' house in Prekmurje. The family cat gave
birth to seven kittens just yesterday. This morning my
grandmother told me that I was old enough: the time had come for
me to do a man's job. It was exciting as there was no other real
man around the house. Well, apart from my granddad, who is
already almost blind and deaf, and spends most of the time just
sitting on the bench in the courtyard. I listened intently as my
grandmother told me that there were simply too many kittens, and
it was my job, as a man, an adult, to take the whole litter behind
the house, kill them with a shovel, and bury them in a hole.

51

All sorts of thoughts and feelings jostled inside me. One side of me thought it was cool to have to do man's work, to be strong and unaffected by emotions. The other side was horrified by the idea of taking the lives of these innocent new-born creatures. I froze for a second, but soon my ability to adapt and my desire to be a real man won out.

As I strike the tiny, thinly mewling, still blind kittens with the shovel, I maintain my cold-blooded attitude because the neighbour's boy Tomi, my younger admirer and personal Sancho Panza, is watching the scene of slaughter. He stares in horror at the bloody mess. I try to smile like Clint Eastwood and say:

"Look, you just don't get it yet. Sometimes you just have to do this sort of thing."

I fill up the hole and level the soil. Total silence pervades the orchard. Tomi and I stare at the shovel.

...

That evening I lie in my bed deeply disturbed; pain, sadness, fear, confusion, horror, all of this is boiling within. As there is no space for these feelings of mine in this world, I bury them too. Deep inside, I know that this scene will haunt me for decades to come.

∞

It's 1980 and I'm 14 years old. My family and I are sitting watching the TV in silence. We're watching a funeral that's being aired live. Tito, the President of Yugoslavia, has died. All my life, I've seen him as a sort of benevolent father to us all. He had heroically brought freedom to Yugoslavia during the Second World War, and since then had diligently made sure that we were all happy.

And we really are happy in this country of many religions, peoples and languages. We're greeted with a smile whenever we go to the Croatian seaside:

"Ah, welcome, our Slovenians!"

We are their Slovenians; they are our Croats, Bosnians, Serbs, Macedonians, Montenegrins. I have the feeling that I live in a country of love and connection, peace and joy. We live calmly and abundantly, relaxed and happy. At least this is how it seems to me. We look down on the Western world, completely obsessed with capitalism and the desire for money. We also look down on Eastern Europe, which we see as lagging behind us, suffering beneath the Russian military boot. It's said that the Yugoslav passport is the best in the world because we can travel both east and west. We're even loved in the Third World for being one of the co-founders of the non-aligned movement.

During the last months, while Tito was in hospital, everyone had whispered that everything beautiful would end when he died. That there would be war. That Yugoslavia would begin to burst apart.

But now we just stare at the screen and watch the funeral ceremony. The commentator reads the long list of world leaders who have gathered in Belgrade. I remember having twice seen Tito up close – the first time in a procession of black automobiles driving past. He had waved out of the window, and our whole school, no, the whole of Ljubljana, had lined the streets with our little flags and waved back at him. The second time was at the station in Kranj when President Tito was boarding his famed Blue Train. He had waved his umbrella happily and we had all loudly applauded on the platform.

Now they show his name carved on the sarcophagus and tears stream down my cheeks.

Three: Spirit Knocks on the Door

I'm about to turn fifteen. I slowly and carefully place one of my favourite records on the turntable: Pink Floyd's 'Wish You Were Here'. I can turn it up really loud because I'm on my own in the house. I sit on the couch and close my eyes. Listening to music has become my world, my private place where I can relax. My thoughts wander, or they focus attentively on the instruments, the composition, the lyrics of bands and musicians like Pink Floyd, Bob Dylan, Jethro Tull, Wishbone Ash, Janis Joplin, Queen, and I think about my life.

My father has moved back in with my mother and me, and at first it looked like everything would be different. He didn't drink. We went on trips together. They bought a house under construction in Kranj. But then he started his drinking again, not like before, but enough so that life shifted to the edge of unbearable.

We've just moved into the newly finished house and now I walk around on eggshells, careful and tense, so I don't give my father any cause to go down to the basement and get drunk. I feel most at ease when I get out of the house and walk for hours with my German shepherd Ari in the nearby forests. Or when I'm on my own at home. Then I almost ceremonially confirm my freedom with masturbation, and afterwards relax and enjoy having the space to myself, usually with music.

I've started to go to high school in Kranj, and it strikes me as more or less a nuisance. I find no kindred spirits there. The teachers are mostly autocrats, ruling with fear. I pretend to study three hours a day at home but mostly I read novels during this time: Kurt Vonnegut, Charles Bukowski and Hermann Hesse. My parents must think I'm pretty stupid since I study so much and still get bad grades.

So what's the point of my life? Just to somehow follow paths already travelled and obey other people's expectations? To adapt to this society, this system, to stop asking deeper questions? Or does some higher purpose exist?

The first side of the record ends. I get up and turn it over. I lower the needle, sit on the couch again, and close my eyes.

∞

The doorbell rings. It's winter break, a cold, snowy morning. My parents are at work. I know who it'll be: Nataša, my girlfriend. I open the door and we kiss. She smiles playfully and says she's come over for a little visit. I step outside. I'm trying to act wise and cold-blooded at the same time but it isn't going very well. I stare into the distance and say:

"Yeah, you know, I was thinking, maybe we should stop seeing each other."

Nataša stares at me in surprise and then quietly says:

"Really? Why?"

My heart pounds in my chest. Her beauty and the tears in her eyes cut into my heart. All the same I manage to answer coolly:

"I don't know, you know, it's just meaningless. That's why."

My heart collapses when I say these words. With tears in her eyes Nataša whispers:

"Well, alright, if that's what you want."

She tries to smile a little through her tears, then she turns and walks down the stairs. I look at her back as she leaves and know that she's crying. I go back into the house, close the door, everything inside me going wild.

What's the matter with me? Am I crazy or what? I love her. We've had a great time these past couple of months. Everything was beautiful. Why did I end it?

I don't know the answer to this. I just sit for a while and stare at the wall. Then I get up, get dressed, and take Ari for a walk in the forest. Only many years later will I understand that it was intimacy that I feared, the exposure and vulnerability of the emotions that had begun to emerge between us. It was what my heart longed for but, because I'd never experienced it, it struck my mind as infinitely dangerous. And similar to my father, who retreated from the vulnerability of openness and emotional intimacy into alcohol, I retreated into the safety of solitude.

To stand in front of another person, stripped naked, in a state of vulnerability, to reveal my heart to someone, with no masks, no defences... As much as my heart longs for it, the world of sincere encounters is so foreign to me, so unknown that it's more comfortable for me to retreat in panic back to the patterns I know, the familiar games where I can be safe.

Ari runs happily alongside me as I swallow my tears.

∞

Slowly, slowly, my disobedient fingers, which feel as if they belong to someone else's hands, finally succeed in pressing down on the right strings. I play the C-chord, and then I begin to move my fingers, stumbling like a dying crab, to the next position, and I manage to play the G-chord. I have to breathe, and relax my fingers for a second, before I go back to C. It goes a little faster after a while and I begin to feel enthusiastic. This guitar that I asked my parents to give me for a New Year's present is beginning to sound at least roughly like a musical instrument.

Pleased with and grateful for my minimal progress, I go into the living room and stand in front of my father, who is reading a book.

"Look what I can do already."

I strum a C and then a G. I look at him with a broad smile. He slowly lifts his gaze from his book and says:

"Well, I can see that so far you don't have much to show."

I look at him astonished. Something breaks inside me. My heart pounds. If I dared I would yell at him. I would scream for at least an hour. All the disgust and pain and disappointment and loneliness would pour out of me. I would scream until my throat gave out, and then I would kick him a couple of times just for good measure.

But instead I just turn around and go back to my room. I decide that that was the first and last time I would ever play for him. I would never again show him anything, ever.

∞

"Born to be wiiiiiiild..... born to be wiiiiiiiiiiiiild....."

I scream. I jump around the dance floor. I go crazy. I skid to the left, then to the right. I fly here and there, bumping into another long-haired kid. We grin at each other, and then fly off each in our own direction.

"Smoooooooke on the water, fire in the sky, smoooooooooooke on the water..."

I jump. I spin. I wave my arms. This is freedom. This is the real thing. I live for these Friday nights at the rocker club in Kranj. My friends and I meet in the city park in the early evening and then the Friday revelry begins. First we put our money together, ask people for change if we have to, and go and buy alcohol at a nearby store, a litre of wine for each of us. We always buy the same wine, the second cheapest, Castle Red. The cheapest one, One Old Man, is for alcoholics and lost souls, and we, of course, are something much more than that. We drink the wine in the park, talking about records and guitar solos. Most of us need to throw up in the bushes by the time we finish the wine but then we're ready for the club. We storm loudly into the place, we yell over each other, we act as if we're more drunk than we actually are. We're totally cool, masters of life. We know what it's all about. We drink a beer, smoke a cigarette, jump around the dance floor, more beer, another cigarette, back on the dance floor. During the occasional slow numbers, we each grab a girl from our circle of friends, hold her close, sway with her, kissing and fondling her, then more jumping and rampaging around. All the anger goes out of me. I scream myself senseless.

Of course all this jumping around also has a practical purpose. The crazier I go, the more alcohol I sweat out of my body, the easier it will be, when I get home, to hide my intoxication from my mother, who usually sits in front of the TV until it goes off the air, and then I can quietly vanish into my room.

∞

The ideal moment arrives at last. I'm on my own at home and my parents won't be back for at least four hours. I settle myself comfortably on the floor, my back against the wall. I unwrap the plastic bag and open the tin can inside. The light brown mass of glue shimmers, its strong odour reaching my nostrils. My heart starts to beat a little faster. I don't really know what I'm getting myself into.

A friend from the neighbourhood told me about his discovery a few days ago. New parquet flooring was being laid in the basement of their house, and he learned from somebody that inhaling the glue can get you really high. When the workers left for the day, he poured a generous amount from their big bucket into a smaller container. He showed me this treasure and asked if I wanted to try it. I leaned towards the container and started inhaling, closing my eyes because the fumes were so sharp. The sound of my friend's dog breathing started to echo in my brain like thunder in a huge underground cave. The familiar physical reality faded into the background and I began to perceive the outlines of something bigger, more all-encompassing. I lifted my head and stared at my friend who was grinning at me.

"What do you say? Good stuff, huh?"

I held my breath for a while and finally the familiar world came into focus again. I let out a sigh:

"Wow, that's crazy. That's the real thing. Give me some."

He told me to go and get a container that could be closed tightly. I ran home for an empty tin can of my father's Borkum Riff pipe tobacco, litre size. It closed really well. My friend poured some of the glue into it, and then I carried the precious stuff home. I put it into a plastic bag in case of spills, and tucked it into a hiding place under my bed. It would wait there until the first possible opportunity.

Which had come now. I slowly put my head into the bag so I'll be fully surrounded by the fumes. I close my eyes and breathe in slowly and deeply. Once, twice, three times… The familiar world disappears, along with space and time. I don't have a body anymore, though I'm still myself. I'm in a sort of infinite void. All of a sudden a loud voice begins to rebound inside and around me. It sounds friendly but also authoritative:

"You have arrived. Welcome! I have been waiting a long time for you. Today we will have our first lesson. I will introduce you to the element of fire. Are you ready?"

I don't have the time or even the ability to reflect on whether I'm ready or not. I don't even know what it means to be ready. Nervousness is rising in me, and I am completely amazed.

Fire with great glowing embers appears before my eyes. It looks like a combination of volcanic magma and flames. It's enormous, glowing, flowing, sending out sparks. The voice speaks again:

"This is the element of fire. Do not be afraid. Everything is alright. I will introduce you to it, initiate you in it."

Suddenly I am in the centre of the fire and glowing magma. I am fire, and the fire is me. Magnificence, peace, spaciousness. My conscious mind disappears…

…

I begin to wake up. My head slides out of the bag, away from the container of glue. I open my eyes wide and stare around. I look out of the window and see that it's almost dark outside. I close the tin can, carefully wrap the bag around it and tuck it into my hiding place under the bed. I sit at my desk and gaze out of the window, slowly returning to myself. Wow! Where was I? What did I just experience? Whose voice was that?

After a while I get dressed and go to get Ari from his kennel. We set out for an evening stroll across the nearby meadows.

∞

I'm walking through the Ljubljana Clinical Centre, supposedly the most modern hospital in Yugoslavia. I'm dressed in a white uniform and jacket, just like the doctors. My long hair floats around my ears and over the nape of my neck. I feel excellent. I have never felt so good about the fact that dozens of people are looking at me. I'm pushing a patient on a trolley. My job is to wheel patients from one unit to another.

At the end of the second year of high school we'd received an assignment in our Technology and Production class to take a work experience placement for one month during the summer holidays and write a report about it. The purpose was for us to learn about the harsh realities of working life, I guess. I push the trolleys up and down the corridors, either empty or with patients, go on cigarette breaks, and eye up the young nurses (one of them, the blonde Božena, provides me with a truly erotic experience and inspiration which I will certainly draw on later in the afternoon when I get home).

Occasionally the work is pretty shocking and I need a longer cigarette break to calm myself down.

For example, the time a nurse summons me on the intercom to the operating theatre. I walk in and she playfully smiles at me and pushes a long oblong package into my hands. She tucks a document into my pocket and tells me to take the package to the morgue in the basement. Slowly I look down at the package.

"What is it?"

She looks at me seductively.

"It's a leg. A man's leg."

She smiles and winks and waddles off in her clogs. All of a sudden the package seems unbearably heavy in my hands. I walk quickly along the corridors and stairways, trying to find the best position for it. In front of me? Over my shoulder? Under my arm? How are you supposed to carry a man's leg? Especially if it keeps bending at the knee?

Or the time I wheel an elderly man to a remote part of the hospital complex. At first he talks a little, then he makes a gesture with his hands, becomes quiet, and dozes off. When I get to the

60

unit, I announce myself in the office and tell them that I'm supposed to bring the trolley back. I go out for a cigarette for ten minutes to wait until the man has been moved from the trolley. When I knock on the office door again, the nurse tells me that the man died during our journey and I need to wait a few more minutes for them to finish the paperwork. Then I can take him down to the morgue. I'm completely shaken, and as I push him to the morgue, it occurs to me that I was the last person to hear his voice. If I'd done something, reacted in some way, he might still be alive.

And then there is the time when the whole emergency room is getting ready because there's been an explosion in a gas refinery in Serbia and they're bringing the burned and wounded to hospitals all around Yugoslavia because the local hospitals in Pančevo are full. The helicopter lands on the roof of the hospital and we hurry along with two moaning victims covered from head to foot with burns. The nurses run next to us, holding up plastic bottles from which they're supplying the victims' blood with who knows what. The man on my trolley is completely orange. His skin looks as thick as the soles of a pair of work boots. He's struggling to breathe. He lifts his head in pain and stares at me with a blank expression, probably because the muscles in his face are dead. He can only roll his eyes, which are almost hidden under their heavily swollen lids.

Or when, twice in one week, I push a teenage girl along the same route from the reception area to the third floor. The first time they told me that she had tried to commit suicide and they'd saved her at the last minute, and that I should watch her carefully so she doesn't escape. And now, the second time, they tell me that she tried again, and they again saved her at the last minute, and once again that I should watch her carefully so she doesn't escape. We're alone in the lift, both of similar age, somehow connected. She clearly wants to die and I'm assigned to be her guardian, while I have just stolen a supply of scalpels in case I ever decide that I want to cut my own wrists. She holds my hand and looks deep into my eyes. We look at each other in silence. There is a sort of camaraderie between us, trust, recognition. I smile at her when the lift doors open. She sighs when I stop the trolley in front of the doors to the unit. We never see each other again. I think about how long she will be alive as I return by the stairs. And what would have happened if I had kissed her in the lift? Would our lives have evolved differently?

But the most valuable thing by far that happens to me during that month at the Clinical Centre is meeting Iztok. Iztok is a medical student doing his summer rotation, and we hang out and talk during our free time. I discover something completely new. For the first time I have a friend with whom I can talk about the meaning of life, not just on an intellectual level, but in the sense of a humble exploration of the unknown. For the first time I have a friend in whom I can confide vulnerable and painful things about myself, and not hide behind the mask of an all-knowing cool guy. It's the first time in a friendship that I experience openness, trust and deep acceptance. It's the first time in my life that I don't feel alone. Our friendship continues, deepens, intensifies even after our jobs at the Clinical Centre are over. I take the bus to Ljubljana to visit Iztok at the medical college every time I have the chance. Or he comes to visit me. We talk about everything. We exchange books about spirituality and philosophy. Spending time with Iztok nourishes my heart with the nectar of hope.

∞

I'm with Iztok in his room at college. It's almost empty today because it's Sunday morning and most of the students have gone home. We're pretty excited because we're about to do a trip together. I've brought a bottle of Flex stain remover that I bought at the store. Some old Kranj hippies had told us kids about this product, which contained ether as the solvent and would get you totally and mind-blowingly high. All you had to do was drip it into a handkerchief and inhale. It was supposed to be even better than glue.

We sit next to each other, leaning against the wall, and each drip a generous dose into our handkerchiefs. We smile and look thoughtfully down towards our hands. We slowly bring the handkerchiefs to our noses, and then press them against our nostrils and inhale deeply. We do it again and again. Suddenly everything disappears: space, time, the whole world…

"Welcome back. I am glad you came again."

I know that voice. I know the energy, the combination of benevolence and calm authority. It's the same guide that showed me the element of fire. I relax. I'm in a sort of yellowish energy of infinite space and pure vibration.

"Today we will have our next lesson. I will initiate you into time and show you the trajectory of your whole existence. Are you ready?"

I'm all attention. I try to understand what I've just heard.

"Are you ready?"

I somehow say that I am. I don't know how I convey the message, but I do. The voice speaks:

"Excellent. We will start at the end and slowly journey backwards through the future until the present moment. Alright?"

This time he doesn't wait for my permission but just continues:

"First I will show you the end; the end of your existence, the end of you as an individual. Look!"

Suddenly I am in a dimension of cosmic expansion in which I both see and experience something that I can hardly grasp. My dissolution as a being, as an individual, as an entity. The outpouring from this body, this tiny container of my being, into unity again, into all, into existence, the cosmos. Even though it's the end of me, the ultimate personal catastrophe, I feel blissful and completely fulfilled. The experience is gigantic and all encompassing. Before I'm even able to take it in, I hear the voice of my guide again:

"Good. Now we will journey backwards through time and I will show you the key event that will bring your existence to an end in this specific way. So, look!"

I quickly see and at the same time experience an event in which I cannot really recognize anything. Am I in this world or in another one? Is this good or bad? And the voice already leads me on:

"OK, now I will show you the event that will cause you to turn in this direction,"

and in a flash I'm transported to new surroundings, new time, a new context. We travel back in time like this and I can hardly keep up, hardly comprehend. Everything is so fascinating and intense it takes my breath away and I barely remain conscious. We've probably witnessed some twenty events through which we move as if in a sort of cosmic spiral down towards the current moment.

Suddenly our rushing along the spirals of time begins to slow down and then we stop altogether. My guide speaks to me:

"And now I will show you the person who will cause you to go on the path that you have just seen. The person who will direct you on this path, the person who will represent the crucial turning point in your life. Are you ready to see this person?"

I energetically nod, giving a sign that I'm ready. Not that I really know what it means to be ready, not that I really know anything at all, if I'm being honest. Once more, my guide, this time with dramatic emphasis, asks me:

"Are you truly ready?"

I feel more and more anxious but still I nod energetically. My guide announces:

"Good. Now look. Because of this person you will embark on this path!"

Everything goes dark for a few seconds. The tension in me grows and then suddenly there is a sort of window in space through which I see Iztok. I'm amazed. He's sitting on the bed, looking at me, laughing.

I open my eyes in shock. I hold my breath and wait a few seconds for my eyes to get used to the light. Then I turn to the right where Iztok is sitting next to me. I'm astonished to see that he's sitting, watching me, laughing in exactly the same way he was when my eyes were closed. I had seen exactly this scene

when I had my eyes shut, and while I was turned away from him.
I stare at him, inhale deeply, and try to understand what has just
happened.

...

That evening, on the bus home to Kranj, I feel a deep calm,
coming from a new level of self-awareness. Something is getting
integrated into a larger understanding: I am not alone. I am one
with everything. I am both myself, Robert, here and now, and
everything, always and everywhere. I am both a small part and
the whole. The world is not as it seems. The world is more,
immeasurably more than it seems.

∞

I'm rolling on the living room floor with my father. We're
pushing each other, panting. We haven't wrestled like this in a
long time, a very long time.

It was something that both of us frequently enjoyed during
my early years of primary school, though especially him. He'd
trained in judo in his youth and it had become an important part
of his identity. He was constantly telling stories from his judo
days, but above all he liked to spar with me. I enjoyed the
physical contact with him too, but it was not so nice that it always
ended with him making sure he would win. When I was a child, I
had less and less desire to play a game in which I was always
defeated, mostly because of the big difference between us in
weight and physical power. Our sparring matches continued over
the years, especially when I was also going to judo classes, but
they just became more unpleasant because of his constant need to
win, even at the cost of being rough with me. We stopped sparring
altogether during the period of heavy drinking and his move to
Kranj.

Yet today it happens again that, almost as a joke, he
challenges me to a fight, and now we're rolling on the floor and I
sense how it's become more serious. I can hear him panting. I can
smell his sweat. I can see him fighting with all his power and

65

struggling with everything he has. And suddenly I notice to my surprise that I'm able to match him. I'm sixteen years old, taller than him, more agile, much more fit, and I experience the shocking realization that I'm in all ways equal to or even better than him. This realization disorients me. For my whole life I've been living with this strong and dangerous father for whom I felt a sense of awe. I'd learned to be cautious and careful with him and now I sense a completely new dynamic. My self-confidence suddenly grows and I wink at my mother who is sitting stiffly on the couch, nervously watching us, from time to time murmuring:

"Oh, please stop, you two, before someone gets hurt."

I slowly take control of the match until the moment when I pin him down in a stranglehold. Wow, this has never happened. I'm firmly controlling my father, he's powerless, and slowly I begin to tighten the stranglehold. I wait for him to tap his hand three times on the floor or on me, and thus to concede, but he doesn't do it. I gradually tighten the hold. I'm implacable and determined. I hear his increasingly forced breathing. I check to see that his hand is free and that he can tap the floor and concede if he wants to. Yes, both hands are free, and he could surrender, but apparently he doesn't want to. He's kicking a bit, trying to shake me off, but there's no way he can do it because my hold is completely stable. I tighten the stranglehold a little more. His breathing sounds even more laboured. Mother says:

"Oh, please, let him go! Please stop!"

I tell my father to concede but he refuses. He gasps. He gurgles. His breathing stops for a moment and then he taps three times on the floor. I release him immediately, move back slightly, and look at him in amazement. He lies on the floor for a couple of seconds with his face turned downwards, coughing and wheezing. He stands up, spits into a handkerchief, and without a word goes downstairs into the basement and slams the door behind him.

My mother looks at me in astonishment. She's stiff with fear.

I feel something I never have felt before in my life: victorious over my father. I beat him, my all-powerful and fear-inspiring father. He couldn't do a thing to stop me. I get to my feet with a feeling of power and freedom that's entirely new to me.

At the same time I feel a sense of pity. Pity for this man who rather than sincerely congratulating his son, rather than complimenting him and graciously admitting his own defeat, being happy and proud about the development of his only son, who rather than all of these more dignified possibilities can only storm angrily away into his basement den. The same thing would happen when he could no longer beat me at table tennis and he would lose game after game. On one such occasion, he broke the bat against the corner of a cabinet in a fit of rage and desperation, and angrily threw it into the rubbish bin before shutting himself in his room to get drunk.

For the first time I perceive my father as a vulnerable, confused, and insecure creature, and I feel a glimmer of compassion for this lonely man.

∞

I get myself comfortable, pour a generous quantity of the liquid onto a handkerchief and glance at my friends seated next to me on the two small benches under a tree.

We caught the last convenience store open in the old part of Kranj right before it closed and bought a small bottle of Flex stain remover. We've settled down beneath the city's medieval ramparts where we feel safe from possible passers-by and above all from the occasional police officer.

I smile and start to inhale slowly and deeply. In an instant the world disappears and I hear the familiar voice:

"Oh, hello again. Welcome. Today I will show you the cosmos, the space. Are you ready?"

As soon as I nod energetically, I begin to rise, at first slowly, and then faster and faster. This rising, this constant acceleration, takes me in larger and larger spirals into the darkness of the universe. Suddenly I'm among the stars. Here I feel completely at home, as if I've at last arrived at some long-forgotten dwelling place. I'm ecstatic. The speed grows, the dimensions are more and more fantastic, and I gradually disappear into the interstellar spaciousness.

...

Suddenly I return to my body, sitting on the bench in Kranj. I raise my eyes and see my friends looking at me, smiling. They've woken up before me. They ask me where I've been, and tell me that I've been sitting on the bench at a 45-degree angle like a motorcyclist taking a curve. I smile and don't even bother to try and describe my voyage.

A good hour later, as I'm walking back home, I'm still feeling ecstatic with my secure knowing that life is much more than what most people realize. Much, much more.

∞

The main theory I have about my mother and her relationship to me is that she is constantly afraid and worried to the point that she has absolutely no confidence in life in general or in me in particular. Although she sincerely tries to understand, she never succeeds in the slightest. Nevertheless, from time to time she does something so brilliant that it shakes the foundations of this theory of mine.

At the end of my second year in high school I failed in Maths and had to do extra exams in the holidays in order to pass. My mother knew that there was little chance that I could correct my grades without some additional help, and she threw herself into finding a tutor for me. As she would tell me later, she studied all the advertisements in the newspaper and called most of the tutors on the phone, always from work, so I wouldn't know what she was doing. She interrogated each of them closely and eliminated all those who she thought had qualities that would bother me: if they were too old, too conceited, too serious or just not nice enough. A young physicist made the final cut, an independent researcher, and my mother decided to meet with him personally in order to be sure that he was right for me. When she set eyes on the bearded, long-haired, smiling young man wearing a hippyish tunic and white trousers, offering her special tea and enthusiastically recounting that he had just returned from five months of travelling around India, she knew she had found the right one for me.

And she was right. I regularly go now and hang out in Andrej's room where he very efficiently instructs me in mathematics, and then we sit a while longer and drink tea and talk about all sorts of things. I explain to him my understanding of life based on the mystical experiences that I've had: that we are all one, that we are all everything and nothing at all, that we exist and do not exist at the same time, that each of us is both an individual and the whole universe. Andrej listens to me enthusiastically and informs me that my conclusions actually capture the philosophy of yoga. He tells me about yoga, about his teacher, and about his research work in which he's trying to prove physically the existence of prana, or cosmic energy. He explains to me the specifics of Indian music, its rhythms and scales. I look at him, smile, nod, and dissolve with happiness. I have a guru now, a role model, a person who has succeeded in combining within himself deep spirituality, scientific knowledge, and worldly experience, a person who glows with inner peace, clarity, joy, and beauty.

I read all the books he recommends to me. I listen to all the records he lends me. I try to be like him. I try to absorb everything I perceive in him: all his wisdom, knowledge, energy, and inspiration. With Andrej I feel seen, accepted, worthy of attention. Like a sponge, I absorb from him the validation that I have thirsted for my whole life but never received.

Andrej will be my mentor, my inspiration and my support for a long time to come.

∞

"Robert, can I ask you something?" asks the middle-aged man who has picked me up as I was hitch-hiking from Ljubljana to Kranj.

"Of course you can," I answer openly. We're slowly approaching Kranj in his big Audi and I'm in an excellent mood. We've had a great conversation all the way. I don't remember another occasion when a much older man had listened to me with so much attention and had seemed to understand me so well. I feel euphoric from the feeling of being seen and respected.

"Will you hold it against me, Robert, if I ask you something?"

"No, I won't. Why would I hold it against you if you asked me something? Of course I won't."

"Really, Robert, because you know you mustn't," he pressed the point home.

"I won't, I won't," I smile, looking through the window at the green fields.

"Good, Robert," he said. "Then can I hold your dick in my hand?"

His right hand is firmly gripping my genitals even before I grasp the meaning of his words.

For an instant I freeze in shock. Then I say:

"No, no, no way!"

Before I succeed in pushing his hand away, he withdraws it himself.

"Okay, Robert, you don't need to get upset. I was just asking," the apologetic voice of the older man continues.

"No, you did not just ask," I mutter with both hands between my legs. I look through the window again, my pulse racing.

"Alright, Robert, alright. I apologize. Don't hold it against me, please."

"Okay, okay. Could you just let me off here please?"

We're still two kilometres from where I usually get off.

"I can, of course, but I can also drive you a little farther. I promise I won't do anything to you."

"Thanks, just let me off here please."

I cut across the meadows and fields to get home. I'm in shock and feel somehow violated. I can still feel his hand between my legs and I don't know what to do with this feeling. I wonder if the girls that I sometimes grab and fondle under the table or at a dance feel the same way. If they do, then this is also horrible, truly horrible.

Deeply shaken, I unlock the door.

∞

Today it's finally my turn and my heart pounds as I hear my name being called. I walk to the front of the class and stand by the blackboard. I'm scared and happy at the same time, full of hope.

At the beginning of the school year, our Slovenian literature teacher had asked each of us to choose a literary work and prepare a presentation about the personal reflections triggered by the reading of the work. For the first time in my entire educational experience, I had actually been inspired by an assignment I'd been given. Following a suggestion from a friend, I had chosen a dark and somewhat depressing poem by Slovenian poet Alojz Gradnik, and the more I had read it, the more enthusiastic I had become, because the work carried my thoughts into ever more existential and philosophical realms. For weeks and weeks I had rehearsed reciting the poem and polishing the text for my presentation, for the first time in my life truly enjoying something connected to school.

And now I'm standing in front of the class believing that at last my time has come. I've hardly functioned during these years of high school, never having the basic motivation and focus to work either in class or at home. I'm considered a pretty cool guy (the senior girls even voted me "the most worthy of a sin" in the whole school), but I'm a pretty sorry case when it comes to grades and academic success. Yet I have the feeling that today I will finally be able to show everybody that I have something to offer in that field as well.

I recite the poem perfectly and then present my reflections. Everything goes smoothly, my initial stage fright fading and giving way to a calm but passionate delivery. I finish, take a breath, and smile slightly at all of my schoolmates who are staring at me dumbly. Then I glance at my teacher who is looking thoughtfully down at her hands. I slowly sit down in my place. Silence reigns for a moment, then the teacher finally lifts her eyes, and gazes at me in her typically superior manner.

"All right Kržišnik. I'll give you a C."

I stare at her without speaking. My pride and good feeling collapse into anxiety. My inner world crumbles. I expected an excellent grade, and I received a merely average one. Somehow I manage to speak:

"Why only a C?"

The teacher answers with a cynical smile:

"Because we both know you didn't write that yourself."

My heart pounds loudly and my voice shakes as I answer:

"I wrote that completely by myself. I swear…"

"Come on, we both know that that's not true…"

The teacher sighs, closes the grade book, stands up and begins to explain some new material. I no longer exist for her.

If I would have had the inner power and clarity, I would have stood up and repeated that I had written the presentation myself, that it was unacceptable for her to so casually accuse me of cheating without proof, that this was the first time I'd ever derived any happiness from learning, that it was wrong of her to immediately destroy that happiness, and finally that she could ask me any question she wanted in connection to the poem and my reflections on it and I would be able to answer.

Maybe I would criticize her even more sharply for how pathetic it was that she'd been abusing her power in such an autocratic way all these years, how she'd exploited us just to stroke her own ego instead of supporting us and encouraging our love of literature, how all she had ever done was to shame and threaten us.

Or maybe I would just scream at her and kick the tables and chairs around the classroom, and keep screaming until the whole world was demolished.

But I don't do any of that. I just stare blindly in front of myself, and return to the familiar world of failure, numbness, loneliness, and alienation.

I have totally had it with school, with the misuse of power by these incompetent teachers and with this whole lousy system.

∞

I'm sixteen years old and I will end my own life today. With suicide. The circumstances are ideal. My parents have left for the seaside and will be gone for a week. I have the house to myself and will be able to prepare and carry out the deed in peace. I just need to drink my morning tea first.

I feel very calm, serene, and satisfied with my decision. I've thought about it for a long time and have finally reached a sense of inner peace. As a result of the mystical experiences I've accumulated already, I'm convinced that life is something much wider and deeper than what we understand. I'm convinced that life is eternal and that the individual enters a higher dimension when the body dies and is liberated from its physical dimension. If this is true, then I want to experience the transformation as soon as possible, not just vegetate for decades in my current pointless condition. If it's not true and life is limited to the existence of the physical body and there is nothing left after the body's death, then it doesn't matter anyway how long I live, since life is a senseless momentary instant in the face of the vastness of the universe. In that case, I have no desire to try to prolong this instant of existence anyway I can. I will end my life for all of these reasons, and the more I accept this decision, the more excited and joyful I become about what I will soon experience.

I've already gone on my morning walk with Ari and bid my dear friend farewell. Now I'm writing my suicide note to my parents: some sincere regrets, some effort to instil a feeling of guilt, a little of this, a little of that. I remember seeing in a film how people sometimes commit suicide in a bath filled with hot water and that strikes me as very comfortable, romantic even. While the tub is filling I get the scalpel ready, one of the collection that I picked up a year ago when I was working at the Clinical Centre. The tub is now full. My suicide note lies dramatically in the middle of the bathroom floor. The scalpel is ready in my right hand.

I slowly begin to cut my left wrist. The sharp sting surprises me. I only make a superficial scratch. I will have to cut deeper and my organism is already in panic. I try again and again, fast, then slow, holding the scalpel at different angles, and in the end I have about fifteen superficial cuts on my wrist and am hardly bleeding at all. I simply cannot cut deeper and inflict so much pain upon myself. What should I do?

I suddenly remember the electric knife we have in the kitchen. I put down the scalpel and head into the kitchen. This will be quick: I'll just press the button and, before I even feel the pain, the blood will be gushing out of me.

But it doesn't go that smoothly. I realize with disappointment that the knife isn't even that sharp, that it's more of a saw than a knife. I try it on my wrist and the electric knife slowly starts to shred my skin, causing considerable pain. It's not going to work. I sit down defeated.

Then another idea comes to me. My mother works at the hospital and has complained for years about back pain. She has a whole pharmacy in a drawer in the living room and I can probably find some pills there that would be effective for suicide. I sit on the floor in front of the drawer and systematically study all the little boxes. About five of them seem suitable: sleeping pills, muscle relaxants and pain killers. How do I know which are the best? I open the boxes one after another, shake half the pills from each into my hand, and gulp them down. I put the boxes back in the drawer and sit down again. Now there's no way back. The excitement within me grows stronger.

I open the drinks cupboard and take two long pulls of whisky just for good measure. I fill the bath to the brim with more water, smilingly take my clothes off and slide into the embrace of the warm water.

These are my last minutes, maybe even my last seconds, in this life. I feel tranquil, satisfied, free and joyful even.

Farewell home. Farewell friends. Farewell Ari. Farewell world. Farewell, you confused, painful, unpleasant, senseless life. Farewell everything. Welcome the unknown. Welcome the beyond.

I slowly sink down towards peace, silence, as if sinking into a dream. Everything is calm, serene. It seems like the light is slowly fading.

Suddenly I am roused by stomach cramps.

Oh no, I'm going to throw up. No, no! I don't want to…

I try to relax, to calm down, but the cramps keep getting stronger. Saliva begins to accumulate in my throat and I know where that leads. I start to vomit even before I manage to climb out of the bathtub and lean over the toilet. I throw up in violent convulsions that seize my body, that practically lift me up, vomit spraying out of my mouth, my nose, my eyes. Even though my stomach is empty, the cramps continue, and a greenish grey slime oozes out of my mouth and nose. Mostly into the toilet, but some misses.

When the cramps and vomiting finally subside, I burst into tears. I slide onto the floor sobbing loudly, and cry and shake there for a while longer.

I can't even kill myself. I fail even at that.

My crying subsides after a while. I wash, and drag myself into my room, lie on my bed, and cover my head. In an instant I fall into a deep, deep sleep, into the darkness.

…

Something familiar, a sound from very, very far away awakens me, but I don't know what it is.

Oh, Ari is barking. He's calling me.

I open my eyes and look out from under the blanket. Evening has fallen outside. I've slept a good eight hours. Dizzily I pull myself out of bed. My whole body is somehow anaesthetized, only slowly coming back to life. Ari keeps barking and whining. The realization that he misses me, wants me, is calling me, and the fact that he loves me triggers in me the will to live.

I get dressed with a sense of vertigo. I drink some water, fetch my dog and we set out on a long walk. Life appears fresh and new, and I feel expanded by something I've not experienced before, some internal vastness. Ari runs happily back and forth in the forest, occasionally stopping and sniffing the air, then racing off between the trees again.

...

The next day I learn from a friend that I shouldn't have mixed so many different pills together, that they react with each other, and that's why I threw up. I should have emptied just one of the bottles.

Oh well…

Four: To Africa for Freedom

I'm standing in front of my collection of LPs on the shelf and wondering what to play. Finally I select Keith Jarrett's Köln concert again. Recently that's practically all I've been listening to. It's the most amazing thing I've ever heard. As if my soul recognizes Jarrett's soul. As if I'm being embraced by cosmic perfection and it's helping me to integrate everything that I've experienced during the last year.

Although I didn't succeed in committing suicide, I've begun to feel a completely new quality in myself, something that reverberates inside me like an intimate secret that I keep from the world: the realization that I am actually entirely free in this life, because I can leave it anytime I want to! I begin to experiment with the first budding growth of this inner freedom and lack of limitations, with this lightness. I can leave anytime. Anytime.

The other thing that's growing inside me is an increasing curiosity about the nature of life, the nature of existence. What is it that I experience as life? How should I understand this life where there are so many realities, in which I can travel among stars and through time, where I can see other creatures and am taught by some kind of guides, where dimensions of space alternate and collapse? This isn't just an intellectual game of ideas for me, because actually such intimate existential questions are what determine my daily experience of life to a great degree. They also provoke a very practical enquiry: what do I want to experience in this life? How do I want to live it?

The more I deal with these questions, the deeper I go into an unknown and ambiguous space. The only thing that's crystal clear is what I don't want. I don't want to live an automatic life within the expected social templates: education – job – marriage – family – retirement – death. I want to be liberated from these patterns and expectations, to be free, but I still don't know what I would like to create with this freedom, what I would like to experience...

Ah, I won't even turn the record over. I'm going to listen to the first side again.

∞

I gaze at the nice bearded young man who is showing us slides in the school hall while he narrates stories about his months of travelling on a moped around South America. My mouth drops open with sheer enthusiasm at what I'm hearing from this amazing man (who I cannot know then will one day become my dear friend) and at the range of possibilities that are expanding in my mind. I occasionally glance over at the teachers who are sitting in the hall with us. I wonder if they knew what they were getting into when they invited this guy to our school. The younger teachers are giggling and even smirking. The older ones are staring dumbly and with dead seriousness at the big projection screen.

Tomo - that's the man's name - is open and relaxed as he explains how he chose a little moped for his travels because he could carry it on his shoulders across fast-flowing rivers and through muddy bogs. He tells us how the moped broke down in the middle of a tropical rainforest and how he was trying to fix it for hours and hours when all of a sudden a jaguar crossed the path about twenty metres away from him, stopped for a moment to get a good look at him, and then soundlessly disappeared into the vegetation. About how he gathered a bagful of psychedelic mushrooms among the cowpats while crossing the endless Argentinian pampas, how he ate them and had many magical experiences while driving his moped, a story which ended with him joyfully embracing and fondling the wife of the captain of police in some village who then threw him in the local jail for two months. And about his many meetings with native people in the heart of the rainforest. About sleeping under the stars and the fullness of each moment. About the enchantment of life. About love. About meaning and meaninglessness. About everything...

I drink in Tomo's words and his slides, and all of a sudden it's clear to me what I want to do with my freedom: I want to travel. I want to taste the world, to get to know it, to enjoy all its manifold forms and possibilities, and then I will be able to decide how I want to live the rest of my life.

∞

I sit at my desk and study a laminated map of the world. I've been poring over this map for months and months now, slowly developing my plan to make a big step into a new life. I'm intuitively drawn to Africa, perhaps because of all the documentaries I've seen about African flora and fauna, or perhaps because Africa has always been presented in school and in the Yugoslav media as a continent of authenticity, joy, honesty, beauty, and purity. Perhaps because I've despaired of the possibilities offered by the first world culture and I long for something more genuine. Perhaps because I see that I can get there overland. Perhaps also because I have a very naive impression about the reality of Africa and am fantasizing about how I will find myself in some paradise of jungle villages far from everything, maybe that I will even be the first white man to visit, and I'll be given some special status as an honoured wise man and will lie around in a hammock with half-naked young women gently waving fans above me. Looking at my map, something draws me to Somalia as the country to head for. It isn't too far to go and it's on the Indian Ocean, so maybe I can continue by boat from there on to Asia…

It doesn't even cross my mind to mention my plans to my parents, like I didn't tell them about my plans to kill myself a year ago – this is an escape plan, another attempt of mine to escape from the meaninglessness of this life.

At last my plan is perfected down to the smallest detail. Well, at least for the first couple of days, and after that things will work themselves out. A schoolfriend who's in charge of our class funds will give me back the money that's been put by to finance the one-week school trip at the end of the year. I'll buy a rucksack and a sleeping bag with that money, and whatever is left over can be used for the expenses of the first weeks. After that I will somehow figure out how to make ends meet. I'll run away from home at the beginning of summer when the Croatian coast is already packed with tourists from all over Europe, so I won't attract attention as I hitchhike south and out of the country. And I trust that possibilities will open up to me as I go, and if not, well, I still have the option of leaving this life.

∞

I nervously look at my watch as I sit on the train, waiting for it to pull out of Ljubljana station. Although it's not really likely, I'm still afraid that I will suddenly run into my father. So far the morning has gone completely according to plan. When my parents had gone to work I packed all the things I needed into a bag, went to my schoolmate's house where I'd left my sleeping bag and big expedition backpack, shoved everything into it, and caught a bus to Ljubljana. I left a goodbye note at home in which I lied, saying that I was going to Germany and the Netherlands, this in order to slow them down if they decided to look for me. And now I'm sitting on the train to Koper, Slovenia's port on the Adriatic Sea, with lots of tourists, and I feel that my big journey is truly beginning. I decided not to hitchhike after all because I was afraid I'd stand out too much. I plan to stick to trains and buses for a while until I'm in the middle of Yugoslavia.

When the train finally leaves the station, I sink back into my seat with relief.

I'm seventeen years old and I'm heading into the unknown. I'm leaving my safe and predictable life, and going – well, who knows where. I have a little money in my wallet, some clothes, some books, some cassettes with my favourite music, my passport, and a healthy body. It occurs to me that my plan is not complete down to the last detail. For example, I don't have a map with me. But all the same, I smile to myself and let out a big sigh.

∞

I'm just beginning to sink into sleep when I'm woken by a quiet rustling across my legs, which are stretched out over the central aisle on the bus. Hajji, an older Afghan man, is trying to pass quietly without waking me, but his long robe brushes over my bare feet.

The first few weeks of my travels have passed in a flash as if on a movie screen. I spent two weeks living on a campsite on the Croatian coast, all alcohol and guitar music, and frequent moments of solitude on the beach when I was overcome with feelings of being lost and uncertain, tears streaming silently down my face. Then in Sarajevo I met a Turkish lad my own age named Kaya who was living in Germany and was hitchhiking to Turkey to visit his parents. We hitchhiked together through the rest of Yugoslavia and now we're travelling across Bulgaria in a convoy of empty buses and trucks that the extremely kind Hajji has bought in Germany and is now taking to Afghanistan. The drivers are German hippies of all sorts. We sleep in the buses along with Hajji's family, and the smile on my face is getting bigger and bigger, with the worries in my heart disappearing. I've begun to have a sense that the world is filled with good people and things will always work out somehow. My confidence in life grows and, at the peak of all this good feeling, I treated myself to a Bulgarian beer with the last change I had.

Hajji's robe once again silently brushes against my legs as he carefully steps over me. He probably was just going to look for something in the back of the bus and is now returning to the front. There is so much tenderness in him, so much care for all of us who are travelling along with him in his caravan.

∞

Somewhere in the middle of Bulgaria I write in my diary:

"Today I'm happy and full of the swing of life. Alone with myself, alone in the whole world, and free, completely free. No more of the bonds which have tied me from birth until yesterday. Now nobody expects anything of me. Even before I was born, my life path was roughly planned out according to the standards of society and also of course the expectations of my parents. I was given the potential for self-determination only occasionally and within limited parameters. I was always the one that had to listen to other people's version of the truths of life and meekly accept them. And the common denominator was that it didn't matter what I thought and felt, that I should hide all of that deep inside me, that I had to prove to those around me that I would fulfil those expectations and only then would everyone be satisfied. Now, for the first time in life, I'm becoming acquainted with authenticity. And I'm beginning to truly live my own life."

∞

I'm walking through a deeply slumbering town somewhere in the south of Turkey at around two in the morning. I have no idea where I am. After countless hours of hitchhiking, this is where my last ride, a truck driver who insisted on calling me Georgie, dropped me off. Suddenly three figures appear in front of me: two in military uniform, the third in civilian dress. The civilian indicates that he wants to see my passport. He looks at it and consults with the two soldiers. Then he smiles at me, and gestures that I should go with them. I hold my hands in front of me, asking if I'm being arrested. All three start laughing and shake their heads. I am to go with them so I can get something to eat and a place to sleep.

They take me to a small barracks and give me some food. They put a few chairs together and indicate I should lie down and sleep there awhile. For a long time I can't fall asleep. I stare at the ceiling and think about the crazy pace of life since I began my travels. I think about how long I tolerated Kaya and his grumpiness, just because I didn't know anyone else and because his parents fed me and gave me a place to stay in Turkey. And how, when I started to hitchhike from Ankara towards Africa, I suddenly realized that I didn't even know what country came next, which border I needed to cross, which cities I should aim for. And how in the lobby of some hotel with a large map of the region on the wall I scribbled on my hand the name of a Turkish town called Antalya on the Syrian border. Later on, sitting in a truck and driving far into the night, the truck driver asked me why I wanted to go to Antalya of all places. It took me a long time and a mixture of languages to answer his question, whereupon he laughed and shook his head:

"No, no, no, Antalya no!"

He stopped at a roadside tavern and, with the help of someone who knew English, he explained to me that if I wanted to go to Syria I had to hitchhike towards Antakya, not towards Antalya, which was in the opposite direction. Well, they always told me at school that my handwriting was a catastrophe. The driver even helped me to find a ride back towards Ankara, then he winked, and roared off into the darkness.

And I'm still moved by the memory of the taxi driver who in the middle of that same night stopped for me when I was standing on a road on the outskirts of Ankara, hitchhiking in the right direction at last. He assured me that he wanted no money, took me to his extremely modest home in the middle of a poor dusty village, and woke his wife to rustle up something for me to eat in the practically empty kitchen. He invited me to sleep for a couple of hours and then woke me at dawn and we set out for the road together, him to work, me to hitchhike towards Syria.

So much goodness, so much kindness and hospitality wherever I've been…

…

One of the soldiers wakes me up with a shake of the shoulder and offers me breakfast, and then they all indicate that I should leave now. The officers are coming and won't be pleased if they find a young hippy sleeping in a military building. I thank them, throw my backpack over my shoulder, and go on my way.

∞

I'm standing on the dockside of the cargo port in Aqaba in southern Jordan, staring at a white passenger ship which is tied up at the end of the dock about two hundred metres away. There's no passenger terminal here though. Perhaps it's refuelling or something.

It's hot, I'm tired, without energy and also without much hope. I've been walking up and down this dockside for two hours. Against all the rules, a kind head of security has allowed me to go from one cargo ship to another to ask if anyone will take me on board as a deckhand to pay my passage across the Red Sea to Africa. Everyone just smiles nicely at me and says that's not the way it works and they can't help me. And now I'm staring at that white ship that's so far away and wondering whether it's even worth walking all the way out to it when I already can guess what the outcome will be.

My journey across the Middle East has exhausted me. First I hit a wall on the Turkish-Syrian border because I didn't have a visa and they told me I had to go back to Ankara and apply for one at the Syrian embassy. I begged and begged, saying that I was only passing through Syria, that I wouldn't be there for even one full day, and so on and so forth. Eventually they had pity on me and sent a telex to the Foreign Ministry in Damascus and, what do you know, the next day a special transit permit arrived, allowing me to cross the country in a convoy of vehicles that was gathering that morning.

But again, when I got to the Syrian-Jordanian border, I was told that I wouldn't be able to cross without a visa. I chatted with the official for a while and we realized that Yugoslavia and Jordan were great friends. So much so that in the end, he gave me a stamp in my passport which allowed me to stay in Jordan for one month. He urged me to come back to him if I wanted to stay longer and he would take care of everything.

I finally decide to drag myself over to that white ship because I'm completely sweaty anyway and I have nothing to lose. Who knows? Maybe a miracle will happen. Because miracles, it turns out, happen to me pretty regularly. For example, that I travelled through all of Syria to Amman in Jordan in a big, brand new Mercedes Benz with an open-minded and pleasant Jordanian. And that I then stayed for a couple of days in Amman in the exceptionally lovely home of another Jordanian. That when hitchhiking from Amman to Aqaba I was picked up by an enormous and brand-new truck driven by Indian Sikhs who half-way there invited me to sleep at the house of one of them. They fed me and even offered me the first joint of my life, which I smoked nervously only to end up feeling nothing special.

Yes, miracles do happen. That becomes obvious to me when I'm finally standing in front of the white passenger ship and watching the sailors jumping into the sea for a swim to cool off, yelling to each other ... in Serbian, a language I speak fluently, and I notice shining on the bow of the ship the name of the Montenegrin poet Petar Petrović Njegoš. They're Yugoslavs! The sailors tell me later that their ship and its crew has been hired by a Jordanian company, and that they will of course take me on board free of charge, and what's more, they'll give me a cabin, food, free drinks, that I don't need to worry about anything, because I'm one of them. I am "their" Slovenian.

I so much appreciate Yugoslavia, where we all belong, although we have four official languages, three religions, six republics. But it doesn't matter: we're all Yugoslavs.

The next day we arrive at the Port of Suez and I step for the first time on African soil.

∞

The raised voices of a crowd not too far away are just rousing me from sleep when all of a sudden a large box lands in my lap. I open my eyes and see that people on the platform of the train station are throwing all sorts of bags and boxes through the window into the compartment, everything flying directly into the laps of me and my Tanzanian friend Joseph, who is also slowly coming to his senses on the bench opposite me. First we just stare dumbly and then we start to catch all the things so they won't hit our knees, stacking them neatly on the floor. All of sudden the people outside start to push an old woman in a black robe through the window. Disbelieving, Joseph and I almost laugh as we catch her so she doesn't fall to the floor. Yes, that's the way it is. People board trains in Egypt through all openings that are available, not just through the doors. They already know that it will be a long night and there are not enough wooden benches for everyone. It's clear that the time for peaceful sleep has passed and that there will be quite a crowd on the train from here to Cairo. Joseph and I smile at each other as the train fills to overflowing and we're squeezed tighter into the mass of bodies.

Life on my Odyssey races forward with amazing speed. It's not the first time I've found myself on my way to Cairo. Six days ago I hitchhiked from Suez to Cairo. For the first couple of kilometres I rode by donkey cart and then travelled a little faster with trucks. I slept at the house of a police officer in Cairo. He told me how much he missed his son, who he saw only rarely since his divorce, and he even slipped a little money into my hand for my travel expenses. I used the money to buy a ticket for a two-day third-class rail ticket to Aswan, where once a week a boat stopped that went across Lake Nasser to Wadi Halfa in Sudan. I hung around in Aswan for a few days, swam in the lake, and got to know the Sudanese and the Tanzanians who were also waiting for the ferry. Unfortunately, things didn't go as smoothly this time and when the boat arrived, they didn't let me on it because I didn't have a visa for Sudan. It didn't matter how much I and my new Sudanese friends begged. And now I'm here on the train with Joseph who has the same problem as me, heading back to Cairo. How I will get hold of twenty US dollars to buy a visa, and then the money to survive waiting for two weeks for it to be approved, in this city of millions is not clear to me. The people I talked to on the train told me that I should look for a job, but the best offer I've got so far is to clean in a guest house for one US dollar a day.

∞

"Come on, man, stop whining and feeling sorry for yourself!"

Diggo raises his voice when I explain to him that I don't know what to do here in Cairo. He stares into my eyes with a slight smile on his face.

"What's the matter with you? Look at this…" he says and grabs the skin of my forearm. "What's that? What's that?"

I stare at my new friend from Tanzania and try to figure out what he's saying.

"That's white skin! White skin! Now look at me!"

He raises his tee shirt and I look at the furrows in the hollow of his stomach.

"What you see on my black skin is my story, boy. Seven months ago I came on a truck from Tanzania to Cairo, on my way to Alexandria to get a job on a cargo ship, and here, in Cairo, only a few streets away, I was attacked by men with knives. They took everything I had and left me in a pool of blood. Passers-by took me to a hospital where they sewed me up. And then I had to figure out a way to get to my mother in Australia, because with these injuries I can't work on any ship. I asked for some money at the Tanzanian Embassy, and for some at the Indian Embassy, because my dead father was from India, and also at the Australian Embassy. Even the British Embassy gave me some, though I don't really know why…"

He laughs and then continues:

"And now I have a British Airways ticket to Australia in my pocket, and a passport with a visa for Australia. If I had white skin like you do, I'd probably have a first-class ticket…."

He laughs again and looks in my eyes.

"So, my friend, my brother, you have time on your hands, so why not make use of it. If you're going to sit around complaining, you won't get anywhere. If you use your brains and your hands and your heart, the whole world is yours. You get it?"

I stare at him with my mouth open. I get it. Yeah, I really get it.

So I go out onto the street. When people talk to me, I tell them, sort of by the way, that I'm hungry. And someone invites me to lunch. And he tells me that he knows a Sudanese guy who studied in Yugoslavia and takes me to meet him. And to this guy I say, over a coffee, that I don't have anywhere to sleep. And he takes me to another Sudanese guy who studied medicine in Yugoslavia but then joined the resistance in Sudan only a few tests short of graduation. When the resistance was put down, he had to flee from Sudan. He lost his scholarship and all his documentation and now he works the desk at the cheapest hotel in Cairo, where he invites me to sleep for free in the dormitory.

This becomes my temporary home and shelter even though the water in the bathroom only runs for one hour a day, which of course is when we fill empty cans to pour water over our sweaty bodies. I figure out that churches are full of money so I decide to focus on them. And, sure enough, after a few frustrating attempts, I find a bearded priest named Father Anastasi in a Coptic Orthodox Church who hugs me – this is after a slightly dramatized recital of my story – and tucks a ten-pound note into my pocket and invites me to come and stay with him and he will take care of me.

In the month that follows, I have many deep conversations with Father Anastasi who I begin to view as my spiritual guide. I get a hundred Egyptian pounds from him, plus money for a visa for Sudan, and full room and board in the seminary. I give a third of the money to Diggo to thank him. He hugs me, winks, and says that I'm actually not as white as he thought at first. Once again I board the train for Aswan, this time in air-conditioned second class, armed with a Sudanese visa and some money in my pocket.

∞

I slowly wake up with a strange feeling of discomfort and slight panic. It takes a few seconds for me to realize that the feeling is caused by a human heel that's stuck in my mouth. I'm lying on the floor of another train, this time heading through the desert night of North Sudan, a crowd of sleeping people all around me, and somehow the heel of a man in a white robe sleeping on a wooden bench has found its way into my mouth. I slowly and respectfully take hold of the sole of his foot, guide it away from my head, and sit up. This isn't going to work anymore. I'm not going to get any worthwhile sleep here. It would be better to go back to the roof of the train where all my Tanzanian friends are. Since I won't sleep, I might as well breathe better air.

As I climb up to the roof of the train, which is slowly making its way through the sandy desert, I put together in my mind the events of the recent past. I waited in Aswan for a couple of days with hundreds of Sudanese and a handful of Tanzanians. I will never forget those beautiful evenings under the shimmering desert stars when the Sudanese made a great circle and sang their traditional songs late into the night.

When the boat finally came, we all crowded onto it and for two days chugged slowly across Lake Nasser to Sudan. I spent most of the time with the Tanzanians who had given up on their long search for employment on the ships in Alexandria and intended to continue looking in Port Sudan. They told me of the beauties of their country, of their dreams of one day returning home with lots of money, to buy a house, get married, open a restaurant or a shop. They gave me the addresses of their relatives and friends who would certainly take care of me if I ever found myself in Tanzania. Well, if Somalia doesn't turn out to be the fairy tale land I imagine, then maybe I will go to Tanzania.

I'm back on the roof. My crazy friends are dancing in the sand storm billowing around the train as it wheezes along, laughing and singing reggae hits. When they see me, they're even happier, invite me to join them, and we all sing together.

I can hardly remember the life I was living only a couple of months ago.

∞

I carefully open the gates and slowly walk through the dusty streets lined with the high walls of Arab courtyards. I feel like Jesus, or at least how I imagine he might have felt. I have long freshly washed hair. I'm dressed in the white dzellaba given to me by the family who have taken me in and at whose house I've slept for the past few weeks in Omdurman, Sudan. I walk majestically along the empty streets. My hair ripples in the wind and I'm certain I look amazing. I'm immensely satisfied with myself until a stone hits me in the back and I hear laughter. I turn around and spot a group of young kids following me and grinning at this strange vision: a long-haired white guy wearing a djellaba.

I continue walking, though somewhat less majestically. I'm even becoming a little bit nervous. I'm wondering how I'm going to get out of this situation. If I try to chase them away, they'll just laugh at me even more. So I can only ignore them. Perhaps they'll get tired of following me… Of course that doesn't happen, so I decide on a discreet and dignified display of power that will hopefully instil some respect in them. I see a two-metre wide and equally deep ditch beside the street. It's filled to the brim with muddy, filth-laden water. I make up my mind to jump over it. That will let them know that a muscular body hides under this shapeless robe, that I'm potentially dangerous.

Calmly, without breaking my stride, I launch myself over the ditch – but once in mid-air, I'm flooded with horror. I realize that I can't extend my leg to land on the other side of the ditch because the djellaba stops me half way.

As I slowly climb out of the ditch, covered in muck, and the kids fall about laughing, I understand why trousers are more suitable for athletic performances.

After my failed messianic walk, I shower, wash my djellaba and hang it over a rope in the courtyard, and sit on the bed. The grandfather of the family is sitting on the bed next to mine. We sleep next to each other in the courtyard because it's a little cooler than in the house. He slowly tucks a cigarette between his lips and rummages around for his lighter. Once again I witness the record-breaking speed-smoking that I watch with amazement day after day. The grandfather inhales the cigarette smoke deeply, coughs his head off until his lungs are emptied, and then once again pulls on the cigarette, exhales by coughing, and inhales once more. In less than a minute only the filter remains. Why in all these years of life he didn't get used to removing the cigarette from his lips when he's overcome with coughing remains a mystery to me. Maybe he's just sick of life.

I lie down and look at the endless sky slowly turning to the red colour of the desert sunset. I'm having a great time in Omdurman. Although I didn't manage to get a visa for Somalia from the embassy in Khartoum, and although the little money friends had managed to collect for my visa application was stolen by someone on the bus, I'm enjoying the warmth of the people and the hospitality of my new friends. I'm enjoying therefore the two things I wanted when I planned this trip at home: total freedom and the chance to travel the world and meet its people. I'm also getting to know the other side of freedom, which is responsibility. I have to figure everything out all by myself. I have no one to cry to when I feel sorry for myself, or to tell sad stories to about my difficult childhood. I have no one to call on the phone and get me out of a pickle.

A small shining light moving quickly and quite low across the sky rouses me from my thoughts. It's not blinking, just slightly swinging from left to right as it moves across the dark red sky. Suddenly it's joined by another light and they move together, silently and rapidly. I jump out of bed with excitement. I want to follow the two lights for as long as I can over the walls of the courtyard. They're certainly not airplanes or helicopters but something I've never seen before. My heart is pounding by the time they disappear over the horizon. Have I just seen my first UFO? Or two even? What else could it have been?

I look towards the grandfather to see if he's noticed the lights. He's sitting bleakly on his bed and lighting another cigarette.

∞

"Hey, mister, heeey, miiiisteeer, heeyyy…"

A distant voice reaches me. I slowly wake up and begin to feel the shaking, the noise, the sense of hanging in mid-air. The next instant I realize where I am: I'm sleeping on the roof of a train. I open my eyes and roll quickly back towards the centre of the roof in my sleeping bag. I had slid all the way to the edge. I smile gratefully to the two other young men who are sitting on the roof and who've woken me just in time. They wag their heads smiling as if to say: what an interesting little guy, in a sleeping bag on a sloping roof.

As I had no money to buy a ticket and was informed that travelling on the roof of the train was free, I've conducted detailed research into train roofs during this five-day trip from north to south Sudan. The cargo wagons have much flatter roofs but they're not springy or soft, and you bounce around an awful lot. And, besides, they're made of metal and get terribly cold at night. The roofs of passenger carriages are slanted and are only flat in the very middle, but they're springy and they're made of wood coated with tar: sleeping on the passenger carriages is more comfortable but also more dangerous. I've heard that on each trip a couple of people fall from the crowded roofs, but of course the train doesn't stop for such trivialities and those who fall usually become food for various wild animals.

During the day I usually sit in the shady space between the cargo wagons, watch the savannah passing by, and sing all the songs I can remember. Sometimes I illegally wander through the passenger compartments despite not having a ticket, and if I do, someone always invites me to lunch – most often soldiers who are there to guard the train, since war has just broken out between North and South Sudan. In the evening I climb back up to the roof of the train with my sleeping bag.

I've grown completely accustomed to this daily life, one that lacks any predictability, where I step into the unknown from minute to minute and move on again long before anything becomes familiar. Somehow life simply flows through me and I watch it all as if I'm watching a film. Calmly, serenely, with curiosity.

After a couple of days we arrive in Wau where hopefully I will get some kind of a ride to the south, towards Uganda. Or I won't. Something will come up. As my grandmother used to say: "It has never happened that nothing happened."

∞

Finally all forty-five of us are settled on the bed of the truck. We're packed like sardines one next to the other and have arranged our bags neatly under our bottoms. We're quite stable and there's little danger that the wild ride along jungle roads will throw us out of the truck.

Already after only half a day of driving – the whole journey will take five days – we've got stuck at a river crossing because the metal bridge is so rusted that it's started to sag. We'll have to wait two days before someone comes to repair it.

The search for a ride to Juba in South Sudan turned out to be much more difficult than I'd expected. Because of the civil war, south Sudanese living in the north were ordered by President Nimeiry to move back to their homelands. Their misfortune was my good luck when, after ten days' wait, I got a space on this UNICEF truck transporting a group of southerners back to the south.

And now we're like a big family. We stop in various villages to eat – as usual everyone is feeding me. We sleep in the open, once in a fairy tale glade in the tropical forest, filled with hundreds of giant fireflies. I talk the most to a primary school teacher, a very peaceful and gentle middle-aged man. I ask him why there are suddenly so many flies and he tells me that we're approaching the region near the Zaire jungle, the home of the tsetse fly which carries sleeping sickness. I wave my hands in a panic, trying to get the flies way, and he calmly smiles and tells me I don't need to wave them all away, only the ones whose wings fold over each other when they land: those are the tsetse flies. Of course I'm hardly calm enough to examine the anatomical structure of every fly that lands on my bare thigh, so I spend the next hours continuing to wave my arms madly.

The truck breaks down two days before the end of the trip. The driver and a couple of men work on the engine while the rest of us stretch out in the shade of the jungle. Now and again a truck or jeep comes by, stops, and people offer to help, lending tools and other things. I get into a conversation with one of the passing locals. When I tell him I'm from Yugoslavia, he smiles and tells me that he knows a Yugoslav who lives in Juba and is working on a bridge-building project. But unfortunately he doesn't know anything about how I can find him, well, only that he has a grey Land-Rover with the registration number EE-7600. All Land-Rovers in this country are grey, so I try to remember the number. Of course I cannot know then that I will remember that number my whole life.

I begin to realize at this time that I can also give something back – I can smile, I can play with a child, help people and luggage on and off the truck – so that not everything rotates around me and the help I need. All the people around me live a much a harder life than me, but still they give and give, and help and encourage and smile.

On the next to last day of our trip, we arrive at a river crossing where two other trucks are already waiting. The river is fast and turbulent and has risen because it's the end of the rainy season. There's no bridge and we will just have to wait until the flow goes down again in order to ford the river. Nobody knows how long we will have to wait, maybe a few days, maybe a week, but nobody is particularly bothered. I also think it's fine, at least until the evening, when the mosquitoes come out.

There are billions of them. They bite in hordes, drinking my blood constantly and it's impossible to get rid of them. The biggest project is to take a dump, because I have no manoeuvring space for defence, and I come back to the truck irritated and desperate. I spend the night soaked in my own sweat, deep inside my sleeping bag, but at least the mosquitoes can't get at me there. By the next morning I know that I won't survive another night here and I arrange with a strong young man from the neighbouring village to carry my backpack across the river, which he knows like the back of his hand, and I will somehow wade after him to the other side. I ask him about crocodiles and he says:

"No, no worries, no crocodiles here. They're much lower down the river, at least two hundred metres."

Very comforting.

And so we slowly wade across, our legs sinking deep into the mud, the surprisingly powerful current reaching all the way up to our shoulders. A few times it carries me away, and I have to swim hard before I can stabilize myself again. All the while, my fellow travellers watch from the river banks and cheer us on. When we finally get to the other side, I wave to them for the last time, gratefully take my backpack, and set out on the track through the jungle.

I will certainly run into someone. Something will happen.

∞

I open the door of the toilet in the courtyard of the police station in Juba – they offered to let me sleep on the floor of an empty office there, which I happily accepted – and I can only stare. I have never seen anything like it: human shit everywhere. It rises proudly from the hole in a high tower, and lies on the surface around the hole, and on the floor all the way to the door. I have no idea where the heroes squatted when they came to contribute the last little piles. Maybe at the open door while having a relaxed chat with their co-worker.

After staring for a moment, I slowly close the door and set off across the village in the hope of finding some hidden place between the mud houses. It's getting dark. My bowels demand almost immediate salvation. I have a piece of toilet paper folded up in my pocket, and I'm walking faster and faster, my desperation increasing because there is no place to go. The courtyards of the houses are all right next to each other. There are people everywhere. It's almost completely dark when I spot a big construction site and quickly turn into the courtyard. After a few steps, I can't wait anymore and I squat down.

My relief in the silent darkness slowly begins to disappear as I hear voices coming along the street. To my horror, about twelve men approach and surround me as I helplessly squat over my newly produced pile. Some of them have flash-lights in their hands and they shine them on my face or on the fragrant shit beneath me. I have never felt so humiliated and powerless in my life.

"Look what you've done!" says one of them, perhaps the leader. "Just look what you've done!"

I stare stupidly into the glare of the blinding flash-lights.

"Yeah, what! I took a shit! Which part of this is hard to understand?"

"Yes! Why did you do that, I ask you, why?"

"Because I had to go. What's the matter with you people? Leave me alone!" I bark back at them as I quickly wipe my arse.

"What's the matter with us? Do you even know where you are?"

95

The leader raises his voice indignantly and directs the light over my shoulder. I stand up, button my trousers, and gaze in the direction of the beam. I freeze: I'm in the courtyard of a Catholic Church, not a building site. I try to keep the indifferent expression on my face as I walk quickly towards the street and in the direction of the police station.

The group of men walk beside me, speaking angrily:

"You defiled our church. You defiled our God. How could you? We're going to call the police!"

I walk faster and at the same time try to act self-confident and calm:

"You don't need to call the police because we're going there together anyway. I have lots of friends there and we'll see …"

This confuses them but they still walk angrily beside me, complaining about my behaviour. When we get opposite the police station I cross the street and walk into the courtyard. As I stride towards the building I glance back. To my relief, I see that they're all still standing on the other side of the street looking at me in disbelief.

I smile pleasantly to the on-duty policeman who is smoking in the foyer and listening to a transistor radio, and disappear into "my" office, where my mortification catches up with me and deepens through the night.

∞

I'm walking along a dusty street in Juba. It's crowded with bicycles, pedestrians carrying loads large and small, naked children racing around, starving stray dogs, women sitting on the edges selling fruit and vegetables. Suddenly I realize that everything has gone quiet and everyone is standing still. I look around and what I see shakes me to the bones. A thin and entirely naked woman with dishevelled hair is slowly staggering through the haze of dust. She looks like she is about thirty years old. She thrusts her hands towards the sky and loudly moans, cries, screams. Everyone stands still and stares at her. All of life comes to a halt and witnesses this pain, this desperation. My skin crawls as she goes slowly past me. I practically stop breathing. She looks at me for an instant, still moaning, and I almost collapse from this brief contact with the pain that emanates from her.

What happened to her? Was she raped? Was she raped a hundred times? Did someone die? Has she gone mad? Has something horrible just happened to her or has she been like this for a long time? Will her pain be alleviated or will she be like this until the end of her life? Does she have someone in this world, or is she alone and abandoned? Does everyone look at her so silently because they know what has happened or are they all as paralysed and confused as I am?

I will never know. Just as I will never know what will happen in the lives of the hundreds of people who are standing with me on the streets watching this unhappy woman. What hundreds: millions, billions? The billions of human stories that are right now taking place in the world… Pain, joy, happiness, longing, disappointment, loss… It's as if I hear in that moment the cries of all humanity. And yet, I am involved only with myself, with my own little life.

The reawakening of life on the street rouses me from my thoughts. Everything returns to its previous state as if nothing unusual had happened. I'm standing there, a little shaken, slowly looking around when a grey Land-Rover rattles past me. Instinctively I look at the licence plate and cannot believe what I read: EE-7600. I run after it and, because of the chaotic scene on the streets, am able to quickly catch up with it and bang on the tin body. The driver slows down. I speak Serbian to him through the open window. Looking as if he's seen a ghost, he stops at the edge of the street.

We chat cheerfully next to his car for about fifteen minutes. I tell him the story of how I learned of him, where I'm from, where I'm going. The man quickly realizes that I have no money and asks if I need some. I nod and he presses thirty Sudanese pounds into my hand, wishes me luck, and drives off.

Thirty pounds! I haven't had this much money for several months. What wealth!

97

∞

Slowly, and with great love, Dennis rolls an enormous joint. Jean-Pierre explains the rules of the game Yahtzee to us young travellers who have gathered in the youth hostel in Juba. It's impossible to remember all the rules he rattles off, there are so many, but it doesn't matter. I'm happy and I'm celebrating life. After about ten days of hanging around Juba, I managed to find a ride through Uganda to Kenya – in a truck driven by a very nice Kenyan named Masange – and we're going to set off tomorrow morning. Jack, an American traveller, and some kind of old hippy, hugs me and gives me five pounds and wishes me a happy journey. Dennis also gives me a warm hug, says I'm a wonderful friend, and hopes we will meet again. My heart is full, joyous.

After half an hour we are nicely stoned and laughing with each other, throwing the dice on the floor. No one knows the point of the game. Jean-Pierre, as if trying to tame a pack of monkeys, faithfully writes down the score and puts the dice in our hands, because no one knows whose turn it is. We laugh and moan that we're getting blisters from sitting on the hard cement floor, and such pain in a game is not a good thing. Jean-Pierre rolls his eyes, says that we're completely spoiled, but goes around the hostel looking for something to put on the floor. We laugh and talk nonsense while we wait. After a minute Jean-Pierre is back with a small rug to sit on, and insists that we stop fooling around and focus on the game. We somehow manage to sit in a circle with all our butts on the little carpet. But however much we try to cooperate with Jean-Pierre, we can't stop laughing. Suddenly Dennis interrupts us with a long, loud:

"Sssshhh, ssshhh, sshhh…"

He shushes us so that he can hear the commotion happening in the hallway of the hostel. We all listen with eyes wide. Agitated voices are looking for something, growing angry, saying they can't find it and will systematically go through each and every room. We freeze. Could it be the police? Suddenly the door to our room is flung open and the receptionist says:

"The Muslim prayer rug that hangs from the wall in the lobby has disappeared. We need it. It's time for prayer. Does anyone know where it is?"

In total silence we stare stupidly at the receptionist. He rolls his eyes and mutters:

"Of course you wouldn't know…"

He goes back into the hallway, closing the door behind him.

The silence in the room continues for a few more minutes as we are all rolling on the floor, holding our stomachs from laughter, unable to breathe, unable to speak.

I suddenly realize that while in Juba I have managed to insult the two greatest world religions. Because of which I laugh all the harder.

∞

"Show me where you have your money!"

The soldier repeats the command with a drunken voice and slowly lifts his dangling rifle to back up his words.

"But I told you five times already that I don't have any money. I don't have anything of value, just my passport and my clothes. I have nothing to show you…"

I repeat this information but am getting pretty nervous. I can't remember how many military checkpoints we've passed as we've driven through the jungles of Uganda, from Sudan towards Eldoret in Kenya. A barrier blocks the road at least every ten kilometres, a few tents containing a handful of more or less intoxicated soldiers who threaten you until they extract some money. And of course when they see a white man step out of the truck, their pupils change into dollar signs just like in a cartoon. They simply can't seem to understand that a white person might not have any money.

"Listen, I'm not stupid. You're not going anywhere until you give me some money!"

He raises his voice threateningly and waves the rifle in the space between us. Then he takes a few steps to catch his balance.

Finally I lose my temper:

"Stop fucking with me. I told you a hundred times I don't have anything. So just shoot me if you want to. But just stop fucking with me because I've had enough."

Let him shoot me. I don't care anymore. They say that whole convoys of trucks disappear in these jungles, including the drivers, so I can also disappear. I've had enough of everything. A couple of other soldiers nearby turn towards us and gloomily regard the scene. My extortionist, still trying to steady himself, smiles cynically:

"You don't want me to put a bullet in your head…"

I'm struck by an idea and soften my tone:

"My friend, I do have something else that might interest you. If you put your gun down, I'll show you…"

The soldier lowers his gun and leans forward with interest.

"Oh-ho-ho! Show me! Show me!"

I pull from my backpack a packet of condoms that I found in a hotel back in Cairo. I start to prattle on about them:

"Look at this! You put this on your penis when you've having sex and it increases the pleasure. It's the latest western technology…"

The soldier looks at the packet with little interest.

"And of course a woman can't get pregnant if you're wearing that. So you can have sex with no worries."

This seems to interest him even less.

"And you can't get infected with sexual diseases if you wear this. Sex is completely safe."

Life comes into the soldier's eyes.

"Oh yes, my friend, now that's a real problem here in Uganda. There's too much disease here, way too much. Can you give me that?"

"Sure, I'll give you the whole pack. I'm so pleased that it will come in handy…"

The soldier smiles sleepily.

"Okay. Thank you, my friend, you and your friends can continue. I'll lift the barrier…"

I get back into the truck. Masange pats my shoulder relieved. I think to myself, I'm only seventeen years old, I'm not prepared for this shit.

∞

"Robert, do you mind if we pay for you?"

The American Christian missionary who picked me up on the Tanzanian border and is driving me towards Nairobi, the capital of Kenya, suddenly asks me this question. With amazement, I look at him from the back-seat where I'm sitting together with his ten-year-old son. The missionary's wife has been silent throughout the drive, in front of me in the passenger seat.

They want to pay me something? But what for? Any money people give me comes in handy, I think to myself, and say:

"No, no, I don't mind at all, thank you very much."

The missionary slowly stops the car at the side of the road, which is almost devoid of traffic, as hardly anybody drives across this border crossing. It's open mostly for foreigners, closed to Kenyans and Tanzanians. He turns off the engine and we sit in silence for some time. Then he slowly intones:

"Our Father, which art in heaven, hallowed be thy name, thy kingdom come, thy will be done…"

Now I realize that he didn't say "pay for me" but "pray for me". Oh no! What have I got myself into? When he finishes with the prayer, he continues addressing God:

"Dear God, we pray for you to take care of our friend Robert. Now he is angry and disappointed because he was unjustly turned away from the border with Tanzania even though he had a visa and only wanted to go there because he had friends who would help and care for him. Robert is very angry with the official on the border who turned him away, telling him he could not enter Tanzania without money and sending him back to Kenya. We trust that it was part of your plan, dear God, to bring Robert back under your protection…"

Motionless I stare through the glass window on my left and wonder how long this will last and what I should say when he's finished.

"We pray that with your loving patience you may encourage Robert to put his life in your hands, to open his heart, and surrender to your greater wisdom. Amen."

For some time we sit motionless and in silence. Then I squeeze a "Thank you" out of my throat.

The missionary smiles mildly, looks into the rear-view mirror, and says:

"You know, Robert, if you give your life to Jesus Christ, everything will change for the better. Everything."

"Thank you," I say again.

The missionary drives on. I stare silently through the window all the way to Nairobi.

∞

"Look at this magnificent bracelet made from elephant bones and the hair of an elephant's tail, all hand-made. The Maasai make them in the savannah and I buy direct from them and sell them for a minimal profit because they're my friends. I just cover my expenses. That's why they're so cheap, much cheaper than in the tourist stores. Here. I'll give it to you for a discounted price of 180 shillings. Or you can pay in dollars, exactly fifteen dollars. What do you say?"

102

I'm walking down a quiet street in Nairobi. The would-be hustler starts to follow me.

"The bracelet is great but I have absolutely no money. I couldn't buy it no matter how much I wanted it."

"Okay, okay. I get it. Then I'll give it to you for 150 shillings. I see you are a good person and I want to help you."

I smile and walk on. For two days I've been living in a Sikh temple in the centre of Nairobi. I heard somewhere that it's a Sikh tradition to let pilgrims stay for three days without asking any questions. They gave me a little room and they feed me, and I observe them and learn with curiosity. I find all of these thoughtful bearded men interesting and I want to understand their approach to life. Maybe it will give me some orientation that will help with the lack of clarity and consistency that has crashed over me in recent weeks. Maybe it will provide me with some guidance as to how to merge my reflections and experience into a meaningful whole. In any case these earnest Sikhs with their turbans inspire me. It seems to me that they don't just blindly believe in certain stories, but rather that their approach to life is intelligent, grounded, and well thought through.

"Look, my friend, I am going to offer you a price I never offer anyone, ever, no-one. A hundred shillings, my friend. Where do you come from? Germany?"

"No, Yugoslavia. And really, believe me, I have absolutely no money and cannot buy anything. You're wasting your time...."

The border official had told me that I wouldn't be allowed to enter Tanzania without money because, if I did, I would surely fraternize with criminals. No amount of persuasion helped. I asked him how much money I needed to have and he said, some, and then I insisted he tell me an exact amount, and he said fifty dollars. When I asked if forty-nine would be enough, he said, no, fifty or more. Okay. At least I have a specific number.

"My friend, seventy shillings, only for you. Look how hard I am trying with you and I will get nothing out of it, absolutely nothing. I just want to make it possible for you to have this beautiful bracelet, do you understand?"

"I understand. I understand. But I have no money, none at all, believe me…"

I laugh out loud. I've been wandering around Nairobi for two days, wondering how I can get fifty dollars, which for me represents serious wealth. I sold a cooking pot that I had in my backpack and used the few coins I got for my immediate expenses. The Sikhs told me that they can't give me any money, they can only put me up and feed me for three nights.

"Okay, okay, you win. Give me forty shillings and the bracelet is yours. You've completely ruined me. I will lose money and have to cover the difference from my own pocket. But, for you, I will do that."

I'm on my way to the Yugoslav Embassy to ask for an official loan. Supposedly it is possible. I'll think up something, some story about how I got robbed and need to get to a relative in Tanzania who will take care of me. It's a pretty tricky situation because I have to make sure that they don't figure out that I've run away from home. I'm not yet legally an adult, and when I become one, I'll be conscripted into the Yugoslav army. I don't know if that's a problem now but it could definitely complicate my life. I will really need to be careful at the embassy, very careful.

"Wait, my friend, wait. Please stop. Look, I'll give it to you for ten shillings. Now, you won't say it's not worth ten shillings. The Maasai made it. It took them a whole day. You won't say it's not worth ten shillings, that's less than one shitty dollar."

"It's worth it. Of course it's worth it. But I really don't have any money," I smile. "You have to believe me."

"You know what? I'm sick of this. I'm trying so hard with you, for an hour in this heat. Here. Give me five shillings and take this bracelet to Chugoslovakia. Take it as a souvenir to remember me. All right?"

Five shillings. That's forty cents. I think I might have that much in my pocket. I reach my hand into my pocket and find two two-shilling coins.

"I don't have five shillings, only four. That's really all I have. I swear."

He looks at me for a moment in silence. Then he takes the coins, gives me the bracelet, and smiles sourly at me.

"Remember this was not business. That was my gift to you."

I shake his hand and smile.

"Thank you."

He winks at me and then slowly strolls away in the direction from which we came.

∞

The pick-up truck that picked me up on the way to Mombasa drops me off, turns right and disappears among the bushes. I'm stuck in the middle of the savannah. The road is empty of traffic. My only companion is an enormous cow with imposing horns. It was grazing the grass but now it's staring right at me. I don't hear any sounds except the chirping of birds. I feel a little nervous because of the cow only a few metres away which is still staring at me. Never before have cows struck me as dangerous, but this one somehow doesn't seem so innocent. I let out a sigh of relief when it eventually loses interest in me and sways heavily away into the low bushes.

I still can't accept that I got turned away from the Tanzanian border for a second time, even though I had fifty US dollars plus 650 Tanzanian shillings that I got for a pair of almost new tennis shoes and a silver chain. The bureaucratic whiz at the border even managed to extract the shillings from me before he handed me a notice that said I was unwanted in Tanzania. Probably because I threw a tantrum in his office.

I've been dreaming for so long about the new life I would begin in Tanzania with the help of the relatives of the friends I had made in Egypt and Sudan. Now everything is ruined and I'm stuck in Kenya. I can't get to my ex-promised land of Somalia by land. I won't go back to Uganda. Ethiopia doesn't seem like a good place to go.

The only hope I have is to go to Mombasa and find work on an international cargo ship. Supposedly they come from India every week and supposedly you can get work on them without a seaman's card. Supposedly, supposedly, supposedly… My options seem to be narrowing and I'm beginning to worry. This waiting by the side of the road for a car to pass in the middle of the Kenyan savannah isn't helping much either.

∞

Slowly and carefully I use my spoon to divide the pile of rice on my plate into two parts and push them apart a bit. I sprinkle salt and pepper on one of them, and dribble salad oil over it. That will be my main course.

I think about my situation while slowly chewing the rice to get all the nourishment out of it. I have virtually no money and for several days have been eating the cheapest item on the menu in this extremely modest hotel: a plate of rice, which costs a third of a dollar. I've struck a deal with the boss to let me sleep for half price on the floor of the room with four other travellers with whom I've become great friends.

Hamish from New Zealand goes out each day to negotiate with a quite dominant local woman to return his passport. She stole it from him during a night of passion and now demands that he is sexually available to her because he is such a tender lover. She also wants him to make love to her friends because they would be grateful to her for such a marvellous experience. Hamish says that he won't go to the police for now because he believes in the power of dialogue and love.

Then there is Andy, an Englishman, who is travelling around the world and who started off teaching English to children on a small Greek island, from which he had to literally escape because he got involved with a beautiful young local woman and the islanders were enraged. Now I help him to translate the letters he receives from this young woman because they're written in such broken English that he can't understand them.

And, of course, Brian, an older man who does reportage and interviews for the BBC, but more as a sideline than something he really takes seriously. What he takes seriously is exercising, so that despite his age he can maintain his slim and strong body and be sufficiently attractive to the young local women. He gradually becomes a sort of benevolent father figure for me.

And then there's Thomas from Switzerland who scuba dives in the Indian Ocean during the day and dedicates his nights to erotic enjoyment with young local men.

I polish off the first pile of rice and now it's time for dessert. I sprinkle sugar on the second pile and, with a faint smile on my face, dig my spoon into it.

I got stuck here in Mombasa. There is no ship that would take me to India or anywhere at all without a seaman's card. I have nowhere else to go. I have no idea what I should try next, where I should turn. I sent a telegram to a friend in Kranj asking if he could send me some money, and now I go to the bank every day to see if it has come.

∞

I sit on the bed, freshly showered. The light of a street lamp falls through the window into the dark room, and I can't believe it is finally happening: I am going to have sex! After all these years of fantasizing and masturbating I am finally going to become a man and taste the beauty of total intimacy, the wonder of sexual union which I've desired for such a long time.

I was sitting with the boys, sipping beers, having fun recounting travel stories in the garden of a simple bar where many locals were hanging out. A local guy was dancing beautifully by the jukebox to the new Michael Jackson hit Billy Jean, eyes closed in ecstasy. Young girls in their late teenage or early twenties paid us visits, laughed with us, sat on our laps, nursed their beers and invited us to enjoy sexual pleasure with them for a very reasonable price. They casually braided my long hair, then unbraided it, and braided it again. In the West they would probably be labelled prostitutes, though in fact they only went with men they liked, and if they really liked someone, they went with him for free.

That's what happened to me. A very beautiful young woman was watching me the whole night from a dark corner where she was sitting drinking a beer by herself. When the bar was almost empty and only Hamish and I were left at the table, she sat down next to us, set her eyes on me, and said simply:

"I like you. Will you come with me?"

My heart beat wildly and I nervously stuttered:

"I would v-v-v-very much l-l-l-love to, but I have n-n-n-no money."

The beautiful girl sighed and dropped her gaze. Then she took a cigarette from her bag, offered one to me, and we smoked side by side in silence. My stuttered response still rang in my head and I thought about the fact that I hadn't stuttered once since I left home. Maybe because of the feeling of freedom, along with the absence of the burdens and strains I had felt my entire childhood.

The girl put out her cigarette, exhaled the last puff of smoke, turned towards me and whispered.

"Forget about the money. Let's go."

She winked, her lips turning into a barely noticeable smile, and stood up. I looked at her in confusion, then noticed Hamish winking at me, smiling, and whispering:

"Go, Robert, just go."

My mind raced in all directions as we walked in silence along the sleeping streets of Mombasa: from fantasies about how great it would be, to panic at the assumption that she was probably very experienced and would quickly realize that I knew nothing. Fortunately, we stopped first at her elder sister's, who lived in the room next to hers. We drank tea, smoked a joint, chatted, and I was able to relax a bit.

And now I'm sitting on the bed and waiting for her to come back from the shower. The light in the bathroom goes off and she slowly glides towards me, wrapped in a towel. I see the drops of water shining on her neck in the half-darkness. She stands in front of me and slowly lets the towel fall. I am moved by the magic of this moment: the beauty of her perfect body, the beauty of this intimacy, the beauty of two strangers encountering each other during a certain moment of their lives and giving themselves to each other. I hold her uncertainly by her hips and gently kiss the place right below her belly button. Slowly she lowers herself to the bed.

…

We make love again in the morning, drink coffee, and smile gently to each other in farewell. I walk along the streets of Mombasa with a smile stretching from ear to ear, ecstatic, and deeply grateful to life for the beauty I have just experienced.

∞

I cannot believe what is happening right now. It's early evening and I'm standing on a street in the middle of Mombasa, passers-by all around. A young Croatian sailor is kneeling in front of me, extending his hands towards me and loudly pleading:

"Please release me! I beg you as I would beg God, release me from your power! I will pay you anything you want, just release me, I beg of you, release me…"

The passers-by stare at us. I nervously step closer and whisper:

"Stop this shit. Come on, stand up and let's walk on."

The young man on his knees widens his frightened eyes and raises his voice:

"Please, I beg you as I would beg God, release me, please…"

What should I do with this guy? I get an idea:

"Okay, I promise to release you, but let's go together to your friends now. I will release you there, I promise."

The young man stands up and we walk on in silence. I think about how the hell I got mixed up in this bizarre situation.

A few days ago I met some Croatian sailors whose ship was in harbour for a couple of days. I drank beer and chatted with them during the evenings. This guy decided, based on my long hair, that I was the right person to ask to get some marijuana for him. He had never smoked before and he wanted to try it, maybe even to buy a little. Sure, I told him, come to my room and I'll roll a joint and we'll smoke a little and I can also give you some to take with you. And so we smoked a joint and I wrapped up a little more in a newspaper. He declined the gift, saying he didn't want any more, but I secretly tucked it into his trousers. Then we set off for the harbour and now this scene.

We arrive and, relieved, I sit down with his sailor friends who are sipping beer in the garden of the bar. He begins to explain to them in a panic that I am a grand wizard, a hypnotist, that I enslaved him and I will also enslave them, that they shouldn't believe me, that they shouldn't even listen to me. The sailors laugh, saying that they already know that I'm a wizard, that all of it is true. Once again the young man dramatically asks me to release him as I promised. I look around in confusion. The sailors wink at me, indicate that I should act it out, and so I make a loud pronouncement:

"Alright. Let it be. I release you. You are completely free."

The young man smiles with relief, thanks me, and then once again warns his friends not to listen me. He walks away into the night. The sailors laugh, saying they never had such a confused young apprentice on the ship as this one, and I retreat into my thoughts. I keep getting myself into these crazy situations…

It all started with a local named Basil who was living in our hotel as he didn't dare to go home for some unexplained reason. We became good friends, often talking late into the night. One day he invited me to go with him because he wanted to show me something as a sign of trust and friendship. We walked along some of the poorest streets in Mombasa and wound up at a half-ruined house in front of which an enormous man sat smoking. Basil greeted him with a smile, they exchanged a few words, and the man opened the door of the house for us. We found ourselves in a sort of warehouse space with around twenty canvas bags, each about a metre high and half a metre in diameter, propped up against a wall.

"You see, Robert, my friend, this is my work. This is my harvest, my business, my love."

Basil opened the nearest bag and showed me its contents:

"Look, my friend, this is the real thing. This is top-quality grass, raised with love."

Astonished, I touched the green wealth. It was immediately clear to me why Basil didn't dare go home. Grinning proudly, he stared around him, grabbed a sheet of newspaper, and wrapped enough grass in it to fill a shoebox. He tucked the package under my tee shirt, making it look like I had a big beer belly, and smiled:

"There you go, my brother, for you and your friends. If you run out, you always know where you can find some more."

And now I have that package in my room and I share grass with my fellow travellers who of course like me very much. I could also sell it. The money would come in handy but somehow I don't feel right selling what I got for free. Besides Basil recently gave me thirty dollars because he made a good deal and was celebrating.

A few days later I meet the Croatian seamen again. They laughingly report that the young man has locked himself in his cabin. They couldn't get him out for two days because he was constantly smoking. He must have found that little package I tucked into the pocket of his trousers.

∞

I have my right arm draped over Brian's shoulder and my left over Andy's, and we're slowly walking from the taxi to the hospital. My body is weak, my head dizzy, my heart moved and grateful that, so far from home, I have friends like Brian and Andy. That same morning I just barely managed to lift myself off my mattress on the floor, stumble and trip to the bathroom where I threw up, and then collapsed. The receptionist took one look at me and said with complete calm and certainty:

"Malaria."

Oh no: so those mosquitoes on the banks of the river before I got to Juba had done their job well.

Andy and Brian jumped up immediately, ordered a taxi, and now we're at the window where they give out prescription medicines. I don't even remember the examination with the doctor a half hour ago. I was mostly lost in my own hallucinations.

The young man glances at the prescription and uses a little scoop to collect a couple of dozen tablets from a huge pile, shakes them into a paper bag, and weighs the whole thing on a scale. He adds a few more tablets, twists the bag at the top, and smiles, and the three of us slowly sway to another taxi. Brian silently pays for everything. I will be grateful to him until the end of my life.

For the next couple of weeks, I sleep most of the time and for the rest of the time I wander through the labyrinth of my hallucinations. Then one morning I am suddenly okay and life continues as before. The only difference is that now I realize my own fragility in this world more than ever before.

∞

I wake with the feeling that someone is sitting next to me on the bed. I've been sleeping in Hamish's bed because he told me that he was going to sleep over with his lady. I slowly open my eyes and look up. Sitting next to me is a faintly familiar young man, speaking to me in Slovenian and laughing awkwardly:

"Oh, hey Robert! We meet here of all places…"

His apparent joy at finding me strikes me as suspicious. Slowly my eyes adjust and I remember, aha, this is the man who works at the Yugoslav embassy in Nairobi, who I met when I went there to borrow money. This doesn't look good. I don't believe this is an accidental meeting. I notice that a very serious-looking Kenyan man is sitting on the edge of Andy's bed on the other side of the room and staring at me.

I smile sourly and murmur:

"Hey, Jani. Good morning…"

Jani answers with a suspiciously cheerful smile:

"How are you? How's life in Mombasa? Great place, eh?"

I sit up in bed.

"Yes, I'm doing pretty well."

Jani gets more serious now and his tone less bright:

"Look, I'll get to the point. This man you see here is a Kenyan plain-clothes cop. Your father contacted us and told us that you ran away from home. He wants us to send you back. This policeman is here just in case you decide to resist. But I don't think that will be necessary, will it? Please cooperate. Pack your things and let's go. We have a car downstairs, we'll drive you to Nairobi and from there you can fly home. Alright?"

I silently stare past him. So, writing that postcard home a month ago wasn't such a good idea. That must be how my father tracked me down. Or perhaps it was in fact a good idea, as I don't see any way out of here anyway. I can't go to any neighbouring country. My Kenyan visa has expired. I extended it once and the official gave me a dark look, saying that he would do it that once but I should not come back. My fantasies about cargo ships have long since vanished. I actually see no alternative. In fact this almost comes as a relief.

I slowly raise my eyes and smile bitterly at Andy and Brian who are looking at me in confusion, as if to ask what is happening, because of course they don't understand my conversation with Jani in Slovenian.

"Alright, Jani, I agree. Let me just go to the bathroom, then pack and say my goodbyes…"

…

And now we're already travelling along the road from Mombasa through the savannah. The Kenyan is driving and I understand now that he's no policeman but one of the drivers employed at the Yugoslav embassy. When I mention that, Jani smiles and says that he had to come up with something, otherwise I would have resisted. And that I shouldn't hold it against him. I just smile and keep looking at the savannah.

I'm saying goodbye to Africa in my thoughts. To all the wonderful people I've met during my adventures, to the hospitality, the laughter and smiles, the joy, the music, the happiness. To all my travel companions, to all the incredibly interesting people who wander around this wide world, and are probably in search of meaning and freedom and happiness just as I am. To the great breadth and depth of life that I've experienced day in and day out.

Must I also bid farewell to my freedom?

Tears run down my face and I try to wipe them away. I think that Jani, sitting in front of me next to the driver somehow senses what I'm feeling and leaves me in peace.

In the evening he takes me to a club so I can go wild and get the confusion out of me. While I'm dancing, someone suddenly hugs me and lifts me off the floor: Dennis from Juba, Uganda! Dear, dear Dennis! We laugh out loud, lift each other up into the air. Tears of happiness and sadness flow down my cheeks. How strange that he should be in the same club in the same town as me, a thousand kilometres from where I last saw him, just on my last night in Africa. It's as if he has come especially to say goodbye to me. Many years later I will learn of his suicide after his return to Europe.

…

The next morning some embassy staff accompany me to the plane. It's January 10th, 1984 and freezing cold when I land at Belgrade airport, where my parents are waiting for me. My father smiles and tries to be funny, acting as if nothing much has happened. My mother watches me silently, hugs me again and again, and wipes away her tears.

That night we take the train to Ljubljana. We have a sleeper compartment and father is already snoring. My mother and I pass a cigarette back and forth from one bunk to the other. Only decades later will I understand how terrible the six months of my absence must have been for her.

∞

I'm lying in a hospital bed, naked below the waist. I marvel at the crazy situation which I've landed in once again. A nurse enters the room, smiles pleasantly, and covers me up to my neck with a green cloth with a big opening in the middle of it. Then she pulls my penis, shrivelling from fear, through the opening. I stare in disbelief and dejection at the ceiling, going through the conversation that I'd had with my mother the night before.

"A doctor at work, a urologist, said he's worried that on your travels you might have picked up an African snail, while wading through a river perhaps or swimming in a lake."

I rolled my eyes.

"Does that doctor have any idea what he is talking about? The illness is called bilharzia, and it's not caused by "African snails" but by flatworms known as schistosomes. I know about it because I read, you see."

The more my mother presented the doctors at work as omniscient demigods, the more I enjoyed making fun of them. But my mother wasn't someone to give up easily. She sighed patiently:

"I'm sure he knows all of that and I just remembered it wrong. But he wants to examine you to make sure you don't have these snails in your bladder. He's on duty all day tomorrow and he

115

said we should just come and he will take the time to have a quick look at you."

It was true that I'd been swimming in lakes and had waded through rivers. Maybe it wouldn't be such a stupid idea to make sure I was alright.

"What does he have to do exactly?"

My mother looked down and said:

"I don't know exactly, just a quick examination, that's all…"

Alarm bells started to ring in the back of my mind – the whole thing reminded me of the painful childhood experience of having my appendix removed – but I foolishly agreed.

Now the doctor enters the room, interrupting my thoughts, and quickly explains what he's going to do:

"Okay. This is how the procedure works. I'll insert this tube through your penis into your bladder. Then I'll pump water through the tube into your bladder until it has completely expanded. Then I will insert a small light into your bladder so I can see the internal walls. Once I'm certain that you have no parasites, then I'll let the water out, and that's it. You'll be sore for a couple of days, there will be some blood in your urine, but other than that you'll be fine. The procedure itself is quite unpleasant but it will be over quickly. Just relax and breathe deeply and everything will be okay."

I close my eyes and feel very grateful to the nurse standing beside me and holding my hand. I squeeze her warm hand, breathe deeply, and think that it makes no sense to say anything to my mother about transparency and trust. Not something she would be able to understand.

Five: A Bird in a Cage

February 9, 1985, my nineteenth birthday. I'm in my pyjamas, standing by the window in a hospital room and numbly staring out at my fellow recruits in their battledress and gas masks, drenched by the cold rain, wearing full military equipment and weaponry, crawling over the wet and muddy ground. An officer walks alongside, angrily yelling at them. He yells louder and, in an instant, everyone is on their feet racing forwards, until the officer yells again, and then they all throw themselves back on the ground and continue crawling.

After my return from Africa, I'd done various temporary jobs for a year and gradually finished high school. The next thing was one year of compulsory military service in the Yugoslav National Army, in my case in Montenegro. Right before my call-up, apparently, I'd caught smallpox from my cousin and had fallen ill a couple of days after my arrival at the army training centre. Now I'm on my own in a segregated room in the infirmary, because I'm still contagious and am not allowed to be in contact with the other recruits. I mostly read books and stand by the window.

What infinite stupidity, this army business. Throughout the whole world, so much energy circulating around armies, nation states, borders, just because we don't know how to live together. And all of this has become such an integrated part of human society that no one even questions it anymore. Before I left home, when my grandmother heard what I thought about the army, she said that I would never be a real man if I didn't serve in the army.

The officer walks up and down alongside the soaking wet recruits, ordering them here and there, back and forth. Masks on, masks off. Crawling, running, crawling again, running again. If I understand correctly, he wants to see greater explosiveness when the soldiers jump up from the ground and greater enthusiasm when they throw their bodies back into the mud.

Utter idiocy. I don't want to waste my life in this way. I must think of a way to get out of this.

The officer arranges the half-drowned and exhausted soldiers into a line, stands in front of them and shouts some more. The boys pant heavily, trying to stand up straight. Even from this distance, I can see the fear and confusion in their eyes.

And I decide at that moment: I will stop eating and I won't start eating again until they send me home. I will think up some emotional reasons, something, anything, but from this moment on I will no longer eat.

∞

"Robert, is it that you don't want to serve in the Yugoslav National Army?"

An officer with a falsely warm voice is asking the question. We're sitting in his office and he's gazing at me motionlessly with his calculating eyes.

"You can tell me the truth. You don't need to be afraid."

I know this trap and I have no intention of stepping into it.

"No, Comrade Captain, it has nothing to do with that. I would very much like to serve in the Yugoslav National Army. But I can't. I just can't."

The officer, who is the military psychiatrist appointed to examine my case, lets out a slight sigh of disappointment, leans back, and asks wearily:

"Well, why can't you? What's the problem? What does that mean?"

"I just always feel so sad, so nervous. It makes me shake all the time."

I say this with my most helpless sounding voice.

"Don't worry. That will pass. But why don't you eat, Robert, why don't you eat just a little?"

Today is the fourteenth day of my fast. I'm only drinking water. A week ago I was sent here to the main military hospital in Titograd, the capital of Montenegro, because they were starting to worry about me. They cannot know that I actually feel fantastic, light, calm, purified even as a result of my fast, and extremely pleased with myself.

"I cannot, Comrade Captain, I really cannot. I feel so very sad that I am actually repulsed by food."

"Why don't you just force yourself to eat a little, for God's sake? You can't do that?"

His impatience is growing.

"I tried. I really tried but I can't. I would really like to eat, Comrade Captain, but I simply can't."

The military psychiatrist sighs in resignation, rummages through the forms on his desk and starts to fill in my data.

"Look, I'm going to defer your military service for three years until you're more mature and it will be easier for you."

He's only going to defer it for three years? I'd placed all my bets on being completely released from military service, which is what I'd heard could happen if you acted crazy enough. If they only defer it for three years, I've accomplished almost nothing. Disappointed, I sneak a look at what he's writing, and see that he's giving me the classic diagnosis that all weirdos get: an emotionally immature personality.

"You'll stay here tonight. Then tomorrow go to the office and get the paperwork to go home. Alright then. Good luck. You can go now."

He looks at me from under his heavy brow and continues writing.

As I walk dejectedly down the hallway, I'm suddenly brought to a dead stop. My mother is standing in front of me. She's wearing a fur coat, her eyes wide open, the expression on her suffering face clearly saying:

"My son, what are you doing to me? Have I not suffered enough because of you?"

We hug and she cries quietly on my shoulder. That psychiatrist was not as stupid as I'd thought. He must have

119

cleverly made a phone call some time ago and woven together a dramatic story for my mother, who is now standing trembling beside me.

Suddenly I realize that I don't want the emotional scene I'm sure to get if I go home: my father completely disappointed by his wimpy son, mostly ignoring me, with occasional lectures, my mother desperate and nervous, all my relatives rolling their eyes and offering advice. Everything in my head crumbles into dust, the scenario before me becoming darker and darker.

I sigh deeply and extract myself from my mother's embrace.

"Everything will be alright."

She looks at me questioningly and wipes away her tears.

I slowly turn around and return to the psychiatrist's office.

"Comrade Captain, I feel a little bit better and I would like to try and serve, if I'm still allowed to."

He leans back in his chair with an air of satisfaction, victory even. Smiling, he stares into my eyes:

"Of course you can, Robert, of course you can. When you go to the office, get the paperwork and return to the training camp in Bar. I am glad you made the right decision."

He crumples up the paper with my diagnosis on it and, as I leave his office, I see him shooting it into the waste paper basket like a basketball player.

∞

I'm standing on a large rock cliff in the middle of the forest among the mountains of Montenegro. I had to get away from everything. I quickly ate my lunch in camp and ran up here for a few minutes alone before we have to continue with the military exercises, which will certainly include running up and down wearing full fighting gear, gas masks on our faces, digging trenches with a small folding shovel that we carry on our belts, throwing ourselves on the ground in front of imaginary bursts of gunfire, attacking imaginary enemies, and, of course, a lot of shouting from the officers.

Altogether the most bizarre and entirely meaningless waste of time that I've ever experienced in my life.

I sit down on the enormous rock and dangle my feet over the edge, which drops away vertically almost twenty metres. Only now do I notice other interesting stone outcrops all around me. Some are only a few metres high while others are probably more than fifteen metres high and look like some sort of ancient stone tree trunks. I'm drawn most by a stone pillar about three metres away from the rock on which I'm sitting. It has a flat top, which is slightly lower than where I am, but it's only a metre across at most.

I begin to think about how I could somehow jump onto that surface, although it's so small that it's not at all clear that I'd be able to hold on to it without sliding straight off again. I certainly wouldn't be able to jump back as I'd have no momentum, since it's lower than the rock where I'm sitting now. The thought of how the officers would react if I did make it onto the little platform amuses me. Nobody would be able to do anything. Everyone would go crazy and no doubt scream at me, but they wouldn't be able to reach me, or I them. The idea excites me more and more. I would be laughing in the face of the whole world, completely free in a way, that is until I fell from exhaustion into the depths, thus ending my futile life.

But at least I would no longer have to be involved in this total meaninglessness. Like yesterday for example, when we all had to lie on our backs, rifles in hand, an officer yelling at us:

"An airplane approaches from the west. It's a hundred and fifty metres high. How far in front of it do you have to aim your rifle in order to hit it?"

I raised my hand to express my thoughts on the subject:

"Comrade Sergeant, it's very likely that the plane would be a jet, which would fly very quickly. At an altitude of a hundred and fifty metres, it would fly over us in a couple of seconds. That wouldn't be enough time to calculate, aim, and fire, and for the bullet to travel a hundred and fifty metres and hit it. Wouldn't it make more sense to save our ammunition and take shelter somewhere amongst the rocks?"

I would have liked to add a cynical comment to the effect that his strategy was probably from the era of biplanes, but I bit my tongue so I wouldn't be given the punishment of cleaning the bathroom with a toothbrush that evening.

The officer dismissed me:

"Private Kržišnik, don't you think too much. We regular officers are here to think instead of you."

Still I can't help myself from thinking, and the more I think about it, the more I like the idea of jumping onto that little platform on top of the stone pillar. Up until now my life has taught me that it's precisely the irrational and almost crazy actions that bring the most vitality to life.

Or, for example, there was the day we were in the field learning how to defuse an anti-tank mine. We were supposed to deactivate the device by lying on the ground and stretching our arms towards it. Working at arm's length was impossible, as we could hardly see what we were doing, with our helmets slipping down over our eyes as well. All of this for our supposed safety.

Again I spoke up:

"Comrade Sergeant, isn't it almost certain that the mine will explode if I poke around in it when I can hardly see what I am doing and my hands are shaking because I have to use my arms to support my bodyweight? Wouldn't it be more likely that I would succeed if I sat upright next to the mine and tackled the task from a position where I could see what I was doing, where my hands could move precisely, and everything was more or less under control?"

"You again, Private Kržišnik. I told you before: first do what you are told and afterwards complain and act smart."

I decide not to jump and I don't even know why. Certainly I'm not afraid. Maybe it's because the life inside me wants to live on. I hear the sharp voice of an officer below, announcing that exercises will resume in eight minutes. I roll my eyes, sigh, and head back to camp.

∞

The bunk bed beneath me finally stops shaking. The heavy breathing of my dorm mate Perica has finally stopped and I slowly sit up in my bed, assume the lotus position and close my eyes. Each night at ten the soldier on duty turns out the lights in our dormitory where twenty of us new recruits sleep. After a few minutes of silence, the bunk bed starts to shake, as Perica apparently has to end each day with masturbation. Fortunately he finishes quite quickly. When it's all quiet again I can begin my evening explorations of pranayama and meditation.

I'm attempting to neutralize the senselessness of military service by using my spare time for inner research. My dear friend and spiritual guide, Andrej, sends me books from Ljubljana, and each day I take advantage of my few free moments to read Ramana Maharshi, Krishnamurti, Sri Aurobindo. I meditate every evening, I focus on developing the skill of dreaming consciously and creating my own dreams. I even discover to my amazement the entire collection of Carlos Castaneda's books in the military library. The previous librarian who ordered the books must have been a kindred spirit. Even though he's not here anymore, I somehow feel less lonely.

∞

I step into the lift and press the button with number ten on it. It takes me to the highest floor of the apartment building in Ljubljana where we lived when I was in primary school. I step out of the lift and stare for a moment through a great panoramic window into the night. Then, exactly according to the planned scenario, I lift my leg and slowly walk through the glass, taking several steps into the emptiness, and stop.

Only now do I fully become aware that I am dreaming. My heart starts to beat nervously, but of course there is no heart, or at least it's not here, here where I'm floating in an ethereal body that is actually my consciousness. Or something like that.

The agitation in me grows when I fully realize that I am actually present in this other world, in this other dimension of existence, liberated from my physical body and my physical identity. I made it.

I suddenly remember the instructions from the book I've been reading about conscious dreaming. The first thing you're supposed to do when you realize you are dreaming is to go and check out your sleeping body. This way you know whether you have really reached the stage of liberating your dreaming body.

Just the desire to see my own sleeping physical body is enough and I find myself floating below the ceiling of the military dormitory. All of the bunks are empty because it's the middle of the day, only I am sleeping in my bed after being on overnight guard duty last night. Still floating, I approach and study my body. I see myself lying on my left side, wearing blue military pyjamas, a blanket covering my legs.

The freedom that begins to fill me is ecstatic. This is real freedom. I shoot up high and perform loops in the universe or wherever I am. I joyfully shout with a new energy that I've never known or experienced before. Then I remember Nataša, my high school sweetheart who I still carry in my heart and instantly I'm in front of the house where she lives. I try to walk around to the other side so I can climb the balcony and peek in her room, and...

... and then I wake up groaning in my bed. I immediately understand how I messed up. I forgot for a second that you move with your thoughts in the dream world, not with your muscles. I was thrown back into my body the moment I tried to walk around Nataša's house.

But all the same: I'm so happy, that I get up from my bed and look out of the window, fully aware of myself. Perhaps more than ever before. I've pulled aside another veil from the mystery of my existence. Or the existence of everything.

∞

"Guys, guys, please, let's do another round, it's about time." I wink and raise my arm up high. "Three, four, go…"

"Hurraaaaah, hurraaaah!"

Cries resound from thirty throats.

Dramatically, like a sort of Herbert von Karajan, I direct with my hands and the hurrahs roll through the surrounding woods. Here and there a soldier yells – "Die, occupier pigs!" – and almost collapses laughing, and then we continue with the chorus – "Hurraaaaah!"

I give a sudden and final wave of my hands and silence reigns.

"Great, guys. We're doing better and better. Now a cigarette break and then someone can take Enes's place on guard duty."

I grin and stretch my legs. We're sitting on the ground on this hill in the middle of the Montenegrin forest, leaning against the limestone boulders, lifting our faces towards the autumn sun, all the while practising our version of an attack on the enemy position. The exercise is to run in some kind of formation up to the top of a hill, and when we get there to let out loud and warlike cries of 'hurrah' as we storm the imaginary stronghold and thrash every last one of our enemies. Then go back down the hill and repeat the whole thing. Over and over.

The strategy that I've developed is to choose a relatively high hill for the exercise, where the officers won't bother to go, but to miss out the physical exertion part of the exercise. We appoint a guard to keep watch over the valley just in case. Every fifteen minutes we all yell 'hurrah' and in between I occasionally yell curses about their mothers and threaten them with courts martial. The guys all smile at me with gratitude.

After the conclusion of my six months' basic military training, the officers decided that I should be promoted as a corporal and sent me on a one-month training programme to earn the higher rank, despite my protests. And now I have to teach and lead a young band of new recruits gathered from all over Yugoslavia: from a professor of literature from Belgrade to a boy from some forgotten village in the hills of Bosnia who explains to us that it's essential to wear rubber boots if you want to have good sex with a goat. Apparently you tuck the hind feet of the goat into your boots so she can't get away. I'm only supposed to supervise a squad of seven soldiers but our ranking officer Lieutenant Tomič is an extremely fat and lazy alcoholic and is always hiding in some corner drinking beer, so I lead the whole platoon of thirty soldiers instead of him. Tomič is grateful to me and eagerly approves my evening outings into town, so we're all happy.

"Okay. Let's go guys. It's time for another attack on the bunkers of the occupier bastards." I smile and wave my hands. Our hurrahs echo through the valley.

I'm learning an amazing amount about human relations and leadership. I'm between two fires – the officers and the soldiers – and am in constant danger of offending either or both of them. So far, at least, I have a good relationship with the soldiers. They trust me and see me as an ally who will always back them up. I learn that integrity and acting as a role model are the qualities that bring respect, trust, and authority. And that's why Tomič has none of that: because he hides his fat butt in the supply truck rather than actually participate in a forty-kilometre night march with the rest of us, potentially even raising our morale along the way.

Only the battalion commander doesn't like me, because he knows that I'm on the side of the soldiers and never on his side, although he cannot prove it. And he also knows that the soldiers will always be loyal to me no matter how much he tries to scare them.

The last hurrah echoes around the mountains. I line the guys up and remind them that they should act very tired and sick of life when we arrive in the valley. We descend the hill in formation. I'm already thinking about how astonished my fellow corporals will be, having listened all afternoon to our yelling in the hills. They'll be amazed at what a beast I am and what discipline I inspire as a leader.

∞

I'm standing at the window and looking grimly out at the sunny Sunday afternoon. Today we have a free day and I see dozens of soldiers in the courtyard, sitting on the grass chatting, or playing volleyball or basketball. A lot of the men took the opportunity to go into town today. Only I remain inside, still in my pyjamas, for hours and hours in this big dormitory. I've had enough of everything. I can't take it anymore. I'm tired, broken, empty. For almost a year now I've been trying to maintain my sanity in this madhouse, to preserve some connection to normality in the midst of this bizarre experience, to remain optimistic and focus on the positive. But now my battery is completely empty. I can't do it anymore. I just can't. I don't even see the point in taking my next breath.

In Africa I tasted so much freedom, flow, and life, and saw beyond the limits that had been presented to me as the only possibility of living this life. But now I've landed in a lunatic asylum, robbed of any sense at all. Maybe if I'd never in my life tasted all so much freedom, it would torture me less. It's like the line in the Bible, which I happened to read one day in Africa out of pure boredom: "The more you know, the more you hurt."

I hear a soft knocking at the door and murmur:

"Yes..."

The door slowly opens and I see the big questioning eyes of my dear friend Nado.

"May I come in?"

"Yes, yes, of course..." I mutter, hoping that he won't want to talk to me. I've already told him twice today that I'm not in the mood to talk.

Nado sits down on a bed by the window, on the other side of the room so he doesn't invade my space. He sets his guitar on his knees and sits in silence for a while, staring out of the window. I feel touched when I realize that this time he's come to speak to me in his favourite language: music.

He slowly begins to touch the strings and to improvise harmonies, gently, attentively, as if he were articulating the atmosphere in the space. My condition, my feelings, the silence of

127

the dormitory. The burdens, the powerlessness, the loneliness and vulnerability: all of that somehow reverberates through the minimalistic and barely audible tones produced by Nado's guitar.

The tension inside me begins to subside, my breathing grows deeper, and Nado's care and gentleness touch me. I feel the black cloud which has enveloped me all day slowly beginning to lift.

Dear Nado, my dear friend, who all of these months has been revealing to me some of the subtler aspects of music, teaching me to play things on the guitar that I never dared to even try before. A friend who combines trust, gentleness, understanding, and respect. A companion with whom I can make music and sing endlessly until we find a flow, a pleasure and connection that feels spiritually intimate and sometimes even erotic.

Nado's improvisation slowly flows into recognizable notes as if he has finally found the song that wants to be played now, at this moment. He quietly begins to sing:

"Hello darkness, my old friend, I've come to talk with you again..."

I smile faintly, sigh deeply, and go to sit next to him on the bed. I wait for the next verse and then sing the second voice:

"In restless dreams I walked alone..."

As always when singing in harmony, an internal space opens in my being.

It is as if through sensitive listening, following, and creating the magical point of harmony, I cease existing as a separate individual and all that remains is the harmony itself, which fills the space with its beauty. The harmony pours through into the space, and expands my heart.

"But my words like silent raindrops fell, and echoed in the wells of silence..."

∞

"I found the right thing, believe me. This is the thing we were looking for..."

I read this sentence in a handwritten letter from Iztok, my dear friend and fellow traveller. Half an hour ago, the duty soldier delivering the post around camp handed me the letter and now I'm reading it for the third time.

Iztok writes to me about Charles Berner, a man who, in the 1960s in California, had combined Zen meditation using a koan with dyadic communication technique, and put the whole thing into the schedule and structure of a Zen sesshin (intensive meditation retreat). In this way he had created an extraordinarily focused and penetrating form of spiritual retreat which he called Enlightenment Intensive. Iztok also tells me about Živorad Mihajlović-Slavinski, a contemporary Yugoslav mystic whose books I'd already read, who brought this method from the United States to Yugoslavia and claims that all other methods are like child's play when compared with it. He writes that the Enlightenment Intensive lasts three days and its goal is nothing less than a personal, intimate, and direct experience of enlightenment, the state of unity and radical spiritual awakening known as samadhi in the Indian traditions and kensho in Zen. Iztok has already attended one Enlightenment Intensive and says that it was the most amazing experience he ever had in his life, radically real. That it wasn't some kind of wishy-washy New Age thing where everyone smiles and convinces themselves and others about some sort of energy and similar illusions. That he experienced the ultimate, the absolute truth, the direct experience of "that" which transcends time, space, energy, and matter. Iztok says that I have nothing to even think about, that he's certain it's tailor-made for me, that it will give meaning to my life because it's a direct jump into the very nature of existence, into the meaning of life itself.

I stare at the distant hills which I can see from the barracks on this clear windy January day and I can't stop smiling. Now it will be much easier for me to hold on through this last month of military service.

And of course, I immediately sign up to the first possible Enlightenment Intensive which is in Koper, only an hour's train ride from Ljubljana, in March, in a little over two months' time.

Life once again begins to have some purpose, it even becomes exciting.

∞

Clack-clack…clack-clack…clack-clack…

The rhythmic and calmly muted sound of the steel wheels of the train carries me from Montenegro all the way back to my home in Kranj. For the last time I say goodbye to the limestone mountains of Montenegro which I've scrambled over wearing full military equipment countless times during the last year, day and night, in heat and cold, sometimes cursing the bizarreness of this world with its armies, sometimes gazing ecstatically at the moon and the stars, mostly wandering through my own thoughts.

Although I hate to admit it, it's been a very valuable experience in which I've learned about relationships and about myself. It's been a great preparation for the next phase of my life.

Yes, I've just turned twenty and I have the feeling that I am now ready to shift my exploration of meaning and the ultimate reality into a higher gear. During my year of military service I've read many books about spirituality and philosophy, and it's become clearer to me where I'm heading: ultimate inner freedom. I don't know how exactly to put it into words but I've started to recognize this inner longing more and more precisely.

The train slowly pulls into the station at Belgrade, about halfway on my journey. About two and a half years have passed since I was hitch-hiking somewhere near here on my way to Bulgaria, heading for the Near East and Africa.

I'll work for about half a year and save money so I'll have enough for another year of backpacking. One possibility is to take the trans-Siberian railway across the Soviet Union and Mongolia and then make my way across China, maybe even all the way to Tibet, en route to India. Another possibility is to go straight to India, which is in any case my main destination. I've heard and read so much about India and its spirituality that I'm utterly certain that that's where I must go for answers.

The hours pass and I enjoy having spent almost the entire journey alone in the compartment, in peace and quiet, sunk in my thoughts. The train hurries across the frozen Pannonian plains toward Zagreb. I'm glad that I didn't take the plane as my mother tried to convince me to do, but chose instead this slow, melancholic, and even romantic way to return to my homeland.

But first, of course, the Enlightenment Intensive. It starts in a couple of weeks and I can already feel the excitement inside me. Fear of the unknown is there, but also hope that there I will discover my path, as Iztok hinted. And also the expectation of something unimaginably ultimate.

It's early morning as I slowly climb the old concrete steps over the railway tracks which lead to the suburb of Kranj where our house is. A bird warbles sleepily from the bare treetops above me, which I can hardly see through the winter fog.

∞

"Hmm, who am I? I'm the one asking myself the question. What else?"

The middle-aged man in a blue track suit sits on the floor directly opposite me, closes his eyes, and goes silent.

I look at him in the silence and at the same time take in the sounds in the space. Twelve pairs sitting like the two of us, facing each other in two straight lines. Half of the people are working on the technique; the other half are sitting motionless and listening. In the ceaseless murmuring of voices, we work through the morning of the second day of the Enlightenment Intensive.

"In essence, I am the one who is aware of myself asking myself this question."

For a moment he stares somewhere above my head.

"Ach, this isn't leading anywhere. This way I can keep taking steps backward and widening my perspective forever. It makes no sense."

He exhales and once again closes his eyes.

131

Everything hurts and we're not even halfway through the retreat. My knees, my back, my head. We get up at four in the morning and go to bed at ten at night. We spend most of the day in the so-called dyads, which are a combination of meditation and communication. I cannot say that anything really earth-shaking has happened but still I have the feeling that I've experienced two months of inner travel in only a day and a half.

"I actually don't know if I'm doing the technique right," he says. "I'll go and ask Alenka."

Alenka, who is leading this Enlightenment Intensive, spends most of the time sitting motionless by the wall and attentively observing what is happening in the room. The man squats on the floor in front of her. Alenka leans in towards him and they start to whisper.

I use this time to slowly stretch my aching spine and become aware of the many voices in the room. On my right a woman is shuddering and crying, her hands over her face, her lap filled with crumpled paper tissues. On my left a man with a bushy black moustache and his eyes closed is screaming up at the ceiling:

"Away from me, Satan, away!"

Opposite me sits another man with a moustache shaking with laughter:

"In my opinion, the question – who am I? – is the greatest mystery in the world. Many years after I have died, people will still be wondering – who was this?"

He twists with laughter. His partner tries to keep his attention on him and not to react, but he also begins to lose it and starts shaking with laughter.

Although at first glance someone might think the room is full of lunatics, I am feeling more and more wonderful in this space. Everything comes out of us: pain, joy, fears, relief, despair, ecstasy… and whatever we express is okay. There is acceptance and space for everything. We are welcome as we are, with everything that's happening in us. A space has opened here for true authenticity and freedom.

My partner sits in front of me again, murmurs that he now knows what to do for the next ten minutes, smiles, straightens his spine, and says to me:

"Experience directly who you are."

Later, during a ten-minute break, the room looks post-apocalyptic. Some participants have collapsed on the floor, others sit hunched staring blankly in front of them. A few are wiping away tears. Two are sitting erect in meditation position with their eyes closed.

Although I didn't know even one person here before the beginning of the retreat, I now feel completely at home as if I have come back to a family full of love and warmth. I've never before got so closely connected to people in such a short time.

All of a sudden Alenka's soft and pleasant voice is heard:

"Nikola, would you come over here please?"

Nikola steps away from the window through which he is looking, quietly giggles, and sits in front of Alenka.

"Nikola, what happened?"

"Uhh, nothing. I'm sitting, working on the technique. Everything's okay," Nikola responds in a low thoughtful voice.

"What does okay mean? How are you actually doing?"

"Yeah, just okay, only the question is somehow always falling apart."

"What does that mean – that the question is falling apart?"

"That it doesn't make sense anymore, the question. No part of the question makes sense. Who. Am. I. None of it makes any sense."

"Nikola, do you perhaps know who you are?"

Motionless, Nikola stares at Alenka, and she asks him the question again with a slight smile on her face.

"Nikola, tell me who you are."

Tears stream down Nikola's face. For an instant it seems that no one in the room is breathing.

"Nikola, who is crying now? Tell me who is crying," Alenka smiles lovingly.

Nikola starts to sob, louder and louder, his shoulders shaking, and then suddenly his sobbing changes into loud laughter. Alenka also starts to laugh, tears streaming down her cheeks. Nikola hugs her, laughing loudly through his tears. He sounds amazingly free, happy, fulfilled.

People are breathing again in the room, some are laughing, and now we hear the voice of the assistant:

"Choose your partner for the next dyad."

...

The next day I sit in a dyad with a young girl who has recently had an experience of enlightenment. Amazed, I stare at her as she wipes tears of bliss from her wide eyes which are shining with a sort of cosmic depth. She speaks almost in a whisper to me and with infinite tenderness and power at the same time:

"There are no words. It is impossible to describe. It is everything, everything, everything..." She folds her hands in front of her. "It's eternity. It's love. It's everything. Everything is one. You, me, before, after... Everything is one. The absolute," she says with complete peace.

When I stare into her eyes it's as if I'm staring into the centre of the universe.

And one thing is totally clear to me. I will keep going to these Enlightenment Intensives until I experience enlightenment myself, even if it takes a thousand years.

Six: To India for Meaning

I'm in my room reading when I hear a knock on the door and my father enters:

"I'd like to talk to you a bit," he says, "if you have time now."

"Sure, have a seat," I say and put down my book.

"Your mother and I can't understand why you're going to India, why India of all places. We're wondering if this is maybe connected with these seminars you've been going to, these Intensives or whatever you call them. I would just like you to help us understand."

"Of course, with pleasure. It's not directly connected, but indirectly, because in both cases, both in the Enlightenment Intensives and my travels to India, the search is the same. The Intensives involve a search for the meaning of life, the effort to directly experience my true nature. It has to do with the experience of absolute reality. The aim of these Enlightenment Intensives is to, right there and then, have the experience of enlightenment."

My father looks pretty lost after these few sentences of explanation.

"Hmm. And have you experienced this enlightenment at the Intensives?" he asks.

It seems that my father is really trying to understand, so I decide to use the opportunity to explain in more detail:

"Not yet, unfortunately. I've been to three so far and I haven't experienced it yet, but I know I will keep going until I do. I've seen people experience it right in front of my eyes and I'm convinced it's an exceptional experience, perhaps the ultimate experience. That's why it's called enlightenment. But we have so many conditioned internal barriers, conscious and unconscious identifications, that it takes us a long time to dig our way through it all. In Eastern traditions people meditate for decades in monasteries or caves in order to arrive at the state of enlightenment. They call it samadhi in India. Now, of course, the enlightenment you experience at these Intensives isn't a permanent state, but, nevertheless, it is a direct experience of the ultimate reality."

My father's gaze wanders around the room and then out of the window:

"Aha, so that's why you want to go to India?"

"Basically, yes. There's an exceptional tradition of spiritual development there, thousands of years old, and I want to go and learn at the source. For example, the book I'm reading right now is about one of the last great Indian wise men, Ramana Maharshi."

My father wakes up a bit. "Aha, I think I've heard that name."

"You've probably heard of Maharishi Mahesh Yogi. He's from Northern India. He's known for bringing transcendental meditation to the West. The Beatles went to visit him and made him famous."

"Yes, yes, I remember. Is the one you're talking about a different guy?"

"Yes, though they have similar names, because in Sanskrit Maha means great and Rishi means wise man, so it's more of a title. Mine, Ramana Maharshi, spontaneously experienced a very deep enlightenment, self-realization at the age of sixteen and it completely transformed him. After that he no longer had any interest in the world, only in the absolute, oneness, the beyond. And he went on to live his entire life on the sacred Mount Arunachala or at its foothills, in a state of oneness. And he taught everyone who came to him to first dedicate themselves to the crucial question: "Who am I?" Only when they directly experience that will everything else be clear."

"Who I am?" my father responds smugly. "I don't need to ask myself that question. It's written in black and white on my driver's license."

I look at him for a few seconds in silence, trying to figure out if he is joking. Unfortunately he's not.

"Yeah, that's your name. What I'm talking about is your ultimate, transpersonal identity. That's something completely different."

"Well, whatever," my father sighs. "Weren't you planning on travelling through the Soviet Union and going to China?"

"Yeah, I was at first. Then I realized that actually only India interests me so I'm going to go directly there."

"And when do you plan to leave?"

"Some time at the beginning of July. I don't know the exact date. I'll hitch-hike to Athens and then fly to India because flights are much cheaper from there."

"July of this year?" my father asks.

"Yes, this year, this year, 1986," I answer with a laugh.

My father stands up to leave and says: "You know, when I was your age, I also dealt with such questions, the meaning of life and that sort of thing. Then I stopped wasting my time and began to focus on more real things."

He shuts the door after him and I sit in silence. He only thought about it then and never again? Because he focused on MORE real things? What is more real than the nature of existence, the meaning of life, one's own identity? These are the ultimate questions about reality. It's obvious to me that my father and I don't live in the same world and never have done. I live in a world with people who never stopped and never will stop exploring the mysteries of life. With people for whom unveiling the unknown, striving for wholeness, is practically the only meaning in life and not only a momentary wave that comes and then quickly retreats.

I lie back on the couch and open my book.

∞

Someone patting me on the shoulder wakes me from a deep darkness. Where am I? Aha, at the airport. An airport official is sitting next to me with my passport in his hand.

"Where is your visa for Pakistan, sir?"

I can't believe this is happening to me again. I take a breath and try to answer as calmly and respectfully as possible:

"Look, I don't need a visa for Pakistan. I have a Yugoslav passport and we don't need a visa for Pakistan. Please, just look at the last issue of the Travel Information Manual, page 56. It says there that only citizens of South Africa, India and Israel need a visa for a month-long tourist stopover in the country."

By now I know this page by heart.

"Alright, sir. I'll check again. Please wait here."

He sighs and heads back to his office.

I rub my eyes and look around the airport where I'd fallen into such a heavy sleep. Images from the last few hectic days streak through my head: the Egypt Air flight from Athens to Cairo to wait a couple of hours for the flight to Karachi, because apparently it's easier to get a visa for India there than in Europe. Endless confusion at the gate before boarding the flight to Karachi. The official at the gate can't find my passport, which I'd been obliged to leave at the counter, even though I show him the exact shelf where his colleague had put it. The rush for the van in front of the building with a second official, who finally found my passport, and a woman wearing a black veil. The driver racing like a madman across the airport apron to the airplane from which they are already removing the stairway. The official goes out shouting, they put the stairway back, and then the official runs onto the plane. After a minute or so, he comes back with an agitated young Pakistani man:

"But my wife is on this plane. My children are on this plane. My luggage is on this plane."

The official ignores the man's protests and guides the veiled woman up the stairs and into the airplane. He returns to the van, telling me that the airplane is full and we go back to the terminal building. An argument ensues with the officials who eventually put me in a hotel room until the next flight the following afternoon. An argument with new officials the next day who realize that I don't have a visa for Pakistan. A hot-tempered debate with everyone, each of whom interprets the text from the Travel Information Manual in their own way, even when I find an Englishman who explains to them exactly what the relevant sentence means. Another night in the Cairo airport hotel. The continuation of the argument the next day. They won't let me stay in the hotel room anymore and tell me they can't let me on the plane without a visa. Going into Cairo city to the Yugoslav embassy where they confirm that I don't need a visa for Pakistan. Then to the Pakistani embassy where they also confirm that I don't need a visa and I ask them to give me a visa anyway so they will finally stop hassling me at the airport. With an attitude of resignation, the official stamps my passport with a visa, writes in some numbers, and tells me that I have to come back the next day so the ambassador can sign the visa, otherwise it isn't valid. Then to Father Anastasi on the other side of Cairo to spend the night in his monastery. My shock the next day when the official at the Pakistani embassy calmly informs me:

"The ambassador said that if you want a visa, you have to go through the whole procedure which takes two months. But you don't need a visa so you have nothing to worry about. Here is your passport. I wish you a good day."

I open the passport and see the word CANCELLED in large letters stamped across the visa. Great. Now I'm in even deeper shit.

Back to the Yugoslav embassy to convince the assistant to the ambassador to come with me to the airport to speak directly to the officials there who refuse to take me seriously. An argument between the assistant to the Yugoslav ambassador and some high-level official at the airport who finally throws his hands in the air and allows me to fly. But since all the direct flights are now full, he has to find another way to get me there. He finds a flight from Cairo to Karachi via Teheran and takes me to the gate. Two officials there stop me:

"Where is your visa for Saudi Arabia?"

Disoriented, I look back and forth from one to the other for a few seconds as if we are in some kind of a showdown with revolvers in the wild west. Then I say:

"My final destination is Karachi, Pakistan. I am only transferring in Iran for a couple of hours."

The officials look at me in surprise, then at each other, shrug their shoulders, and let me board the plane. I realize when we land that we're actually in Saudi Arabia, not Iran, in a city called Dharan that I've never heard of in my life. I had thought it was their peculiar way of spelling Teheran, Iran.

And now I'm sitting in a building in Dharan airport, waiting for another official, and shaking my head at how my spiritual pilgrimage to India has begun. The official comes back, sits down next to me, and says:

"Alright. We'll let you on the plane but you have to sign here, agreeing to pay any expenses that might be incurred if you're turned away at the border."

I sign everything he puts in front of me and try to doze for a while but the flight to Pakistan begins to board almost immediately. After a few hours, in the early morning, I'm standing completely disorientated in an endless line at passport control at Karachi airport. When my turn finally comes, I hand my passport through the window and the official flips through the pages, finally asking:

"Where is your visa for Pakistan?"

Oh no, not again. I slowly take a breath and begin to speak:

"Well, I don't need a visa for Pakistan…"

"But you have a visa for Pakistan, mister," he interrupts me, looking at my passport with a smile. I realize that he's looking at the visa and somehow not registering the enormous word CANCELLED stamped across it.

"Oh yeah, in fact I do, yes…" I stammer uncertainly.

He happily brings the entry stamp down on the page and hands my passport back to me.

"Welcome to Pakistan."

When I try to find my luggage, which arrived three days ago from Cairo, I'm told that it's a holiday and the person who has the key to the storage room is away and will return in two days' time. If it's a holiday then the Indian Embassy where I have to go for a visa for India is probably closed as well. Dispirited, I stagger out of the airport, ignore the taxis, and look for a bus into the city to find a cheap hotel for I don't know how many days. If it carries on like this, I will go crazy before I even take a step on Indian soil.

∞

I'm sitting on the bus taking me from Delhi to the north and the foothills of the Himalayas: my destination is Rishikesh, a pilgrimage site and centre of yoga and spirituality, one of the holiest places in India. It's a city of saints on the holy River Ganges, close to its source where the water is completely unpolluted. It's hard to even count all that is holy in Rishikesh so of course it must be my first stop in India.

The bus is just perfect, the way I remember them from Africa: with no glass in the windows, dented inside and out, the seats so close together that there's no room for my legs, so I extend them into the aisle and place my feet on a metal suitcase. The driver of course is going crazily fast, constantly honking at bicyclists and pedestrians, cows and goats and pigs. My mouth is stretched into a big smile because I'm so happy. Back on the road again!

The future seems endlessly bright and full of hope. I will go straight to an ashram where I will meditate myself unconscious, until I find enlightenment. Nothing will be too difficult for me to do in order to accomplish my aim of letting my ego disintegrate completely. I will carry shit with my bare hands if I have to, submit to any test by the wise men in the Himalayan caves, give up everything: predictability, dignity, pride, my own identity, absolutely everything, let it all fall apart as soon as possible, so that only the underlying ultimate remains, my absolute true nature.

At that moment I feel someone patting my shoulder. I look up and see two women in saris sitting diagonally across from me, gesturing with irritation that I should take my feet off their suitcase.

I immediately move my feet and look outside resentfully. Where should I put my feet when the dimensions of this bus are made to the measure of these tiny Indians? Not to mention that my feet are bare and probably cleaner than their suitcase and everything else on this bus. How can they be so annoying and inhospitable?

All of a sudden life becomes dark and India senseless. There's no point in anything. I have nothing to learn from these Indians.

A couple of hours later the bus arrives in Rishikesh. By then I'm calm again and I smile to myself: so much for transcending my ego.

∞

"Where are you from, you gorgeous young man?"

I hear the soft voice behind me and turn around. The ashram librarian, with whom I exchange a smile each day when I come to browse through the books, is standing in front of me. She is probably around seventy years old but an extraordinary beauty and tranquillity emanates from her. Her eyes glow. A calm dignity resides in her physical posture. Her braided hair has the aroma of coconut. It won't be long before I start believing in the genetic superiority of the Brahmin caste.

"From Yugoslavia. Have you heard of that country?"

"Of course I have. It was one of the founders of the non-aligned movement, along with India," the lady smiles. "How do you like our ashram?"

"It's interesting. It is the first ashram I've ever been to. I'm still getting used to it. I go to meditation and hatha yoga. I talk with a lot of people. I go to another yoga class at the Sivananda ashram and for walks along the Ganges. And in the evening to lectures with the swami, although I have trouble understanding him, he speaks so fast. But, in short, I find it all very interesting."

"Wonderful," murmurs the lady, peering into the book I'm holding in my hand. "I see you are always reading Ramana Maharshi," she says, coming closer and speaking in a whisper. "Listen to my advice: stick to people like Ramana Maharshi. Those are the real saints. That is real spirituality. Our swami here is nobody special. He was completely unprepared to succeed our previous teacher who died five years ago. You won't learn anything worthwhile from him. I stay here because I am old and I have found my own rhythm and spirituality but it would be a waste of time for you. Go to Mount Arunachala, go to Ramana Maharshi. As you know, his body died in 1950 and he returned to eternity, but his spirit is still very present there."

"Thank you," I smile and bow slightly, her glowing eyes still embracing me. I return to my room enchanted. Do I need a clearer sign than this?

∞

Slowly, very slowly, I open my eyes slightly and look around me. I'm sitting in the glow of a candlelight at the centre of a small room with eight other people, five men and three women, all somewhere between thirty and seventy years old and all sitting in the lotus position, completely erect, motionless, eyes closed. I am by far the youngest, and there are no other westerners here. We have certainly been meditating for half an hour, and, okay, that's not so long, I can handle it. I close my eyes again, straighten my spine which had started to sag, and direct my attention back to the point between my eyes, which Rajpal had gently recommended to us at the beginning.

I heard about Rajpal from a very nice woman from New Zealand staying in the ashram in Rishikesh. She told me that he lived in the hill station of Mussoorie, only a couple of hours' bus ride away, and that he was a true wise man, a true yogi, not some kind of charlatan of which there were so many around here. Although the woman had given me precise directions, I couldn't find him at my first attempt, despite walking around the whole town and asking many people that I met. Disappointed, I returned to the ashram late in the evening. After getting even more precise instructions on how to find the place, I packed my stuff the next day, left the ashram in Rishikesh, got back on the bus for Mussoorie and finally took a room in a cheap little hotel opposite Rajpal's house.

Again I open my eyes slightly and start to turn my wrist slowly, very slowly, so I can secretly look at my watch. I don't want to cause the slightest sound because the room is so quiet that even the occasionally fluttering of the candle flame can be heard. Oh no, we've been meditating for more than an hour, entirely motionless. Before we began, Rajpal had said that it would be a relatively short session tonight because we'd started so late. My legs have gone completely numb in the lotus position, so I slowly, very slowly, lift my right foot and ease it off my left leg and onto the floor, into the half-lotus position. I feel with relief the blood beginning to flow back into my foot.

After I'd settled into my little room at the hotel earlier that day, I had gone out with the intention of going on an afternoon walk and getting something to eat before visiting Rajpal. To my surprise an older gentleman with short white hair and beard, wearing white trousers and a tunic, was already waiting for me in the hotel's courtyard. He smiled pleasantly, put his palms together in front of his chest, and spoke gently:

"I heard that you were looking for me so I came to you. My name is Rajpal."

I looked into his enormous and endlessly kind blue eyes and my heart began to beat faster.

"Yes, yes, it's true. My name is Robert and I heard that you're a teacher of meditation and yoga and spirituality. You were recommended to me and I would like to study with you, if that would be okay…"

144

I stuttered nervously as we sat together on the bench in front of the hotel.

"No, I am not a teacher. I like to meditate with friends and to share what I have learned through meditation, but I'm not a teacher," he smiled gently.

"Well yes, exactly, I would like to learn from your experience if I might. I have so many questions that torment me, that constantly spin around in my mind. For example, I don't know how to recognize my authentic will, how to tell the difference between the impulses that come from the depths of my authentic being and impulses that come from my ego, my fears, my patterns, but are well camouflaged. Or, how can I figure out what to focus on in my life? Should I dedicate myself entirely to spirituality, or is my karma something else, that I don't want to see, that I run away from? Or, perhaps…"

Rajpal interrupted me with a gentle smile.

"I understand, yes, these are all big questions, very important, and very difficult. If I had some supernatural spiritual powers then I would gladly bring clarity to you and give you perfect peace of mind. Yet I don't know any other way but to meditate, and slowly things become clear as your mind becomes calmer and more serene. If you like, you can come with me now to my home where my wife is cooking dinner and also thought of you, so there is enough for everyone, and then a few of my friends are coming and we will meditate together. If that is what you would like to do."

I gratefully accepted his invitation. As I walked beside the light-footed Rajpal, I wondered whether I had perhaps found my guru, since our meeting was so similar to other seekers' meetings with gurus that I'd read about in books. There was something miraculous about it. And Rajpal looked just like Ramana Maharshi…

My knees are burning with unbearable pain and my watch shows that we've been meditating for over two hours. Everyone is sitting completely motionless, seemingly in a state of perfect attention and harmony. Only I am in agony. I tense and relax my butt and slightly shift the angle of my position in the hope that at least a tiny bit more blood will flow into my legs. I think each cubic centimetre of my body is hurting. There is absolutely nothing even slightly like meditation going on here. I am just trying to survive, while secretly checking my watch every five minutes.

I almost cannot believe it when I finally hear the sound of the little bell with which Rajpal announces the end of meditation. I open my eyes and discreetly glance at my watch again. We've been meditating for two and a half hours. That's what he calls shorter meditation.

Rajpal smiles kindly at me and asks:

"How did it go, Robert?"

"Okay, everything was okay. It was great. Thank you."

I babble nonsensically as I slowly and nonchalantly try to extend my legs, which have long since lost all sensation.

Rajpal mildly asks:

"It seemed to me you were having difficulties and I am sorry if that was the case. I thought I understood from our conversation at dinner that you were used to meditating and that you had a lot of practice?"

"No, no. I didn't have any difficulties. It was fine. Maybe the floor was harder than I'm used to but, aside from that, everything was great."

I speak with an artificial smile on my face, praying that some sensation will return to my legs before it's time for me to stand up and leave the room.

Rajpal gently smiles again.

"That pleases me. Tomorrow we get together at eight in the morning and we will have a real meditation, four hours from eight to twelve, then lunch, and then we will continue in the afternoon with another four-hour meditation period. You are warmly invited. It would please me very much if you would come."

Somehow I manage to maintain a calm expression on my face.

"Oh, wonderful. Of course I will come. I look forward with great pleasure."

As I slowly hobble across the street to my hotel on my numb legs, I think that Rajpal is a hard-core adept. I could not imagine a better guru: modest, gentle, loving, attentive, glowing with a bright energy, a sort of loving light and inner peace.

...

I sleep very little that night and at six in the morning I'm sitting on the first bus out of town, to the south, back to Delhi. The whole way back I try to find reasons and excuses for running away like this, and I realize that in Mussoorie my fantasies had collided with reality.

∞

"How did your retreat go?"

An older gentleman asks me the question. We're leaning against the railing of a terrace and gazing down at the Bodh Gaya, the holy place where the Buddha found enlightenment after forty-nine days of motionless meditation beneath a tree. I came here to the source for a ten-day Vipassana meditation retreat with a traditionally strict regime: intensive, but in a more manageable format for me, with six one-hour sessions of meditation each day, plus two meditative walks and conversations with the teacher. Each minute of the day, including mealtimes, was supposed to be permeated with complete presence and meditation.

"Okay. It went really, really okay," I respond.

Though I know it actually did not go all that well. I stuck to the schedule for the whole ten days and sometimes even had wonderful and slightly cosmic experiences of total inner silence and presence, but most of the time during meditation I just had more fantasies and made plans about the future. How I will meditate fantastically in the south, at the Maharshi ashram, and at

147

holy Mount Arunachala, pretty much constantly and with extraordinary depth of course. And how things will be when I get home, how I will order my life in the spirit of a sort of contemporary asceticism. When I will wake up in the morning, which meditation and which exercises I will be doing, how I will set up my room so it will be as spiritual as possible. I thought about everything down to the tiniest detail.

The man smiles with generosity and respect and asks me:

"How old are you, if you don't mind my asking?"

"I'm twenty."

I turn towards him with a smile, hoping he won't immediately peg me as some dumb kid.

"Twenty years old? Only twenty? Unbelievable. What fantastic karma you must have that you started on your spiritual journey so early. I'm sixty-five years old and I come from Thailand, which is a Buddhist country, and I was born into a Buddhist family. But it wasn't until two years ago, when I retired, that I truly found the spiritual path and began to meditate, and now I'm here and I'm going to stay. And you are only twenty! What fantastic karma!"

He looks at me with admiration.

A little later I'm in a rickshaw on the way to the train station, feeling dispirited and confused. It's bullshit, not karma. My spiritual practice is a farce, more meant to make an impression on others than anything else, and in truth I am completely lost in my fantasies. I even fantasize about how one day I will make a complete break and stop fantasizing altogether.

∞

My whole body stiffens when I realize that a macaque monkey has jumped on the back of my right leg and is holding on with its little claws. I somehow manage to control my instinct to kick it off and slowly stop and look down at the little brown owner of those tiny claws. In the meantime, a few other monkeys pause nervously, looking at me suspiciously, baring their teeth. One quickly reaches out its paw and pulls the smaller monkey from my leg. I sigh with relief as it seems that they don't want any trouble, that we're somehow on the same side.

I continue my slow ascent of Mount Arunachala surrounded by around fifty macaques and wonder how to safely extract myself from this group in the middle of which I have found myself. All of a sudden they had bounded in from the right, swarming all over the path, and now we're walking together. It seems to me that we're all a little nervous but we act as if everything is normal. I'd like to go a little faster but I don't dare to push my way through them. The monkeys are not big but their teeth and claws are sharp. They're quick and strong and above all there are a lot of them. Suddenly I notice with relief that the monkeys at the front of the pack have turned off to the left onto a slope and I am alone again.

Hmm, finally the south of India and Arunachala, the holy mountain, supposedly the supreme chakra of our Earth, the seat of planetary energy. Everything is calm and silent and the sky is red as the sun is about to come up. I somehow feel that this is the climax of my travels through India. As I reach the peak, the sun is just beginning to appear and lying before me, as if in the palm of my hand, there's a gorgeous view of one of the greatest temples of Shiva in India, in the middle of the little town of Tiruvannamalai which is just waking up now. In a short while the town will be wrapped in a cloud of dust from the hustle and bustle of the day, but at this moment everything is crystal clear.

Suddenly, in the midst of this silence and peace, I sense the presence of something behind me. I instinctively turn and stiffen. A man with long, matted hair, wearing only a lungi around his waist, is gliding silently past about two metres behind me. He's carrying a stick in one hand and in the other a vessel of some sort. His age seems indeterminate. In fact he moves past me like a ghost, with an otherworldly softness. For the briefest instant he looks into my eyes and I almost shit my pants. His eyes are like the blackness of the universe. The next moment, he disappears into the bushes and I'm alone again as if nothing had happened.

Except that my heart is beating so wildly that it's actually moving my whole chest in and out.

Finally I start to breathe again and my pulse grows calm. I slowly make my way back into the valley towards the ashram where I'm staying. But I get another shock on the way down when a pack of six langurs, big white monkeys with black faces, race past me. They look as if they're from another world or perhaps from the Ramayana, the great epic which features Hanuman, the monkey god. They're so big that it seems as if the ground shakes when they jump across the path in front of me.

I've had enough shocks for one day, I think, when I finally step into the safe haven of the ashram.

...

Later I learn that the man I saw at the top of the mountain was an ascetic who has been living there for decades and who practically no one ever sees, since he only comes down to the ashram at night for food and water, otherwise spending all his time meditating somewhere among the boulders and high bushes at the top of Arunachala. Wow, I think, he's the real thing.

∞

I'm standing in front of a little red-painted house that was built near the entrance to a small cave at the foothills of Arunachala. It's the place where Ramana Maharshi sat and meditated for many years. Or perhaps it would be more accurate to say that he sat absorbed in a state of oneness, in the state of samadhi. Many of the stories that I've read about him happened right here.

I approach the little house built around the cave just as a young guy dressed in white steps out. He's just finished sweeping inside the house and is now beginning to carefully sweep the area around it. He smiles broadly, puts his palms together in front of his chest in greeting, and bows slightly. I greet him in the same way and look towards the doorway of the house to ask if I may go in.

"Yes, yes, please, please…"

He smiles and moves aside to make room for me.

I step slowly and respectfully into the little house, and continue into the little cave itself where a large black stone with a flat top draws my attention. The smiling young man returns to his job of sweeping the courtyard and leaves me alone.

I approach the rock on which Ramana Maharshi used to sit in this small space and am drawn to sit on it myself. My legs seem to slide on their own into the lotus position, my spine straightens, my eyes close – as if meditation is the only thing that it's possible to do in this tiny space in which the energy is so extraordinarily concentrated.

Here there is only presence, only awareness.

…

Later, as I walk down the slopes of Arunachala, I realize that the meditation practices of Ramana Maharshi and Enlightenment Intensive represent the same path, the same focus. And however much I enjoy the environment here, however much I feel Ramana Maharshi close to my heart, I now feel increasingly drawn back to the Intensives. I sense that extraordinary discoveries still await me there.

∞

"Everything very clear. You have a big and open heart. And very good dreams that you must trust. Truly: very strong and good dreams. Great spirits always on your side, always support you. You have much divine power."

This is what the old and extremely kind bearded Indian man says to me. Every day as I walk from my room through the park in Pondicherry to the Sri Aurobindo ashram's cafeteria for breakfast, lunch, and dinner, he greets me pleasantly and offers to read my palm.

"Standard reading ten rupees, special reading fifteen rupees."

Up until today I have just smiled and said "Perhaps another time", but today I responded differently. Somehow his kindness and his sparkling eyes have grown on me and so I stopped beside him and said:

"Okay, what do the standard readings and special readings include?"

"Standard reading everything, special reading more."

It was obvious that I wouldn't get any more details from him, so I made an offer:

"Okay, I'll start with the standard reading and then, if I'm satisfied, I'll add five rupees for the special reading. Is that okay?"

He smiled and invited me to sit next to him on the bench. He looked intently at my hand, closely tracing the lines on my palm with his fingers.

"You must be very independent. You must live a very independent life. Your father won't help you very much. You will have very many difficulties, yes, indeed, very many difficulties with women…."

Great, I think.

"You will have two sons. You will live to be eighty years old but you will only be really happy after fifty."

"I'll only be happy then? After thirty more years? Until then I'll be unhappy?"

"No, not unhappy, but true happiness will come only after you are fifty. And the year 1987 will be very, very, very good for you. Very good."

"So, next year if I understand you correctly."

"Yes, 1987 will be an exceptionally good year for you spiritually."

He studies my palm for about twenty minutes, comes to various conclusions, and I write everything down. Then he says that that is all.

I thank him, give him ten rupees and then another five.

"Here. Five more rupees for the special reading. If you could now do the special reading and tell me what you see."

He smiles, takes the money and puts it away, holds my palm again, and stares into it for another few seconds.

"Very, very special hand, very special hand."

He smiles again and lifts his gaze to me.

"Okay, got it. Can you please do your special reading now?"

"Yes, yes, very, very special hand, very special hand," he smiles.

"So this is your special reading?" I ask incredulously.

"Yes, yes, very, very special hand, very special."

He is still smiling. I look at him blankly and then I can't help myself. I start laughing and we laugh together. I don't even know what we're laughing at. Perhaps it's the sheer joy of connection with this sweet man with his sparkling eyes, a connection in which we both reach beyond the roles we play, beyond the drama and seriousness, and get a glimpse of this cosmic joke called life. I shake his hand and cheerfully say goodbye and he, still laughing and with playful eyes, repeats one last time:

"Very, very, special hand. Very special."

∞

I'm sitting in front of a moustachioed official with carefully combed and oiled hair. He's wearing a white shirt and has a sophisticated expression on his face. The office is also a waiting room and there are four other men in the queue behind me. Today I actually managed to be first.

"How can I help you?"

153

The official raises his eyebrows.

"I would like to extend my Indian tourist visa for an additional three months. I have everything with me..."

He interrupts me:

"It is not possible. You cannot extend your visa."

"How is it not possible? I looked into it and a three-month extension is completely routine. I checked. Look, I have everything with me: my passport, two photographs..."

"Two photographs are not enough. You need four," the official interrupts me again and looks through my passport.

"Why four photographs? If I checked and only two photographs are required," I say, becoming agitated.

"Here in Tiruchirappalli we require four photographs. Where is your visa for India? Ah, here it is. I see. Where did you get this visa?"

"At the Indian Embassy in Karachi, Pakistan."

"In that case this visa is not valid," concludes the official with satisfaction.

"What do you mean not valid? It's an official visa. How could it not be valid?"

At this point I'm getting visibly upset.

"It is not valid because it was issued in Pakistan. India and Pakistan have no diplomatic contacts. Therefore it is not valid. Only visas issued in India are valid."

"What are you talking about? I couldn't enter India without a visa. You have to get one in advance, before entering the country, and that would be at an Indian embassy which is the official representative of India outside of India. And I applied for one at the official Indian embassy in Karachi and received one."

My patience is vanishing. The official slowly turns the pages of my passport as if he cannot even hear me. Finally he looks at me:

"Where have you travelled in India for these past three months?"

"Lots of places. I was in the north: in Rishikesh, Haridwar, Mussoorie, Dhera Dun, Bodh Gaya, Delhi of course, Agra, Mathura, Mumbai, and then I came south by train and visited…"

"All right, here is a piece of paper. Write me a list of all the places you have been, the dates you were there, the names of the hotels where you stayed."

He smugly places a sheet of paper and pencil in front of me.

"Are you kidding? That's a lot of information. I can't remember it all."

I look at him dumbstruck.

He returns my look calmly. "Well, you'll have to. Otherwise I can't extend your visa."

"You want the names of hotels. Do you also want the room number in each hotel?" I cannot suppress my sarcasm.

"Yes, exactly, also the hotel room numbers. I have to go and look for something and I will come right back. In the meantime you write it all down."

He walks smugly out of the office. Incredulous, I stare after him and then I stare at the paper in front of me. The man behind me in the queue approaches me, a tall middle-aged Sikh. He leans in towards me and speaks to me in a quiet voice with an impeccable British accent:

"My friend, that official has no idea what a visa is. You will get nothing accomplished here. Go to the neighbouring city and arrange matters there. It will be much quicker."

I thank him and a couple of hours later I am stepping toward a smiling official in his office in the neighbouring city of Dindigul. He addresses me with a smile:

"Good day, my friend, how can I help you?"

I take a deep breath and with all my strength try to speak in a relaxed manner:

"I would like to extend my tourist visa for three months. I have everything with me: two photos…"

"Okay, okay, no problem, no problem."

He quickly looks around him and speaks to me under his breath.

"I give you visa, what you give me?"

I smile with relief. "How about 50 rupees?"

"Very good, very good, my friend. Come back in one hour only."

He smiles and I quickly push the money across the counter and walk out through the wide corridor outside. Sometimes life can be so simple.

∞

Something inside me grows calm, relaxes, opens. I begin to notice it in Shantivanam, an ashram in the south of India, which I like the most of all the ashrams I've visited up till now. It's an ashram where many philosophies and religions have found a place and coexist like the same message in many different languages.

Not only am I calmer inside but the meditation and the hatha yoga is finally working for me. It all becomes a natural part of my everyday life.

It also becomes clear to me that travelling around India is not going to solve anything, no matter how many ashrams I visit, how long I stay in them or how many saints I talk to. I carry myself with me all the time. Whatever I experience I am always the same one, and the manner in which I experience life will remain the same until I transform things within. I actually determine my life experience from moment to moment regardless of where I am and what I am doing.

Spirituality is here and now and is expressed, or not, in each moment. In how I interact with people. In my own self-pity and self-praise, in my presence and absence, in my urgent blabbering or my frightened stuttering. I'm always expressing my true level of maturity and spirituality wherever I am and whatever I'm doing. It's reflected in how I encounter the experience of human life here and now.

It's time for me to go home.

∞

Using a big silver spoon I take a full measure of the gelatinous yellow-brown mass from the kitschy silver bowl on the pedestal in the middle of the table. I'm flying back to chilly Europe tomorrow and I'm treating myself to a better class of restaurant today after half a year of eating in the cafeterias of ashrams and simple vegetarian places around India. I will end my travels in the spirit of celebration.

Although this restaurant is way above my level, I try to give the impression that I belong here, that I always eat in such places. I try to look very sophisticated, serious and distant. Two well-dressed and courteous waiters have just placed several plates of sauce and side dishes on the table and that mysterious bowl in the middle of everything. I decide to start with precisely that one.

As I slowly bring the big spoon with the gelatinous mass towards my mouth I notice a young waiter out of the corner of my eye. His eyes widen. He raises his hand and is about to rush over to me but is stopped by the older waiter standing next to him, who indicates with a dark expression that he shouldn't go anywhere. He should just let me do what I'm going to do.

I realize in that instant that this doesn't look good but somehow I don't have the power to stop, to smile perhaps, and simply ask:

"I see that you were about to tell me something, and it's true that I actually don't know what this dish is and what I should do with it. Could you help me by providing some information?"

With friendliness, with candour. Ah, if only I was capable of such maturity. But because that is not within the realm of my possibilities, the only choice that remains is to open my mouth

157

with apparent dignity and a sort of pride, with the cool reserve of Clint Eastwood, and put the contents of the whole spoon in it and then set the spoon back on my plate.

A volcano immediately explodes in my mouth and hot lava begins to fill the space where my throat used to be and slowly drip down to my stomach, which also catches fire and begins to burn. A nuclear meltdown is taking place in my body but I try hard to maintain a calm expression, despite the fact that sweat is now beginning to leak out of every single pore of my skin.

Of course everything becomes clear to me in that instant. The contents of that bowl were intended for the whole restaurant, for the whole evening. I could probably have taken a quarter of a spoonful and it would have been more than enough for my whole dinner. It's also clear to me that the chief waiter would have helpfully told me what was in the bowl, if I'd been more relaxed and polite with him, but as it was he probably thought; let him burn, the spoiled brat. Now he's probably looking at me with satisfaction. Absolutely everything is clear to me but nevertheless I try to maintain the old masks and calmly continue with my dinner, observed from the side by the smirking waiters standing against the wall, while hiding the inner collapse of my digestive system.

…

The next day on the airplane, where I have to visit the toilet very often, I think that perhaps this last day provided me with the most essential spiritual lesson that India had to offer me during my half year of travels. That the direct manifestation of spirituality in this world is perhaps pure authenticity, sincerity, openness, rather than all those layers of self-satisfaction which make up that finely finished and well-polished mask. That spirituality is merely stripping ourselves down to the authentic nakedness, instead of dressing ourselves up in new and more sophisticated clothing. It has to do with an encounter with ourselves, with others, and with life in a state of radical authenticity, despite our fears.

Yes, the journey is going to be a long one, a very long one, I think and gaze out at the clouds beneath me.

∞

I'm sitting at the table at home, trying to smile. The house is full of relatives and neighbours, coming and going. My mother is busy cooking and serving food, stopping every now and then to hug me again. My father is sitting smoking his pipe and making wisecracks. There's a lot of laughter, everyone is talking over each other.

We're celebrating my homecoming from India after half a year away, and I'm sinking into depression, completely unprepared for this scene. Everyone is toasting my return with wine and beer, which I no longer drink. Everyone is asking me superficial questions and answering them for me before I even have time to open my mouth. In this supposed celebration of my return, I myself have virtually no significance.

Yes, it's time for me to start searching for a new home.

Seven: The Time of Illuminations

I slowly open my eyes... and close them again. Something is disturbing me, but I'm not sure what. I open my eyes again and look at the person sitting opposite me in the dyad. He's looking back at me, relaxed and silent. It's the third day of an Enlightenment Intensive, and suddenly something seems rather different, and I'm not sure what it is. Everything is the same, familiar, and yet completely different. I close my eyes in order to pull myself together. In my thoughts, I ask the question again: "Who am I?"... and... then... I slide... into... timelessness...

...

There is nobody at all that would be experiencing
and nobody to be experienced...
There is nothing to merge because I am already whole...
I am... one with all.
I am in everything and everything is in me.
I am all and there is no me.
There is only the presence of the true self,
which is eternal.
I have always existed and always will exist.
No thought can capture the truth,
wholeness, infinity, eternity.
There is no time, no energy, no matter;
and this is also not true, these are only images.
Only pure boundless self-awareness exists at this source.
Here I am at home,
and I am always present at home, I never leave.
Only an image of myself exists in the world,
leaving the impression that I am there.
Only this moment exists, and my presence in it.

I am constantly in this moment.

Outside of this moment, there is no time, no duration:

the illusion of time is created in me and moves through me.

This moment is my entry point into this reality,

nothing more and nothing less than this moment,

which is, and also is not.

...

I feel a gentle touch on my right shoulder. I open my eyes and hear one of the assistants gently whispering into my ear:

"Alenka would like to speak with you, if that's alright."

I nod, slowly get to my feet, walk across the room to Alenka, and sit down in front of her. She looks at me inquisitively.

"Hey, Robert, what's going on?"

I smile mildly. "Hmm, I'm not sure, nothing, I think…"

Alenka smiles.

"Robert, you were with me at your first Enlightenment Intensive and now you are with me again and this is your sixth one. We know each other well. So we can skip the games, right?"

Still smiling, I take a breath and nod.

"Yeah, it's true. So, something did happen, I think."

Alenka grows serious and asks:

"Okay, Robert, tell me how old you are."

My mouth tries to give the automatic response but stops in the middle because the question actually makes no sense when it meets my inner reality:

"How old am I? Hmm.. I'm not… I mean I'm not old… I mean that it doesn't exist, age and time, I am not…"

I struggle to capture the essence as my whole being sinks backwards into a sort of infinite vastness.

"Alright," Alenka smiles. "Well, try and tell me how tall you are, if you happen to know."

Another veil falls from my consciousness and a deeper reality speaks through me, on its own, without the volition of my conscious mind:

"I have no size. I have no physical dimensions. I am not tall. I am not short. I simply am."

I break into relaxed laughter: "Alenka, you're asking silly questions."

A deep happiness bubbles up inside me.

"Okay, Robert, now tell me if you happen to know who you are," Alenka smiles at me with tears in her eyes.

I hug her, tears running down my cheeks and onto her shoulders, my lungs breathing more deeply than they ever have before.

"I know, Alenka, I actually know who I am in truth, yes, in fact I know…"

…

When I sit back down in front of my partner, I take a breath and open eyes which before now had never truly seen. And I smile for the first time in my life.

I have only now been born.

∞

When the alarm clock rings, I automatically reach out and turn it off so I don't wake my parents. It's four in the morning. First I write down my dreams, which I remember extraordinarily well these days and which have been increasingly complicated lately, and, yes, crazy. Then I perform the Jala Neti, the cleaning of the nostrils with salt water. Then a series of pranayama exercises, then asanas. At five I am ready for meditation – first twenty minutes of Shiva yoga, which I was initiated into at the

Kumaraswamy ashram at the end of my travels in India, then Vichara, Ramani Maharshi's meditation. At six, when my father gets up to go to work, I'm already making tea and getting ready for my study of spiritual literature.

After my first experience of enlightenment, it's become completely clear to me what interests me in life and how I want to live. In any case I have no intention of wasting time in a senseless manner. My goal in life is to transcend life itself, to attain oneness, and I don't want anything to distract me from that path.

And I'm looking forward to the next Intensives, which I've already registered for. And – how unusual this is for me – I'm also looking forward to life, to the future.

∞

"Stop talking to me about horrifying children with crystal eyes, I told you already! It's too much for me! Stop saying all this crazy stuff. I don't want to listen to this anymore!"

These words slowly awaken me. I begin to realize that I'm in a small room, fiercely walking up and down between two beds, up and down, up and down, in almost complete darkness. Only the faint glow of the street lights penetrates the window.

And then I realize that it's me speaking these words.

Surprised, I stop in the middle of the room and go silent. I look down and see that I'm naked and covered in sweat. I stare around me. A little room, a bed on each side of it, and then I gasp: on the bed, which I recognize as mine, there sits...

...a little creature. A humanoid about the size of a six-year-old child but who otherwise looks very, very old. Somehow I know it's a male. He's a dark blue colour and has huge eyes like two polished crystals. The creature looks at me calmly, completely calmly.

At this point, I begin to remember: the creature had been speaking to me in my dreams or wherever I was. Somehow communicating with me telepathically. And this upset me. Now

163

we look at each other. I'm afraid, even though I know he doesn't want to do me any harm. We look at each other for about a minute, then the creature starts to become transparent and finally somehow evaporates, vanishes. I keep looking at the bed and begin to breathe more easily.

I look at the other bed and I see Nado there looking at me, eyes wide open, his blanket pulled all the way up to his nose as if he had completely frozen from fear, watching me apparently raving like a lunatic. I walk to the window. Now my full awareness returns: I am at Nado's, my good friend from my days in the military. He came with me to one of the Enlightenment Intensives in Zagreb and then we went to sleep in his room in the student dorms. And now he will probably never want to hear of Intensives again.

I sit on my bed, sigh, and say:

"Nado, look, what can I say except that everything is okay and you have nothing to worry about. I'm still spaced out from the Intensive. I had such deep experiences, you see. And many different realities are somehow oozing into one another. So, it's a bit confusing, but it's going to settle down and be fine."

Nado lies motionless and stares silently at me. I slowly lie down on my bed and roll onto my side. This intense internal life in which I've been existing recently, what with all the Intensives and meditations and exercises, fills me completely, the exploration leading me on fantastic journeys to unbelievable worlds. But I'm starting to worry that I'm going a bit crazy.

∞

Dinner is over. It's dark outside. We take our torches and slowly make our way up the pass to the top of Mount Ajdna, a half hour's climb. The night sky is starry, the mountain air incredibly pure, and I feel happy. I'm living a perfect life. Everything is centred around the three-day Enlightenment Intensives, as I'm participating in a new one every few weeks, and that's where my inner journeys reach unforeseen depths, with frequent enlightenment experiences. When I'm not at the

Intensives, I spend five days a week at an archaeological excavation of old Slavic settlements on Mt. Ajdna, a thousand metres above sea level, in the Karavanken mountain range of Slovenia. Eight of us are assisting two archaeologists at the digs. We're mostly friends who met at the Intensives, and the head archaeologist likes to hire us because we're so positive and full of energy.

I spend long days here in the exceptionally pure air, surrounded by the mountains and forests, and immersed in silence. We dig, push wheelbarrows, carry material here and there, and all the physical exercise helps to ground me, preventing me from being carried away by all my spiritual experiences. Most evenings, we get together to practise various meditations and other exercises, because we can't do without it. I could live like this forever: Intensives, nature, physical labour, wonderful friends.

Good. We've reached the top. We put our sleeping bags in the middle of the foundations of the old Slavic temple that we've been excavating during the day. We light a few candles and lie down. Today we will have a rebirthing session, a therapeutic and also spiritual method we like to use a lot and which is always an incredibly powerful experience, and will be even more amazing in this special place.

∞

Tears are running down my cheeks in a constant stream. I stopped wiping them away long ago. Tears of feeling so deeply touched that my whole body is gently trembling. It's just the pure awareness of all of us who have been sitting silently in this circle for several hours now, the awareness of all of us on this planet, all of our explorations and journeys, the awareness of our nature, our vulnerability, and our shared eternal search. It's not pain, not sadness. It has no quality. And yet it cracks my heart wide open.

Outside, night has long since fallen when the timer rings. Four hours have passed. Four hours of sitting silent and motionless in a circle, our attention focused on the whole group.

165

Four hours of meditation. Not long ago in India, I ran away just from the thought of such a thing, but now it's the greatest pleasure for me.

I love our little community of Enlightenment Intensives enthusiasts here in my home town of Kranj. We've become a real little family. We're together during Enlightenment Intensives, we're together on Mount Ajdna, together during the weekends. The sense of belonging, the connection and safety heals my wounds and nourishes the parts of me that were so rarely nourished in my family.

∞

I'm flying in the sky and spot an old monastery below. I decide to visit and land in the courtyard. Waiting for me there's a tiny white-haired old man with lively eyes which regard me playfully and seem to know everything about me. I realize that he's the abbot of this monastery.

We speak about Zen. He smiles that it makes no sense for him to explain anything to me, because I already know it all. I say that's not true, that I know almost nothing, while he cheerfully keeps smiling that I know, of course I know. I tell him that I would like to live with him at the monastery and he says I can stay and care for his large and quite difficult horse. I accept the work. The temperament of the horse doesn't worry me. I will manage somehow. The abbot shows me around the monastery and I understand that he's my spiritual teacher. He is calm, beautiful, warm, content, and I love him.

All of a sudden, he stops, looks at me and says that he has sold all his books about Zen Buddhism because they only raised ideas about having awareness without thoughts. He looks at me playfully and says: "Well, you must have at least one thought, mustn't you, the thought of God." He looks at me enigmatically, still smiling.

I wake up from the dream. I turn on the light, reach for my diary, and begin to write it down. Recently I've been dreaming so much and my dream diary fills up quickly. I often remember six or seven long dreams when I wake in the morning. Sometimes it's too much to write them all down, it takes so long, and the dreams are becoming increasingly complicated. I have the feeling that the channel between these two worlds, between this reality and the dream world, is wide open. Many nights I seem to be in both worlds at the same time. It's hard for me to be aware of everything that happens during these long nights but it's definitely getting crazier and crazier.

Most of my dreams belong in one of two categories. The first are dreams in which a group of five to fifteen of my closest friends from the Enlightenment Intensives travel through out-of-this-world realms, exploring other realities, contending with complex phenomena, from a big silver sphere that arrives on earth from a distant part of our universe and we are trying to figure out what it wants, to finding ourselves trapped in an instant outside of time. The feeling that we're a spiritual tribe is constantly present, a holy fraternity, together exploring the mysteries of existence.

The second category are dreams that begin with meditation, or even more often with sitting at an Enlightenment Intensive, when all of a sudden I start being pulled into some other reality. The world around me disappears, energy begins to spiral, carrying me around. I slowly start moving through various realms and finally I myself begin to disappear entirely, to vanish. I sometimes wake up from these dreams as if from a nightmare and at other times completely calm. Often, after such dreams, I feel the presence of something in my room, some energy from another world. And sometimes some part of my body burns with a dull yellow heat, usually the area around my pelvis and lower back.

Okay. I record my dreams and put down the pen and notebook. I turn off the light, lie back on my side, close my eyes and think: the night is still long. Where will it take me?

∞

I lie on my side, turned toward Olja. We have just made love and now are lying naked, facing each other, looking into each other's eyes, motionless, silent.

Time has disappeared.

I am melting in love. In cosmic, infinite, limitless love. Only our connection here and now in the field of love. There is nothing else.

We are like two magnets which have been waiting for the whole of eternity to merge with each other. Two halves of one sphere. During the night, after we made love, I was saying something and suddenly went silent because I realized I didn't know if it was me or her talking. It's as if we were one essence expressing itself through two physical forms.

In the few weeks since we've been together, we've created our own world of magical connection in which there is only perfect love and nothing else. We can be completely open with each other. We don't need to play games or try to fascinate each other. Total acceptance.

Not only did the Enlightenment Intensives give my life meaning but I met this love of mine at one of them.

We're still motionless, looking at each other, and drowning in each other's eyes. There is no need for me to do or say anything. It is just love.

∞

I step slowly, placing one foot in front of the other with total presence: slowly, with attentiveness. Everything around me stands still, the whole of nature, the whole of the earth, even the silence itself. I'm on an afternoon meditative walk on the sixth day of a fourteen-day Enlightenment Intensive. It's my first fourteen-day Intensive and I've been waiting for it for a long time. Actually my whole life. To completely submerge myself in this river.

I stop, take a breath, and look around at the hills bathed in the warm light of the sun that will soon go down. I open myself to the mystery of Life, and disappear…

…

I am home.

The true I is home.

The spark of life,

this manifestation of what I perceive as myself,

is home, home in the absolute.

Nothing exists,

nothing except this eternal foundation.

Everything else is dreams,

a cosmic game.

Only existence exists.

Only oneness exists,

which cannot be put into words,

cannot be rationally understood.

And life.

The material that comprises what we experience as life,

is eternal love.

Not love that yearns for action and expression,

but the silent calm nature of it all,

the omnipresent essence of this manifestation

which connects us, all of us.

I can never hate anyone,

because we are all one.

One.

…

When my consciousness returns to presence in this place on this forest trail where my legs are still standing and my eyes are still staring at the hills, I remember the words of a Zen master:

"Before enlightenment, mountains are mountains and waters are waters; at the moment of enlightenment, mountains are no longer mountains and waters are no longer waters; after enlightenment, mountains are truly mountains and waters are truly waters."

I smile and slowly take the path back.

Oneness is omnipresent.

∞

Click-clack, click-clack, click-clack: the familiar sound of the wheels of the train is somehow meditative. How often have I taken this train from Ljubljana to Koper and back on my way to and from the Enlightenment Intensives. They usually take place in an isolated old stone house in the middle of the Mediterranean hills which we've rented just for this purpose and which has now become a sort of second home for us. Or even a first home.

Today I'm travelling from Koper back towards Ljubljana and then on to Kranj, back home from a one-week training for leaders of Enlightenment Intensives. I don't have a clear picture about when I will run my first Intensive but I'm very sure that I will do it at some point. I know that this is directly connected to my mission in life. I know deep in my gut that I have a calling for this, that it's an important or maybe even crucial part of my life path.

And I observe how I'm already flooded with a multitude of internal reactions. Fears about whether I will succeed, whether I will know how to do it, whether anyone will even sign up, what will happen if I mess the whole thing up, doubts about whether I'm good enough, whether I'm competent, whether I'm perhaps too immature…

Well, once again I'm getting myself into something quite radical, trial by fire. I will open my arms and step naked in front of everyone. I will expose myself voluntarily and offer my vulnerability on a platter…

Hmm….

∞

I'm walking beside the sea in the pitch-black silence. I'm accompanied by the barely audible splashing of the waves against the fishing boats and yachts anchored in the harbour. I don't know where I'm going and I don't know when I'll be going back to the apartment in which Olja and I have been living over the summer in Rovinj on the Croatian coast.

What I know the least is what I want from us and our relationship.

There is still an incredible amount of love between us. Actually it's much deeper and wider than it was at the beginning. Magic, spiritual connection, beauty.

But at the same time there is also more and more pain. I long for reciprocity, for us to mutually care for each other. It seems to me that I'm constantly the target of criticism, exposed to her search for the negative, her complaints because I'm not fulfilling her expectations. It seems that I constantly have to protect and defend myself.

I would like to know that my feelings also count, that I'm worthy of respect, that I matter. But the way it is, I have the sense that I just give and give, that I must always be available to provide support when it's needed of me, and then in the next moment I become irrelevant.

Of course I know that my thoughts are biased and very subjective but still I cannot deny that I'm longing for more mutuality, more warmth and care.

This is not the manifestation of love as I want to experience it. Love is attention, giving and not only taking. Love is shown in relation to the other, even when we get out of bed on the wrong side, even when we're both in pain. Especially at those times, in fact.

But actually I don't even want to be dealing with all of this, with a relationship, with all its patterns, dynamics, and conflicts. I just want to focus exclusively on Enlightenment Intensives, to dedicate myself to my path and my mission.

And yet with Olja I'm experiencing a dimension of love that I've never experienced before and I don't know if I ever will again.

I sigh and turn slowly back towards our nest where Olja is probably already sleeping.

∞

Tears flow in two continuous streams. Tears of love. Love that is sweet but also hurts because it recognizes divisions wherein essence there is oneness.

I'm sitting in the work room as an assistant on a fourteen-day Enlightenment Intensive. Dušica is running the Intensive with an extraordinary combination of clarity, depth, and gentle love. And I'm looking at thirty people sitting in dyads and doing the Enlightenment Intensive technique.

I love them all, love them infinitely. I want to give them everything I have, my entire self, even if this means that I die of exhaustion after the Intensive is finished. There is no higher meaning in life than using all my power to help other souls to wake up.

I observe all of these beautiful people going through torment: getting angry, screaming, crying, squealing. And I know that this is a manifestation of love, that all of this is only love which is searching for a way through them.

And I also understand that I have only one responsibility in my life: the responsibility to my path, to the absolute, to light…

∞

I'm standing with several of my fellow-travellers from Enlightenment Intensives on a veranda and we look towards the distant hills. The sky is milky white, and it's somehow crazed, like it's gently breaking into pieces. An enormous pale red sun rises and covers a quarter of the sky. The sun is also crazed, dull, and appears to be slowly going out. This is the last sunrise, the last day on earth. When the sun goes down, it will be the end of the world.

Silence is all around. We calmly regard the scene. There's a soft vibration, a gentle trembling in everything, in ourselves and in the world dying around us.

...

We're in the time after the apocalypse, alone in the world, darkness and silence all around. My friend Silvano has returned from his travels into the collective unconscious. He tells us that we'll soon have insights into new knowledge because we're not returning to our planet yet, as new tasks await us here.

Silvano looks at me with a weary gaze. He looks old, sad, melancholic. He suffers because he knows something that I don't know, but he's not allowed to tell me.

His tired and frightened look is terribly familiar to me.

The alarm clock pulls me from sleep and I automatically reach for my dream diary. I can barely keep my eyes open as I write down my dreams. I'm completely exhausted on what will be the twelfth day at this Enlightenment Intensive. Being an assistant is a round-the-clock job, as intensive as being a participant, and energetically way more draining. It's 3:45 in the morning. I slowly start to get dressed. I have to put on the water for tea and begin to wake the participants.

∞

"I love you so much, so much, but I can't do it anymore. I just can't. Our dynamics just hurts me so much. I'm completely destroyed all of the time. I go through the whole cycle twice every day: from total cosmic love for you to my heart disintegrating from pain and desperation."

I'm sobbing in a telephone booth in Kranj.

"Yeah, I know. It's like that for me too. I feel wrecked from it all," Olja answers.

"I love you, Olja," I whisper into the phone.

"I love you too, my darling," I hear from the other side.

"So is this really the end? I can't believe it. I really can't believe it at all."

I speak in confusion.

"I also think it's completely crazy, but we both know it's the right thing to do."

"I know. It's true. I love you."

"I love you too."

"Goodbye, Olja," I whisper for the last time.

"Goodbye, Robert," I hear, and then beep-beep-beep-beep…

I slowly close the door to the telephone booth behind me and go for a walk in the forest. My tears dry up and it seems strange but there is soon a calmness in me, a deep tranquillity.

I had a perfect, total, otherworldly love with Olja. Magic and depth to the extent that words seemed almost useless since they could never capture it. Even thoughts and consciousness itself began to disintegrate.

At the same time it was also clear to me that in order for the beauty of perfect love to be manifested in this life, on the human level, one needs to be remarkably down-to-earth. One needs to have true maturity. As hard as it was for us to accept, we weren't ready for it now. Each day we voyaged between divine love and unbearable pain. At least twice a day from paradise to hell and back again.

I don't have the capacity to sustain all those ups and downs. I don't have the capacity to hold heaven and hell at the same time, combined. I can't do it. Maybe one day I'll be able to. I hope so because I'm not interested in other kinds of relationships. I'm not interested in a relationship that doesn't strive for totality. But for now I'm just not capable of such a thing.

I slowly return home.

∞

February 1988. I'm back in 'my' phone booth again. I'm holding the phone receiver in one hand and resting the other against the dial, while trying to stay calm, but not succeeding very well. How can I be calm when I'm gathering the courage to call Živorad, the leader of our community, with whom I trained to lead Enlightenment Intensives, and to ask him a question that will be so important to me and my life's work?!.

Finally I dial the number and, when I hear his voice on the line, I mumble in a shaky voice:

"Hey, Živorad, it's me. Robert."

"Hey, Robert. Great to hear from you," he says cheerfully. "What's up?"

"Uh, hmm, I was thinking," I can hardly even talk, "that I would like to run my first Intensive."

"Excellent, Robert, excellent. You say you're thinking about it? Did you decide or not?"

"Well, um, I guess I did decide, yeah. I checked and I would like to reserve a date in March. Now I'm checking with you to see if it's alright."

"Excellent, Robert, excellent. Look, you have my full support. I've known for some time that you're ready for this and I have no doubts about you. I'm completely with you. But listen: from this moment on there is no space for hesitating. From this moment on, the leadership of your first Enlightenment Intensive in March begins. From this moment on, you're running your first Intensive. Do you understand?"

That's Živorad, energetic as always.

"Yes, I understand, Živorad. Thank you."

My head is spinning from the realization of what has just happened.

Živorad continues:

"Robert, be careful not to waste any energy on doubts about the correctness of your decision. Direct all your energy into doing a great job. That is now your only responsibility. If you need something, you can contact me. Otherwise, good luck. You made the right decision and I'm with you."

"Thanks, Živorad, thanks so much. Take care."

I end the call and hang up the phone. I can't believe what I've just set into motion. On the one hand, I'm so bursting with enthusiasm, I could shout for joy. On the other, I'm so scared I could shit my pants.

I'm twenty-two years old. I've never led anything in my life, not a workshop, not a seminar. And now, for better or for worse, I've thrown myself into running such a terrifyingly intensive thing as an Enlightenment Intensive, where literally anything can happen and the only predictable thing is that it will be unpredictable. What will come up for me and for the participants, will I even understand what's going on, let alone be able to guide others through it?

When I get home I put on my running shoes and go for a long run to release the energy that's beginning to build up inside me.

∞

"Robert, everything is ready. All the participants are in the workroom. We can start."

My friend Tatjana is one of my three assistants at the Enlightenment Intensive.

"Okay, thanks, Tatjana. You go on in with the others and I'll come in a minute. I just have to go and pee," I respond, slightly nervous.

When I'm finally standing outside the workroom and holding the door handle, I hear many people, chatting in a relaxed fashion while they're waiting for the Intensive to begin. I press down the handle and slowly open the door. All the voices stop, as if cut off. In that instant silence reigns and thirty-three pairs of eyes turn towards me. My feet automatically step backwards away from this pressure. I scratch my forehead as if I've forgotten something and disappear back into the kitchen.

I stand there, breathe deeply, knowing I have nowhere to go but back to the workroom, although every cell in my body is urging me to escape to the other side of the world. I finally take a deep breath and, giving into my fate, walk into the workroom, sit in my chair, look at the group, and say:

"Good evening. My name is Robert Kržišnik and I will be leading this three-day Enlightenment Intensive."

And then I disappear.

Minutes pass, hours pass, days pass, and I am practically not there. Only occasionally for a moment am I aware of myself. Other than that I hardly exist. Only this Intensive with its thirty participants, each journeying by themselves through the thorns to the stars, from hell to paradise and then back again, experiencing deep pain as well as moments of ecstasy, experiencing oneness and the absolute, and also total alienation and isolation. All of life flows through them and through the whole of the Intensive, and I just serve this path. As if I'm merely providing a body through which this Intensive can be led by some higher wisdom. I am not the person I normally experience myself to be.

And at the same time I have the deep knowingness that I am here, in this life and in this world precisely in order to support this path to ultimate authenticity.

∞

I calmly place my legs into the lotus position, straighten my spine, and look around one more time to check that I have enough space, because I don't want my physical body or my energy to be restricted. It's the eighth day of my second fourteen-day Enlightenment Intensive and forty of us are getting ready for midday meditation, which always means a sort of acceleration into the rest of the day.

I close my eyes, slow down my breathing, relax into my own identity... and all of a sudden I am sitting at...

...

the source,

the source of all of us,

where there is no division into individuals.

Where there is an undivided and indivisible oneness,

the total absence of everything.

Peace.

Timeless peace.

The cosmic cradle of souls,

innocent, undivided,

one cosmic organism

where we are all one.

From here we rise and are formed into individuals.

Still we are all one and the same self.

This is the fundamental, primeval, true condition.

The only condition that is true

is that of omnipresent love,

eternal, infinite.

This is my true home

and a home for all of us.

Oneness

...

∞

"OK, now tell me one more time what kind of event will you be having?"

The police officer sitting at the table is speaking. He glances at his colleague who's standing next to the table and staring at me in silence.

"A religious ritual," I respond, amazing even myself with how calm I am.

"A religious ritual. In the evening or what?" the seated policeman asks with a hint of puzzlement.

"Not only the evening. The ceremony lasts three whole days."

"A religious ritual that lasts three days? What kind of ritual is that? Tell me again what religious group you belong to?"

"We're called the White Gnostic Church," I respond and almost start to laugh at how shocked they look.

"What Church? White what?"

"Gnostic. Gnosis means self-knowledge. We don't believe in an external God, but try to come to ultimate self-knowledge. You could say we are trying to realize our divine nature."

The two policemen look at each other, then down at the papers that I'd placed on the table in front of them: documentation about the registration of a religious community and the list of people registered for the Enlightenment Intensive. I stand in silence and wait calmly, while thinking about how bizarre this whole thing is.

Because in Yugoslavia any gathering of larger groups of people was considered suspicious and a potential threat to the system, we had been required to notify the authorities in advance whenever an Enlightenment Intensive was scheduled, and there were many questions and checks. Sometimes the police would even come in person to see what was happening. Sometimes they wanted to stop an Intensive from going ahead. Eventually we had registered as a religious community and from then on everything became much simpler. We still had to notify the Intensives to the police but it was dealt with more or less routinely without any serious complications. It only required a little patience.

"And where do the participants come from?" asks the standing policeman.

"From all over Yugoslavia, from everywhere, although this time most are from Slovenia because that's where the ritual is taking place."

"And what are the professions of your participants?"

It appears that the two policemen are running out of relevant questions.

"All different professions. We have doctors of science, professors, judges, medical doctors, physical labourers, students, teachers, all different professions. Even a police officer may attend sometimes," I smile.

"Really? Even police officers? And you're saying you're a bishop in this church of yours?"

"I will lead the ritual, and, yes, I have the title of bishop."

I feel most uncomfortable saying that. When we registered as a religious community, we had to present a hierarchy as expected in mainstream Christian churches, so we have our patriarch, archbishops, bishops. I, as a certified leader of Enlightenment Intensives, have the title of bishop. At twenty-two years old. Pretty ridiculous.

"Hmmm," says the seated policeman. "Well, I don't have much to say. You brought the documents. Everything looks all right, so good luck, and that's that. If we have any additional questions, we'll contact you."

"Good. Thanks very much. Have a nice day."

I smile and walk back to the street, amused with the thought of what the two policemen will be saying to each other now, but then my thoughts carry me in a different direction, to the second Enlightenment Intensive I'll be leading, in two weeks' time.

∞

The palm reader in Pondicherry was no charlatan, it seems. He obviously knew what he was talking about when he predicted that 1987 would be a very strong spiritual year for me. It really was and it looks like it will continue into 1988.

My participation in Intensives, both three-day and fourteen-day ones, then assisting and then leading them, and all the enlightenment and other experiences, has triggered many evolutionary transformations in me.

Perhaps I'm most content because I'm in constant contact with the multiple dimensions of life, of the mystery that we call human existence. Doorways leading in many different directions, and to different realms, open to me, from experiences of oneness and universal consciousness, to crazy journeys in my dreams, to interpersonal fields full of unprecedented dimensions of love, authenticity, vulnerability and connection, to all the new understandings about the nature of existence and the integration of mystical experiences I have had in the past. All this incredible richness and complexity addresses a very core longing of my heart and fulfils me immeasurably. I feel so deeply alive.

It's true that most of my nights are crazy and I'm often very confused during the days too, but somewhere in my gut it has become much clearer what my life is about and where my path is leading. This clarity is not intellectual but somehow deeply embodied and integrated.

At the same time I notice in myself, almost all of the time, a certain peace and stability that I've not known before. It's as if, through all of the inner experiences of the previous year or two, a strong gravitational centre has developed in me and is giving me a stable presence in the moment, as if I'm always in a sort of slight meditative state of greater awareness.

I become more selective in my relationships. Everything that is loud or artificial quickly creates resistance in me. I need sincerity, authenticity, gentle presence. Otherwise I prefer to be alone. I can't help but wonder if that kind Indian palm reader has read the rest of my future with equal precision.

∞

Did he really say this? Really? Did I just now hear Živorad, my beloved teacher and mentor, turning towards Zoran, my dear friend and the Slovenian representative of our White Gnostic Church, saying:

"Zoran, I don't love you anymore!"

I stare in deep bewilderment.

About 16 or so of us, senior members of our community, are sitting in Zoran's living room having an urgent meeting. Harsh words are being said, accusations, blame, often with raised voices.

No trace of eternal love here, I think to myself as I observe the scene in confusion and shock.

These last months things have been getting more and more baffling in our Church. It seems that along with my beloved Yugoslavia breaking up, my beloved spiritual community is going in the same direction as well. Politics and nationalism have found their way into our group, and with those ideas have come demands, accusations, pressure. While we keep crying together at the Enlightenment Intensives, overwhelmed by divine love, outside of the events themselves it seems to be all about divisions – us versus them, right versus wrong…

I love all these people, but there is also more and more sadness and concern in my heart. Behaving like this, are we really the harbingers of a new world, as we like to see ourselves?

Dark clouds are slowly covering the sky.

∞

I'm feeling divided to an almost unbearable degree. Pressure in my chest is making it difficult to breathe, my awareness is narrowed. I'm at a regular meeting with members of our community in Ljubljana. We were doing some sort of communication exercises and now we're relaxing, socializing, chatting, and soon we will each go on our way. I feel that the anxiety and division are not just in me but in the whole atmosphere, because some people in the group know what happened and others don't.

Namely, a few days ago Mirjana and I spent the night together and now I'm acting as if I hardly know her. During the last few months we've become closer friends, spending an enormous amount of time together, and a few days ago, when I was sleeping at her place in Ljubljana, we became sexually intimate. In the morning I went home to Kranj and thought about it for several days.

On the one hand, it's obvious that we are friends first and foremost. Of course a certain polarity is present and the energy between us would be completely different if Mirjana were a man. But despite that, I experience her above all as a friend and there is nothing like the deep dimensions of love and magic that characterized my relationship with Olja.

On the other hand, it strikes me as terrible, truly terrible, that I would be like all those other men who, after having sex once with a woman, lose interest. I would be ashamed not just to see myself in that way but also be seen in that way by the community and by Mirjana. In my integrity I long for a different kind of relationship with women. Yes, I feel guilty for the past and even for the future, imagining how it might influence her life if I walked out on her now...

If I had the strength to be entirely sincere and direct, I would say to her:

"Dear Mirjana, I'm afraid that what I'm about to say will hurt you but nevertheless I believe that sincerity is more important than such fears, and I also believe that you want sincerity as much as I do. What I'm trying to say is that I don't love you in the way I would like to love a romantic partner. I love you as a dear friend, a very dear friend, but with you I don't experience the depth and magic of love that it's essential for me to feel. I think it would be reckless of me and not in accordance with my integrity to assume that a single sexual encounter must constitute the beginning of a love relationship. I take responsibility for my actions and regret them but I want us to return to being just friends. What do you think about it all?"

And I would have received her feelings, her pain and disappointment, and stood by her side as a friend. But I don't have that strength. I don't have that maturity. I simply cannot do it. It's not within the range of my abilities at this time.

So, instead I take a deep breath and step towards Mirjana:

"Hey, do you have some time next week for me to come for a visit?"

∞

I'm at the community meeting and the ritual act of surrender is taking place. We slowly approach the altar in a line. Each of us kneels individually in front of the altar and makes an internal shift towards total surrender. When we finish, we kneel, and then leave space for the next person. When it's my turn, I kneel down and suddenly start crying, feeling deeply shaken and touched. Then I make the internal shift towards surrender and begin to be carried off to a wider reality, beginning to disappear.

After the ritual is over I go down to the cellar under the building. Stone walls, darkness all around, like the cellar of some old manor. In the beginning I'm afraid because I sense an invisible entity hiding in the darkness. I slowly relax and begin to explore the gloomy space. I find myself in a big dark chamber and suddenly a yellowish light appears in front of me, moving and slowly coming together into the form of a human figure.

At this moment I realize that I am witnessing God incarnating right in front of me.

Now this transparent human shape slowly solidifies about two metres away in front of my eyes. God begins to slowly and majestically walk, or perhaps even glide, around the cellar. I somehow know that the body I'm seeing is not made from the same material as normal human bodies. It's not the same atomic structure, but exists on a different frequency, much more refined and subtle.

I witness this scene and weep, sobbing, feeling deeply touched. I notice there is a telephone attached to one of the walls.

184

I know I can reach the whole world through this phone. I pick it up, still sobbing, and begin reporting, through my tears, to the whole world that God is within us, although I'm now seeing him in a physical form, God is above all an internal subjective experience....

I wake up gasping and need some time to completely return to my body and to this reality. Then I turn on the light and open my dream diary.

∞

For God's sake, what's the matter with us? We are really total Balkans! We just throw ourselves into the unknown, convinced that we can master it right away, that we know everything. It's a sort of crazy, forceful belief in ourselves.

These are the thoughts racing through my head as I hold the torch in my trembling hand. My body is shaking from excitement. I look at Silvano, holding a lit torch, slowly walking around our circle of about twenty people. He pauses in front of each of us for an instant, looks in our eyes, and ceremoniously lights our torches. When all the torches are burning, we raise them high in the air and stare at the neat stack of one-metre long logs in front of us. Tonight we're going to walk on fire.

We're about to try this for the first time in Yugoslavia. Two of our friends participated once in a fire-walk, one in Germany and the other in Italy, and now they're already facilitating it here. That's how it goes in this region, I smile to myself. We're already gathered at the secluded retreat house where we've been holding Enlightenment Intensives and other events, so it's the perfect opportunity. Along with all the others, I take two steps towards the stack of logs, our flaming torches extended in our hands.

At that moment the air at the centre of the circle explodes in one huge flash of flame.

There are screams as we jump back in horror. A few logs are thrown into the air, others roll around on the ground at our feet. We start to tend to a few people whose hands and faces have been burned. People with rakes push the burning logs back into the pile while the fire crackles wildly.

Later we discover that an assistant, wanting the fire to burn well, had poured about twenty litres of petrol on it before we started. So that was where the peculiar smell was coming from, I think to myself.

After the fire is burning safely, we spend several hours in the house, lying down, doing some relaxation and visualization exercises. This makes us drowsy as we've just finished an Enlightenment Intensive and are quite exhausted already. It dawns on us that we don't really know what to do while waiting for the burning logs to turn to embers, that we actually don't really know how to prepare for the experience of fire-walking.

When we finally stand barefoot in a circle around the carpet of embers, now raked out into an oblong bed around five metres long and three metres wide, the sight of this pulsating red surface pulls me into an almost hypnotic state. I'm afraid but also entranced by excitement and expectation.

And now it's my turn. I step right up to the embers. The heat that hits me is shocking. I wasn't expecting this. I stare at Silvano at the other end of the glowing bed of embers and he seems impossibly far away. Both of us open our arms and it seems to me that Silvano smiles slightly. I take a breath, lift up one foot, and surrender: to the unknown, to life, to death, to everything.

In this entranced state I walk slowly along the glowing path and realize that it doesn't burn at all. It's as if I'm walking on soft, warm sand. I smile as I ecstatically fall into the arms of Silvano who's waiting for me at the other end. It's crazy, completely crazy.

Of course I immediately set out to walk across again. What else?

∞

"I never looked for a guru. No, not really ever. And I never looked for a spiritual community. Or a spiritual path. I only ever looked for one thing: the truth. I was only interested by the question of the ultimate, absolute truth about life, about reality. That's all I ever looked for."

I'm listening enthusiastically to Skanda who is explaining his journey with a slightly dramatic voice. His words resonate deeply with me, very deeply. Yes, I'm also looking only for that: the ultimate truth about the nature of existence. The ultimate truth about the meaning of life. To some degree I've found it already but, at the same time, it's clear that the path to ultimate realization is a very long one.

Skanda and Satyavati are an American couple, the leading disciples of Charles Berner, the creator of Enlightenment Intensives as well as the transpersonal psychotherapeutic method called Mind Clearing. They live with Berner in Australia in a spiritually focused permaculture community but once a year they go off on a two-month world tour, leading retreats and spreading his teachings. They've stopped for an evening in Slovenia and all of us who are serious about Intensives have come to the event.

The more I listen to them and enjoy their presence, openness, and charisma, the more I realize what my next step will be: a trip to Australia. It will probably be the next stop for both of us – for Mirjana and me – to learn Mind Clearing and everything else right at the source, from Charles Berner himself, who in recent years has taken the spiritual name Yogeshwar Mouni.

I approach Skanda after the formal part of the meeting and ask him if it would be possible to come. He answers with a smile:

"Absolutely, Robert, you're very welcome. You can already go ahead and buy tickets."

So, Australia it is. My whole internal being smiles happily as Mirjana and I walk home that night.

∞

Slowly, very slowly, I put together the sentences in my head and then type them. It's very hard for me, in fact it tears me apart, to write this letter to Živorad, telling him that I'm leaving the

White Gnostic Church. It's been obvious to me for some time that the community has many of the properties of a cult or a sect: a powerful hierarchy dominated by Živorad at the top, an exclusivist ideology, the belief that we are the only ones who have attained the way to redemption while others are stumbling through the darkness, a policy of threats, pressure, secrets, lies, and attacks. On one side elevated words about eternal love, and on the other an everyday reality which resembles dark political intrigues. I know that I no longer want to be a member of a community in which there is so much division.

But at the same time, this is the family in which I have had some of the most wonderful, deep, and magical experiences of indescribable dimensions of life for which I will always be grateful. As I also will always be grateful to Živorad for his support, trust, and belief in me. We've been like brothers and sisters exploring the mystery of life, crying and laughing together, showing our naked hearts to each other.

How can I leave this spiritual family of mine, for which I was searching for so long?

After many hours of thinking and slowly writing the letter, I lick the edge of the envelope to seal it. I have given everything that I have to give here. I have received everything that I am capable of receiving.

It's time for a new step.

Eight: Grounding Down Under

"Good morning, Skanda. It's Robert. I'm in the phone booth where the bus dropped me off. Can you come and pick me up? It's pouring with rain, as you probably know."

I rattle off the words with relief because I'd been so worried that Skanda wouldn't answer the phone so early in the morning, or that I'd have the wrong number or something like that.

"Hey, Robert, good to hear from you. So, you managed. Great. You're in the phone booth near the Mt. Barker highway exit?"

"Yes, I believe so."

"Okay. I know where you are. It'll take me about twenty minutes to reach you, so hang on," says Skanda.

Then I'm alone again in this little phone booth which is being pelted on all sides by a powerful storm. It's six-thirty in the morning and here, in the Australian winter, it's still dark. I'm a pile of misery: soaking wet, cold, under-slept, jet-lagged.

But, okay, I'm finally here in Australia, very near to Yogeshwar and his closest students. As if I'm about to step into the promised land. I've been making sacrifices for around nine months just so I could be here now. I moved back to my parent's house, together with Mirjana, so we could save the money we would otherwise have used for rent, even though it was an emotionally difficult and frustrating experience. I worked the morning shift as a switchboard operator at a big company, while Mirjana worked freelance on various editing and proof-reading jobs. In the afternoons, Mirjana and I had an extra part-time job cleaning offices. In the evenings, I translated, edited and eventually self-published a book about Ramana Maharshi. And now it's April 1990 and I'm finally here. A grey Nissan Sunny stops beside the telephone booth and I get completely wet again in the time it takes to throw my backpack in the car and right after it my body. Skanda laughs and shakes my hand:

189

"Welcome to Australia! It's a watery baptism, right? Don't worry. A day will come when the rain will stop and you'll see a magnificent blue sky. How come you're alone? Didn't you say you were coming with your wife? What's her name again?"

"Mirjana, and yes, that was the original plan, then she wanted to finish the last of her university exams which she'd been delaying for several years. So now the plan is that she'll come in two months' time."

"Ah, well, by the time she comes you'll have got used to everything," Skanda smiles.

"And it's also true that I got sick of waiting and adjusting to all the many delays. I'm always for action and movement, while she lives, well, much more slowly," I mutter bitterly.

"Ah, the pleasures of married life. Here: this is our house. Come in for breakfast. Satya has prepared something and then I'll take you to the mobile home that I've arranged for you. It's located in a very nice place on the estate. You can rest for a while there, and then in the afternoon I'll come and get you and take you to the community meeting with Yogeshwar so the two of you can meet."

I get out of the car. The rain has let up, everything smells lovely, and this afternoon I'm going to meet the legendary Yogeshwar who up until how I've only read about in books.

∞

"Nothing about me is real. Nothing, that is, except myself. Everything else consists of aspects, viewpoints... Therefore I am not transforming and developing because I cannot be changed. I am, I always was, and I will always be the same. I only change my relationship to life and other entities. I slowly harmonize this relationship with the absolute, I evolve it."

Entranced, I watch this tiny old man with white hair, a long white beard and big blue eyes. He's dressed in a sort of black robe and is sitting on the floor calmly speaking these words, a faint smile always on his face. Around twenty of us are gathered in a

190

half circle around him. Most are his students who live in the community here. Two or three of us are just visitors. Yogeshwar either answers questions or shares his thoughts as inspired by the moment. Each day he's available to the community for about an hour. Other than this, he lives in isolation in his amazing solar-powered house which is completely adapted to the natural environment and to the climate of the hills of South Australia.

More than by the meaning of his words, I'm astonished by the space from which the words come. Not from books, not from reflection, but from a deep direct experience of underlying reality. Tomorrow I will come with a notebook and write everything down. Or maybe I can bring a cassette recorder and just record this amazing wealth of understanding.

"All of this, everything in this world, all of our life is, from the standpoint of the absolute, only a game, a game with no reason. Testing possibilities, playing with creation. A game of the gods who are so involved in the play that they sometimes forget who and what they are. But it's a game with no reason and as long as we search for a reason for each of our actions and make an effort to do everything we do for important reasons, we're not living in accordance with absolute reality."

∞

I sit in my trailer and write a letter by hand to my dear and everlasting friend, Iztok.

I write how enthusiastic I am about Yogeshwar, his wisdom, his lovingness, the serenity that emanates from him. I write how excited I am about life in the community, where there's a lot of contact with nature, work with the soil, a focus on energy sustainability, both a great spiritual connection and friendship and space for the individuality of each person or family. I write how I'm beginning my training in the Mind Clearing transpersonal psychotherapeutic method and about everything that's coming to the surface as part of this training, which includes me attending sessions as a client. I write to him about all of these things but I don't have the courage to write about the thing that torments me the most.

Even within myself I don't dare to fully face this.

Now that I'm so happy in Australia all alone, without Mirjana, I'm constantly wondering why I am with her at all. Now, in my solitude, I see quite clearly that I don't really miss her and that in fact I enjoy being without her. Once again I realize that I experience her as a friend and that our relationship is very far from the depths of love for which I long. Everything is okay, we function well together as friends and fellow travellers through life, but there's no magic, no connection that reaches deep into other dimensions of life.

One part of me realizes that I have a good opportunity now to bring this clarity out and to end our relationship at the right time.

But I can't. I simply can't. I don't speak to anyone about it, not even at the Mind Clearing sessions, because I'm afraid of what will happen if I express what's in that hidden place. Something forces me to suppress it, to clench my teeth, and to keep the relationship going regardless of my own feelings. There is this strong imperative to not wreck a relationship.

∞

"So, would anyone like to go first?"

I ask the question with an artificially happy and light voice, looking out at the circle with a smile on my face. All of the eighteen people present look with concern at the thick carpet of embers in front of them, bursting with heat. No one makes a peep. Only the menacing crackling of the flames can be heard. I try again.

"To be the first one to go across the fire is a special honour and so I offer it to you. Would anyone like to be the first to cross?"

The embers crackle, pop, and sizzle, but everyone in the circle is silent. Some of them glance at me quickly as if they think

I'm crazy. Others actually take a step backwards. Just to make it very clear.

Okay. It looks like I'll have to do it myself. I'd been hoping that someone else would want to go first because today I'm more afraid than I've ever been before. I've walked on hot embers many times. In fact I've led fire-walks five times already but I've never experienced anything like this. These embers look ten times worse than any I've seen before. It's probably because eucalyptus wood has a much higher heat value than beech wood, which is what I've used back in Yugoslavia. Once again I've thrown myself Balkan style, without collecting any information first, into something I know nothing about when I announced the fire-walking workshop in the hills above Adelaide.

I step up to the embers pretending to be relaxed.

"Alright, then, I'll go first. I'm actually looking forward to it," I say, trying to fake it.

The heat pounds into my whole body, my face. I feel as if I'm standing in front of a huge pool of liquid lava. This is where my game ends. This is where all my games end. I've no more cards to play. If I step away, everything dies: my dignity, self-respect, integrity, my entire self. If I step forwards, everything indicates that my body will die.

I stand motionless, inhaling the hot air, my body turned to stone. I look up – at the stars, my beloved friends. There are so many of them and they're really glittering tonight, winking down at me from the black sky.

It strikes me that in the worst case I will die and that's really not so terrible. My consciousness expands. I remember all my out-of-this-world experiences. I remember who and what I am, and what life is. From somewhere in my memory rises the story of Jesus dying on the cross and, inspired, I open my arms and say out loud:

"Oh God, into your hands I commend my spirit."

I lift my foot in an act of total surrender and step onto the molten lava. And soon I realize that I'm walking on a soft warm carpet. I start to laugh in relief and amazement. The participants in the circle also laugh. The stars laugh. The whole world laughs.

When I get to the other side, I drop down on my knees. Tears of gratitude flow down my cheeks. Gratitude for the miracle of life.

∞

"The difference between the spiritual and the material is entirely artificial, apparent. Even the idea to have two different expressions – spiritual life and material life – is a step down a dead-end street. Because in reality it is all one. Existence is all of this. We all exist in our interconnectedness and that is all that there is. You cannot arrange your material affairs in one way and your spiritual affairs in another. The two are one, a holistic reflection of the divine."

I listen to Yogeshwar during his daily darshan and eagerly write down all his words. Somehow this listening helps me to understand and to ground all the other-dimensional experiences that I have had during the past two years. It helps me to integrate all the different realities I've experienced, although I believe that total integration will take many years.

I don't miss a single darshan, also not a single one of the longer Sunday gatherings where we also sing, eat together, and celebrate life. I bathe in Yogeshwar's wisdom, love, and light.

Perhaps I've finally found the father that I've been looking for.

∞

I sit in my trailer on the estate, open my diary, and start to write:

"Today I had my tenth Mind Clearing session and many things opened up, came to the surface, and became clear. I've been functioning with the deeply engrained conviction that I'm not good enough, that I don't deserve goodness, love, happiness.

Of course all of this is connected to my childhood and my relationship with my father. I experienced this feeling again and again when I compared myself to other boys who were stronger, faster, manlier than me. I always found myself too soft and weak, too gentle, too clumsy. I always had the feeling that I wasn't meeting my father's expectations, that he wasn't proud of me, that I disappointed him, that I was a nuisance to him. From all of this, I developed my patterns of behaviour based on the idea that I had to fulfil the expectations of others, and that the more I fulfilled these expectations the more likely it was that I would be accepted and loved. Beneath this, deep inside, was my unmet need for acceptance and love."

Working on these patterns and on my core beliefs through Mind Clearing is incredibly useful. I already feel ten kilos lighter.

And I've also come to understand that I want my children, when I have them, to be enfolded in a sense of acceptance, with the knowledge that they are wonderful the way they are, that they don't need to be something other than that in order to receive my love, respect, and acceptance.

∞

The whole group of my Yugoslav friends from Enlightenment Intensives and also the whole community from Australia are gathered around Yogeshwar who has announced that he has something important to tell us. We are all silent and Yogeshwar calmly and formally announces that he will soon depart this world, will leave this level of existence, and will not return. His personal assistant adds that for a while she will lead the group, but only for a transitional period, during which she will be preparing everything for me to take over the leadership of the whole community and its spiritual voyage. When I hear this, I stare in astonishment.

Yogeshwar smiles tenderly and says that she wasn't supposed to say that out loud, that I wasn't supposed to know right away, but that it is true, that I am to take over his role. He looks at me and smiles lovingly.

I feel confused – how can I be the teacher and leader of this group? It doesn't make any sense.

I wake up and look at the ceiling for a while. Then I write down the dream in my dream diary. When I'm finished, I lie back again and turn towards Mirjana who's sleeping next to me.

She has also arrived in Australia now and we've moved into the wonderful eco-house where Skanda and Satya usually live. They've recently left on their annual tour around the world, and we're taking care of the house, the garden, the trees.

I'm getting on well with Mirjana. We share friendship, harmony, even love, and everything is actually nice. Maybe I've been expecting too much from relationships, searching for something special, magical, cosmic. Maybe Yogeshwar is right that it makes no sense to complicate matters with a search for some special kind of love, if this life is anyway just a kind of a dream in which, in the great scheme of things, nothing is more important than anything else.

I close my eyes. I'll sleep for another hour. I'm in no hurry.

∞

I stop swinging the pick-axe that I'm using to dig a hole in which to plant a tree. I rest for a moment, breathing deeply, then angrily toss the pick away, straighten my back, look at the sky, and prepare to say some strong words to God.

For the whole week, while I've been working to earn money for my life here in Australia by planting trees, gardening, cutting wood, I think about the letter that I got from my acquaintance Brane who moved to New Zealand last year to join some Christian community in Christchurch. He's completely changed during this time and now I feel like I hardly know him. He writes about how it's necessary to unconditionally accept God, the Christian one of course, and to submit to his will, to surrender to him. He writes that all other spiritual paths, including yoga, Zen Buddhism and new-age spirituality, are the devil's work, part of his evil plan to tempt us away from God. He writes about how we will all burn in hell if we allow ourselves to be tempted by the devil in this way. He writes that God is merciful to all of his children but that his mercy has limits and that a terrible punishment will await us at the end if we don't follow him.

Of course I think this is all nonsense, that Brane has stumbled into some kind of sect from the Middle Ages, but I don't know for sure. In reality I know nothing. In the past years I've learned so much new that I can only say that I know that I don't know much. There have been so many ideas that I've strongly believed in, so many understandings I could have staked my life on but which soon proved to be untrue and disintegrated right in front of my eyes. I'm continually evolving my understanding of life and witnessing my old models falling apart. I cannot be truly convinced of anything anymore. I can't truly stand by anything. Everything might collapse tomorrow, or be transformed into something else.

So it's also possible that everything Brane says is completely true, although the way I see things at the moment, that strikes me as completely absurd.

Anyway, it's clear to me that his God is not my God. It's not a God that I would recognize as some sort of superior being. My God is love, oneness. This other neurotic God doesn't touch me at all, even if I get to burn in hell because of that. Fuck him.

I take a breath and begin to speak loudly and provocatively to the sky:

"Fuck off, do you hear me, fuck off! If you're so egocentric, such a neurotic maniac, that you demand total obedience, that everything has to be your way, and you punish anyone who isn't unconditionally faithful to you, then that's your problem, not mine. Maybe you need therapy. What do I know? But I'm certainly not going to be subordinate to you. You can strike me with lightning, fry me. I don't care. But as long as I'm alive, as long as I move, I will resist you. I will not obey you for even a second. Actually, I will fight against you with all my power until the end. Fuck you and all your childish, immature, neurotic shit. Fuck off!"

I wait a little while to see if something happens to me and of course it doesn't. With a smile, I pick up the pick-axe and continue digging the hole. I feel greatly relieved, calm. The hell with him, I think, and my smile becomes wider and wider.

∞

"Robert, I'm pregnant. There's no doubt about it."

Mirjana and I look at each other and smile. Two months have passed since our decision to have a child and, what do you know, it's already happening.

We'd been toying with the idea for some time and recently, encouraged by Yogeshwar's teachings that it made no sense to complicate things and wait, that it was actually good to start a family phase of life as soon as possible, we'd decided to take that step.

Hmm, I'm twenty-four years old and will become a father in eight months. Am I ready? Could I ever really say that I'm ready? What does being ready even mean and how should I know if I am? I know that at least I feel a lot of trust in life and I begin to look forward to welcoming this unknown being who is now travelling towards this world.

∞

Today Linda is visiting us. Linda is a member of the community who is currently not living on the estate, but in Adelaide where she has a regular job as a social worker. I'm helping to build her a little house on the estate and all three of us have become good friends in the past eight months. We're always happy to see her because she is somehow more lively and easier to get to know than the others. This evening, the after-dinner conversation goes in an interesting direction.

"My dear friends, I don't want to dampen your enthusiasm for Yogeshwar and this community and I agree that there is much that is very beautiful here, much that is very deep. But I need to warn you that not everything is as perfect as it appears at first glance. I wanted to tell to you about this before you make some dramatic decision such as moving permanently to Australia."

"What are you trying to say, Linda? Can you be more specific?"

"Yogeshwar is not quite as holy as he seems. I'm talking about sexual abuse and the abuse of power. The community is quite hierarchical, as you've probably noticed. There are inner and outer circles, and certain "spiritual" secrets that are accessible only to specific people. The men have much more power and enjoy more tolerance than the women do. People who are same-sex oriented, like myself, are side-lined. It's very much a personality cult. These are the things I wanted to tell you. I'm not sure I want to talk about specific names but I can if you like. Actually why not? In any case, I'm seriously reconsidering whether I want to finish my house at all, or perhaps just sell it as it is."

A gloom falls upon me, a heaviness, weariness. Not just because of Linda's warnings, but even more because I've started to realise myself that all is not perfect here. I have often noticed the cult of personality, for example when Yogeshwar says something that he pretends to know and I have first-hand knowledge that what he says isn't true, but everyone nods and accepts everything he says as if it's pure gold. If he says it, then it must be true. And how sometimes he just runs over someone he doesn't agree with. Suddenly divine love disappears. And, indeed, we have also heard whispering about these spiritual secrets and about sexual abuse too…

Dark clouds have begun to gather in the sky. The whole situation with Yogeshwar is suspiciously familiar to me. An older male teacher who appears to be spiritually brilliant and inspirational but who, in his relations with the people around him, slips towards the abuse of his own power and of the trust his followers place in him. I cannot believe that I've again fallen into a cult system as I did with Živorad. I seem to have a pattern of just deciding that someone is the absolute and all-knowing authority in my life and beginning to follow him blindly. I am actually playing the child who knows nothing and gives all the responsibility for his life into his father's hands.

How hard it is to see everything clearly, to take what is worthwhile and not to touch what is rotten. That night Mirjana and I go to sleep with heavy hearts.

∞

I'm sitting at an Enlightenment Intensive in a dyad and suddenly I'm flooded by the premonition of the presence of another dimension of existence, the recognition that the reality in which I live is superficial and illusory, and that there is a deeper reality, a deeper world that is always there but that I cannot perceive. The more this realization deepens, the more the world in front of my eyes begins to fade and various beings begin to emerge.

First I perceive beside me a sort of child with powerful energy, staring at me intensely, maybe even challenging me. Then I see beside me a seated old woman looking thoughtfully at the floor. There are more and more of these figures that I begin to see and at the same time I realize that these beings are always here, beside me, moving through me, but that they exist at a different frequency. They have a constant influence on my life without me knowing it.

I want to drive them away, I'm horrified by the constant disintegration of everyday reality, and the revelation of something deeper, something unseen until now.

I wake up screaming. I need time to calm down in order to write the dream down in my diary. When I lie down again, I'm still filled with fear, uncertainty, because I realize that anything can happen at any moment. At any moment the reality in which I believe can prove to be a mere illusion, can disintegrate. At any moment I might come to the realization that everything I believe to be real is essentially just a fleeting occurrence. Anything can happen at any moment. There is no predictability in life. No certainty.

∞

"Good day, my good friend, may this be a good day for you. Tell me, what seems to be the problem with your handsome body, my good friend?"

The white-haired man wearing a white tunic and a nicely groomed white beard smiles at me. It's the official doctor at the Ramana Maharshi Ashram in Tiruvannamalai in southern India. After nine months in Australia, we were going to fly back to Europe but decided to make a six-week stopover in India and visit two of my favourite ashrams: this one beneath Mt. Arunachala and the Shantivanam Ashram, also in Tamil Nadu. We don't dare to do any more adventurous travelling through India now that Mirjana is pregnant.

"A week ago, I jammed my finger in a heavy door in Singapore and it's in a really bad shape now."

I explain the situation while unwrapping the bandage on the index finger of my right hand. The finger is entirely black, twice its normal size, and hurts so much that I have to hold it up in the air all the time, like some kind of preacher, so the blood flowing through it doesn't throb so forcefully.

The doctor examines my finger with interest, not touching it, and then says light-heartedly:

"Hoho, my good friend, you stuck it into the wrong hole, is that it?"

Surprised, I looked into his cheerful face, waiting for him to say something more serious, but he just laughs and smirks.

I offer a sour smile: "Hmm, yes, ha-ha, perhaps you're right. Can you tell me what to do about it?"

I am trying to push our conversation in a more medical direction.

"My friend, you surrender it to God only!" he smiles.

"Hmm…. That's it? Any other way you can help me with my finger?"

I look at him in the hope that he will get serious and tell me something useful.

"Surrender it to God only, nothing else."

I smile bitterly again, wrap my finger back in the bandage, thank him and leave.

After a while, my disbelief and frustration turn to relaxation and even joy. After all, what else can I do in this life? Just surrender, let myself be carried by the flow of life. That's what it's all about, isn't it?

By the time I'm back in our room with Mirjana, I know that everything is alright, and that everything will be alright. With my finger, with life, with everything.

∞

Mirjana and I are standing on the shores of a wide and slowly flowing river, surrounded by eucalyptus trees, near the Shantivanam Ashram. I stand behind her, all four of our hands on her belly. We smile in silence and enjoy the moment.

A few hours ago we felt the first kick of our child. At first it surprised us, even frightened us, then we were overcome with happiness, rapture even at the miracle of life. This child, this being who is coming into the world, is alive and it's our sacred task to surround it with all the love we can.

It's true that our relationship is not as magical as I might like. It's true that our energies are not so very much in harmony. Sometimes it seems like I'm pressing on the accelerator and Mirjana on the brakes. But at the same time it's also true that today I have entered the miracle of life. That I'm happy. Deeply moved. That I feel a connection and companionship with Mirjana because of the care and love we share for this unborn child.

In the silence and with our hands covering the little being in Mirjana's belly, we stare at the river which flows calmly, serenely, yet powerfully past us.

Like the river of enchanting life.

Nine: When Children are Born...

"What on earth are you doing in here? Stop this nonsense, what is wrong with you?"

The short middle-aged red-haired doctor brays at us in her deep rasping voice. Standing legs apart in the doorway of the delivery room in the Ljubljana maternity hospital, she flicks on all the switches. The room is filled with the cold and blinding glare of harsh neon lights.

We all stop what we're doing and are silent: Mirjana, sitting with her legs spread on a special pillow on the bed, me standing beside her and holding her hand and shoulder, the midwife between Mirjana's legs feeling how dilated she is, and a young doctor in training who's here to provide help and support. The calm atmosphere of half-darkness and gentle whispering that we'd created in the delivery room has been suddenly and brutally interrupted. That's not how we'd planned it, or what we'd agreed with the hospital.

The midwife and trainee exchange glances and silently continue their work. I stare at this red-haired doctor and think about how I would like to pull her out of the room by her hair and let the security staff deal with me afterwards. All I can think is that I will not allow this woman to ruin the birth of my son. Mirjana squeezes my hand and whispers:

"Let it go, Robert, don't make a scene, we'll manage..."

The doctor marches up to the bed in her high heels, looks between Mirjana's legs with no expression, and barks:

"Okay, she's going to give birth soon. Did you give her an epidural?"

The midwife responds softly:

"No, she didn't want an epidural. She also doesn't want to have labour induced."

The doctor brays:

"Ha-ha, she'll beg you for it. You'll see. She'll beg for all of it."

I hiss at her: "You must be kidding..."

I feel Mirjana squeezing my hand again. She looks at me beseechingly:

"Robert, please..."

Motionless, the doctor and I size each other up. A sense of tension reigns in the birthing delivery now.

Suddenly a hospital cleaner walking along the corridor stops in front of the open door to our room. She looks kind of sleepy and spaced-out, observes for a moment the tense scene within, and then extends her hand and turns out all but one of the lights. She regards the cosy atmosphere she has created with satisfaction, smiles slightly, and dreamily continues down the hallway.

Apparently, this action, entirely outside the realm of what seemed possible, has reset the mind of the doctor, who flinches slightly, then exits the room without saying another word, shutting the door behind her.

Mirjana, the midwife, the trainee and I exchange glances, and the birth continues peacefully. Miracles still happen.

When the birth enters its final phase, the sunny afternoon outside suddenly transforms into a powerful summer storm and Filip cries into the world amidst wild lightning, violent thunder, and raging wind. He is very tiny and wrinkled, and at the same time the most beautiful creature I have ever seen. I kiss Mirjana and hug the trainee. I'm laughing and crying at the same time, shaken by the wonder of life.

After a while, I look out of the window and – what do you know? – it is a calm and sunny afternoon again.

...

The next day I read in the newspaper that "Filip's" storm had blown down one hundred-year-old oak trees just outside Ljubljana. My boy, you sure know how to make a spectacular entrance!

∞

"And there goes the rest of your mind…"

Says Yogeshwar, with his deep blue eyes smiling gently at me. We're sitting on the floor next to a big sheet of flip-chart paper, scribbling on it with felt tip pens and talking about my favourite topic: the nature of existence. He's just explained and drawn a diagram to illustrate his concept of time. My mind has begun to melt because I somehow understand in my gut what he's saying: that our mind creates the illusion of linearity so it can process in pieces the infinite potential of oneness.

Yogeshwar patiently waits for my mind to put itself together again so I'll be able to continue our conversation. He smiles lovingly. I have never before felt such recognition and happiness in my life. But, nevertheless, I sense that our story is slowly coming to an end.

Yogeshwar has come to newly independent Slovenia as part of a world tour, his first for many, many years. I've organised a workshop and a big public presentation for him here in Ljubljana. He was practically forced to go on tour because not long after Mirjana and I had left Australia, the whole classic cult situation of abuse of power, sex, and money had exploded, the community had quickly disintegrated, and he no longer had any financial support.

I feel an enormous love and respect for him. After all, this is the man who created the Enlightenment Intensives, which saved my life and gave it meaning. And Mind Clearing, as well, which is now part of my professional practice, in addition to running Intensives and other workshops also based on Yogeshwar's work. For all of his warmth, love, and spiritual knowledge I will be forever grateful from the bottom of my heart.

But, at the same time, I simply do not see in him the integrity that for me is so precious, so crucially important. On several occasions in the course of this event, he has lied to me directly, probably not knowing that I'd already been informed of certain things. Or he's lied to the workshop participants. I was translating his words for the audience, while knowing that what he was saying was untrue. And I've heard him repeatedly denying any responsibility for the break-up of all three of his past communities, which also doesn't quite fit with what I saw in Australia.

And so, my dear Yogeshwar, I will always remember you with a warm and grateful heart but we will probably not see each other again in this life.

∞

A high, piping cry wakes me up. I find my watch in the darkness: 2:30 a.m. So it's my turn. I have an agreement with Mirjana that I get up at night when our little boy wakes before three in the morning and she does if it's after three. I gently lift the crying bundle, hold it in my arms, and begin to walk up and down, sleepily humming a lullaby.

Parenthood is exhausting and there is hardly time for anything else, but nevertheless it's filled with beauty, tenderness and joy. Mirjana and I cooperate well. I support the family by offering individual Mind Clearing sessions. I advertise them under the label of transpersonal psychotherapy, in order to make it a bit clearer what it's all about. I also regularly lead Enlightenment Intensives and various communication workshops. In fact I'm often exhausted from work because I'm getting more and more clients for therapy. I'm working five days a week, sometimes even six, seeing two or three clients per day, but I have the feeling that I'm helping them, that my work is valuable, and this fulfils me.

Mirjana and I successfully provide support to each other so that each of us can do surrender meditation for ninety minutes a day, a practice which we were initiated into in Australia.

207

And then there is Filip, this little creature with big eyes and huge curiosity. He's a source of constant joy and happiness and now he's relaxed and fallen asleep in my arms. I gently put him down and go back to bed to get a couple of hours of shut-eye.

∞

"Good evening, everyone. Thanks for coming to my lecture. There are so many of you. I apologize for starting late but as you can see there are not enough chairs in the auditorium and we had to bring them from a neighbouring hall. I'll talk a little faster to make up for lost time... ha-ha..."

I feel fantastic. I'm standing in an absolutely full-to-the-rafters auditorium in Ljubljana and giving an evening lecture which was only announced a couple of weeks ago. How incredibly cool I am! I just stick a couple of posters in bookshops and health food stores and look how many people have come.

Feeling full of myself, I proudly begin the lecture. I speak with self-satisfaction about communication, human relations, married life, parenthood, the structure of the mind, about subconscious patterns and mechanisms, about spirituality and the meaning of life...

And then four people stand up, slowly make their way down the row of seats, and leave the hall. And right after them two more.

It's impossible for me not to be affected by this. I smile at them, as if to say, it's okay, I love you no matter what, but my equilibrium is upset. I seize at what seems to be my best option. I will bring more of Skanda into the lecture. He's always really fascinating and charismatic. I become even more vehement. I make thoughtful faces. I nod to myself just as Skanda does. My self-confidence returns. I must be fascinating them now.

Then, all of a sudden, six people get up and start to move toward the exit. Before they even get there, four more stand up and follow.

I'm starting to panic again. I grab the next lifesaver: Judy from Scotland. Six months ago I was on a visit to the Findhorn Community in Scotland for a one-week retreat and then running my own workshop for the community. Judy, a community member who presented something to our group, charmed me and all the others with her candour, authenticity, and modesty. I'll put a pinch of Judy in my presentation. That will surely captivate them.

I continue the lecture, smiling and laughing, nice and cute, sweet and modest. Very, very sweet.

And four more get up and leave.

And then two.

And then three.

And then four more.

I somehow make it through to the end of the lecture in a state of complete internal confusion and discombobulation. I comfort myself that, all the same, more people stayed than left and I'm eternally grateful to everyone who smiles pleasantly at me as they leave as a way of saying that it was all nice.

Later, in the silence of the city night, as I return to my car, I feel like a piece of shit. I lecture about authenticity, while being completely fake. About sincerity while I'm hiding behind my own masks and games. I pretend that I know everything about life while actually I'm only a twenty-seven-year-old kid. I act smart about parenthood when I hardly have any experience of it myself.

Modesty, sincerity, authenticity, humility – I value all of these virtues but don't know how to live by them. I know I won't get to them by pretending I'm modest, by pretending I'm sincere, donning a mask of authenticity, and playing the humble spiritual guy. I will only get there by actually stripping down to the essence and revealing myself and my heart to the world.

I sigh deeply and start the car.

∞

"Mum, we have to settle something."

I'm having coffee with my mother in the sunny garden of a café in Kranj. I've been preparing for this conversation for a long time and know it won't be easy. I'm nervous because I'm perennially scared of spoiling relationships. I have such a deep need inside to always smooth things over, to keep relationships in good condition, in a sort of harmony, even if only on the surface.

"Almost always when we sit down to have a coffee together, you start to talk about Dad, what he did, what he didn't do, what kind of relationship you have with him, how you get angry with him…"

I begin the conversation slowly and cautiously.

"Well, it really is difficult with him. You know yourself how he is, especially when he's drinking," my mother rushes to explain.

"Of course I know, it's very difficult. Yet it's becoming clear to me that I no longer want to hear about all of this from you. I've been hearing about it since I was a child. It was unpleasant then and it's unpleasant now. Actually it's very unpleasant for me, because I don't know what I'm supposed to do with all of this."

"It's also sometimes very unpleasant for me to be with him."

"I know. Of course I know. And I wish for you to get all the support you need. But from your own friends. I am not your friend. I'm your son. These conversations burden me and they also burden my relationship with Dad."

I'm trying to remain calm. My mother puts out her cigarette. There's a dark expression on her face.

"Fine. I won't say anything about it again. I'm sorry if I have burdened you with this and if my presence is such a burden to you as well. I'm sorry if I was a bad mother and if I've caused you pain in your life."

She speaks slowly, looking down at the floor.

This is the way it usually goes. Now this drama will be followed by several months of cold relations and hurt feelings. It would help if I could say at this point that she is a good mother and that I'm grateful for everything. But I don't know if I want to go on playing these games. I'm fed up with them.

∞

"Robert, come here, let's look and see if the placenta is intact..."

The midwife whispers to me. Throughout the whole birth she had noticed my enthusiasm and tried to include me in the process. I stand next to her, leaning over the bloody placenta on the white sheet, observing her fingers gently exploring it, carefully examining the edges.

"You have to look very carefully to make sure the whole placenta came out, that it didn't tear, in case some small piece remains inside because that can be very dangerous..."

Her voice starts to sound very remote and fades away, echoing as it does so. I begin to see twinkling lights and geometrical shapes in front of my eyes. I'm losing my balance and realize that I'm about to faint. I take a deep breath, straighten up, open my eyes wide, and nod enthusiastically, hoping that I won't black out in the middle of the room. Apart from me there are three happy women here: Mirjana, the midwife, and a friend who provided homeopathic assistance at the birth. Well, actually four women, because now little Lucija is with us as well, calmly sucking on Mirjana's nipple and looking entirely content.

Little Lucija, created nine months ago during a passionate night filled with beauty and joy, and now born in the warmth and serenity of our bedroom. If Filip came into the world amidst thunder and lightning, Lucija slid in with peace, serenity, tenderness and love.

I have a daughter.

I take another breath, and wipe away the tears, feeling deeply touched. And I feel a sense of relief: the placenta is whole and I did not faint. I go into the kitchen to get a plastic container, put the placenta inside, carefully close the top, and place it in the freezer. The only piece of meat in our kitchen. And no living creature had to die for this piece of meat, instead it came with birth, with the miracle of life. When everything calms down, I will go and bury it somewhere in the forest, in the earth, under the trees. My friend Tomo, after his daughter was born, made himself a meal of placenta fried with eggs, and I was also considering that option, but in the end decided on something less radical.

...

The next morning Filip shuffles in with my mother. He's now three-and-a-half years old and has spent the previous night at her house. He kicks off his shoes and looks at me very seriously:

"Where's the baby?"

"In the bedroom. With Mummy."

"Is the baby awake or asleep?"

"I don't know. We can go in and check," I smile tenderly. "It's a girl. Her name is Lucija."

"Okay, but first I have to get something."

Filip goes decisively to the cutlery drawer in the kitchen and pulls out a big two-pronged fork, the kind used for serving roasts and that sort of thing. I don't even know why we have it since we don't eat meat. He marches towards the bedroom with the fork in his hand. Feeling tense, I walk right behind him, ready to jump in case it turns out he has some dark plans. My mother is behind me, rigid with fear.

Filip stands in front of the bed and holds the fork out towards Mirjana who smiles in loving confusion, and also towards Lucija who is calmly suckling, her eyes facing the breast through their half-closed lids. Filip speaks:

"Look, baby, this is a fork. It's very sharp and pointed and you can stab yourself with it. That's why you mustn't play with it yet..."

I smile and my shoulders relax. My mother next to me starts breathing again. I kneel down and hug the little imp:

"Filip, my boy, you're worried that your little sister might hurt herself. How sweet, Filip, how very thoughtful…"

"I am, because the baby's so little, she doesn't know what's dangerous."

Filip hands me the fork, slowly steps closer to the bed, and pats Lucija on the head. Mirjana and I look at each other with tears in our eyes. How much love and tenderness is in all of us.

∞

"Hello, Robert Kržišnik speaking. May I speak to Marko please?"

"Hello. I'm sorry but you can't speak to Marko."

It's a woman's voice on the line, quiet and hesitant.

"Okay. When is he coming home? I can call back."

"Sir, Marko committed suicide a month ago. He is no longer with us. I'm sorry," the woman's voice on the line articulates the words slowly.

After a brief silence I find my voice:

"Oh my. My sincere condolences. Thank you for telling me. I am sorry. Goodbye."

I put down the phone.

Marko committed suicide. A little less than a year ago he came and asked if I would be his therapist. I told him that I was all booked up but that I kept a waiting list. He could get on the waiting list and his name would come up in about nine months or maybe a little more. He said that his situation was really urgent. I told him I believed him and that I would really like to help him, and suggested that he could contact a colleague of mine who trained with me and in whom I had a lot of confidence, and she could provide the support he needed. But he said he wanted to work with me, asked if I could take him right away, said again that the situation really was urgent. I said that I didn't want to make a judgement about which case was more urgent than another and to push someone else back in the line so that I could take him. He said that he would think about it and left.

And now he's killed himself. A heavy weight falls on me. Even though I know that I'm not responsible for the actions of others, that I cannot save each and every person that I come across, it doesn't help much. I sit down on the couch and the whole situation torments me.

This responsibility for the emotions of others, for their happiness, their lives, is slowly exhausting me. I give three two-hour therapy sessions five to six days a week, and the weight of responsibility is always there, somewhere in the background, that I have to save them, that it's all on me. And I still lead the occasional workshop, I take care of the kids and Mirjana, and also provide psychological support to my mother, and my friends.

I'm exhausted. And I don't have any place to go when I need support myself.

∞

"What's going on, do you have no intention of ever calling me again or what?"

I hear my father's voice on the other end of the line. My entire internal system goes on alert. I hold my breath and slowly answer:

"Hi, Dad. We both have each other's numbers. We can call each other, right?"

"Yeah, yeah. But it's only decent that you call your father, not that you completely ignore him…"

My father is speaking sharply and tension in me is rising rapidly. I try to answer calmly:

"After the way our last conversation ended I didn't look forward to talking to you again, if I'm completely honest with you."

Half a year earlier we'd spoken on the phone and his behaviour, like so many times before, had been nasty, humiliating, and domineering, and I just lost my cool. It was the first time in my life that I'd allowed myself to react to my father. I'd yelled at him:

"I don't want you to talk to me that way anymore. I've had enough. Goodbye."

I'd slammed down the phone, my heart beating wildly. I'd never done anything like that before. He was always the one to end our conversations. I was always the one to adapt, to submit, to retreat. On this occasion my anger had overrun all these mechanisms and I had finally reacted. I'd been upset for many hours afterwards, flooded with a sort of primal fear, as if the whole world as going to fall apart because I'd done something so radical. But at the same time I had a very clear feeling that I was behaving in accordance with my own integrity. That I simply didn't want to have that kind of relationship anymore, that I wanted to be treated as an equal, as a human being worthy of respect.

For six months we didn't talk even once. My mother begged me to call him and I said no, I won't, I'll call him when I want to, he has my number and he can call me if he wants to.

And today he called.

"Well, whatever, I think we should bury the hatchet and start talking again. What do you think?" my father asks.

"That's fine with me. But first let's meet and go for a long walk somewhere outdoors."

…

And that's exactly what we do a couple of days later. A walk during which I stand up for myself, where I clearly state what I want, clearly express my thoughts and values. It is the first conversation with my father where I actually have the feeling that he is listening to me.

Maybe this year, 1996, when I'm already thirty years old, I've finally begun to grow up.

∞

"Look, Filip. Yesterday you asked what happens to people when they die. Well, their bodies are buried here."

I'm walking slowly with Filip though the village cemetery in the afternoon calm. We're alone, not another living soul.

"But where exactly do they put the dead bodies?" Filip asks.

"Let's go and see if there is an open grave somewhere. There's usually an open hole ready to receive the coffin of someone who has died recently. Ah, yes, here's one. They put the dead body in a hole like that."

We stand in front of the deep pit in the rows of neatly ordered graves.

"They just throw the body in there?"

"Well, first they put it in a nice wooden box called a coffin and then they slowly and respectfully lower it down and then they throw soil over it."

Filip looks thoughtfully into the hole.

"Oh, I know. It's like when we plant a tree, but here a new body for a new person grows," he announces.

"Hmm, that would be both interesting and simple if that was the way it really happened. It would be quite nice to plant new people, but actually things happen a little differently. Let me explain…"

I smile and we continue our walk.

I endlessly enjoy my little boy: his beauty, his desire to understand life, his lively and inquiring eyes. And, of course, the endless hours we spend playing Lego together. I'm deeply moved by how much love and trust I receive from him.

Sometimes it actually frightens me.

∞

Summer 1996. Mirjana and I have been living apart for almost two months without anyone else knowing. We decided to take a little break, well, it was mostly my decision, but we're not telling anyone else about it. We're thinking and exploring our options. One of us stays in the apartment where we've been living together near Kranj and the other in the house in the mountains which we rent for running retreats. The children are sometimes here, sometimes there, always with one or the other of us.

I'm feeling trapped by the relationship with Mirjana, it's pressing in on me from all sides. I'm not fulfilled. This isn't the love that I long for. The flame of my life is slowly going out, though everything looks fine on the outside. We cooperate, we care for our two beautiful children. But the on-going frustration, along with the life in me searching for air and fullness, is bubbling up in me very strongly. Yet I can't seem to be able to make the decision to leave her because I'm so overwhelmed by fear: that I'll be condemned, just look at him, a couples therapist yet he can't even hold his own relationship together, that the whole world will reject me, that everything will fall apart.

I can't. I simply can't. There's some powerful mechanism in me which makes me clench my teeth, retreat and adapt, and do everything possible to preserve the relationship, to preserve harmony.

And so I do my best to strengthen the relationship and invest my energy in our family life.

∞

I'm standing next to a tree in the forest and staring into the eyes of a lion lying not far away. It's enormous, the size of a cow, and incredibly majestic and calm. The longer I watch it, the more the fear disappears from me and is replaced by peace and trust. All of a sudden, slowly and silently, a black panther the size of a horse glides past me. I freeze for an instant and then quickly relax. I know he's not dangerous, that he wants nothing from me. I admire his beauty.

217

I look around and see that there are six more big cats near me, lionesses and black panthers padding about in all their immeasurable grandeur, power and beauty. Some people run out of the forest towards me. They're frightened, overwhelmed by panic. They don't know where to run with all these great cats prowling the forest. I calm them down, tell them that I know the cats well, and that they're peaceful, that they're not a threat to anyone, that everything will be alright.

I write the dream into my diary and wonder why I'm having so many dreams recently that involve massive big cats – tigers, lions, black panthers, all at least as big as horses. I start off somewhat frightened at the beginning of the dreams but this always shifts to respect, admiration, and finally trust.

When I talk to my friends about the dreams and also mention that big cats have always struck me as the most beautiful creatures, they say that these dreams have to do with the awakening of my inner power and that it's time that I begin to accept and ride it rather than being afraid and hiding from it.

Intuitively, I think I know what they're talking about, but I have no idea what specifically I should do. I put down my pen and close my eyes.

∞

"Wahoo!"

I call out at this spot in the valley because I know the mountain wall in front of us makes an especially loud and clear echo. We're on one of our frequent family trips to the forests and mountains of Slovenia, enjoying the beauty of nature.

"Who was that?"

Filip and Lucija both ask in astonishment when they hear my call repeated.

"That's an echo. The sound of my voice travelled up to those mountains and bounced back to us. That's called an echo."

"What is a sound?" Lucija asks thoughtfully, still staring toward the snow-covered mountains.

"That's something you hear, like when I am speaking now. The sound travels from my throat and mouth to your ears. And the sound of me yelling also travels from me to the mountains and back again so we can hear it."

"Who throws it back here?"

Lucija is looking at me while Filip is giggling in the background. He always seems to thoroughly enjoy these kinds of conversations with Lucija.

Life with the children is incredibly fulfilling. I so much enjoy when we sing together in the car, when we do silly dances at home and laugh like crazy, when we draw and go on walks. So much happiness, joy, and trust.

I'm especially happy to see the kind of companions they are to each other, how gentle they are, how they care for one another, how much love and trust there is between them.

∞

"Look, Mum, I spent my childhood and youth with an alcoholic father and that had a huge impact on me and now I'm so sorry to see that you have started to drink. It worries me, and your sisters are worried too."

We're back at the café in Kranj. I have something very difficult to say to my mother today.

"Maybe I can try and get close to him that way, get to know him better," she answers. "What do I know? I can't think of any other way."

As my mother speaks, she plays with a little bag of sugar on the table. I take a slow breath and try to smile:

"Yeah, okay. I understand your desire to get close to him, and, well, if you really think this will get you close to him and you two will meet somewhere in the fumes of alcohol, well then OK… I'm a bit sceptical but what do I know either? All I know for sure is that I don't want to expose Filip and Lucija to this, not even a tiny bit, not at all in fact."

My mother lifts her gaze and looks into my eyes in surprise:

"Nothing's ever happened when the children have been with us. I take very good care of them. Has anything happened?"

"Look, Mum, things happen on different levels. Children sense everything, perceive everything, they're very sensitive, more than adults are, and these changes in behaviour confuse them. They don't feel safe. They feel nervous. They've told me that many times. So I've decided that I'm not going to leave them alone with you anymore until I'm completely sure that neither of you will be touching alcohol while the children are with you."

I speak slowly, looking into her eyes to make sure she understands what I'm actually saying.

"Oh, that's the way it is then? You're going to stop me having contact with my own grandchildren? And I love them so much, so very, very much…"

There are tears in her eyes.

"Oh, Mum, please just try to listen to what I'm actually saying. By no means do I want to prevent you from having contact with the children. Both of them love you very much, Dad too. And I know how much you love them. And it's very important to me that you have a good relationship with them. You're always welcome to visit and spend time with the children. Or to take them on a walk. Or we can all go on trips together. And we'll still visit you regularly. But I'm not going to leave the children alone with you until the situation changes."

My mother looks at the table and slowly nods. It's hard for me and for her, but at the same time I'm very satisfied. I've finally started to stand up for what is important in life. I've finally begun to shift the patterns of the past.

∞

I hear the sound of a splash in the water and stiffen. Where is Lucija? I was standing on the pier talking to a friend and Lucija was playing nearby. I jump to the edge of the pier and see little bubbles floating to the surface from Lucija's submerged body about a metre under the water. I jump into the sea after her, reach her easily, and pull her out. She spits and coughs, laughing at the same time.

"Lucija, please don't jump in the water without telling me beforehand. You still don't know how to swim and I need to be with you..."

I try to explain the situation calmly, gently, sincerely.

"Ha-ha," she coughs and laughs as she spits out more water. "I do know how to swim, ha-ha..."

"Lucija, you don't know how to swim. I will teach you, but you're only two years old and you don't know how to swim and I do have to be with you, to watch you and help you. Really."

I keep talking as I hold her hand and we step onto the shore together.

"But you do help me."

She calmly responds as she picks up little stones from the beach.

"Of course I do, but I need to see you. If I don't see you because you don't tell me where you're going, that can be a problem. You could have drowned while I was just calmly chatting on the pier."

"Ha-ha, that would be really funny."

Lucija giggles as she places little stones in her bucket.

I admire her infinitely relaxed approach to life and her immeasurable confidence in it. But at the same time it terrifies me. It seems to me she has way more trust in me than I can actually justify. With a laugh, she throws herself from the top of the stairs down to the bottom where she trusts I will catch her. I always have done up until now, but when I tell her that there may be a time when I don't see her coming, she just laughs.

And, although I try to convince her not to trust me so completely, I also admire her. There will be no obstacles for her with that kind of trust in life. Where would I have got to if I had had anything close to that kind of trust?

∞

Dr. Eleanor Arroway sits strapped to her seat in the capsule on top of a huge structure made out of three spinning rings which begin to spin faster and faster, creating a kind of powerful energy vortex. When it's at the peak of its three-directional spinning, the capsule drops into the centre, and it's the beginning of a fantastic voyage for Dr. Arroway, played by Jodie Foster in the film Contact.

She finds herself in a worm-hole in space, a tunnel that connects two different points of space-time that are millions of light years apart. She's being pulled through the wormhole at unimaginable speeds, and now and then she stops briefly at one of the intersections of the wormhole before she's pulled onwards again. She witnesses fantastic phenomena at these intersections – constellations of stars, black holes, supernovas. Poetic beauty of cosmic dimensions…

All of sudden emotions boil up in me without me knowing from where they come or why. I look at those stars and I start to cry, to sob. I don't know what's happening but it just keeps coming out of me. I wipe my nose and my eyes, trying to keep this catharsis somehow under control and not attract the attention of everyone in the cinema.

My friend, Tatjana, who I've come to the movie with, while our partners are taking care of the four children, looks at me questioningly from the side to see if I'm okay. I don't know if I'm okay. I only know that something very primal and very deep inside me is responding with agitation to the vastness of these intergalactic scenes. Something very deep and subtle is resonating inside me and causing a very powerful emotional response.

When the action of the film finally returns to Earth, my shaking and sobbing gradually subside. What remains is the feeling that something in me has opened up or that some fundamental connection to the stars, to the cosmic expanse, has re-awakened, and is reverberating inside me like an ancient memory or a recognition of something I've forgotten long, long ago.

This connection has awakened so strongly that it will never again entirely be forgotten, even though I still don't know today what it actually means.

∞

"Filip and Lucija, can you please cooperate, so we can finally go out. Come on, please. Oh, you kids, why is everything such a struggle with you two…"

I grumble impatiently as I gather the things we need to take with us on our nature trip. The children stop chasing each other and laughing at the tops of their voices and Filip starts to get his backpack ready. Lucija stands in front of me thoughtfully, looks right into my eyes, and slowly speaks:

"Why did you decide to have children at all, if it's not any fun, if it's only a struggle for you?"

I stand up, stunned, and look at her, but she just continues calmly:

"And you see, now you're mad at us, and tomorrow you'll be apologizing to us for getting mad."

My mouth broadens into a smile as I watch my four-year-old angel, who calmly, clearly, and with a sort of inner satisfaction, regularly imparts this kind of wisdom. She's light years ahead of where I was at her age. Nothing will stop this girl, I think, as I answer her:

"Lucija, you are absolutely right. I have nothing to say."

We both laugh and continue getting ready for the trip.

Of course I won't stop saying I am sorry: to be honest, critical of myself, to take responsibility for my words and my actions, and, when I sincerely regret something, when I do something that's not in harmony with my integrity and my values, to apologize… all of this is very precious to me in any relationships with other people, but most of all with my children.

Not long ago I realized that during my childhood what hurt me most about my father was not what he actually did or said. All of that was possible to take and also to understand. What hurt me the most was the fact that somehow he wasn't really in our relationship. He didn't have the capacity to be with me, to listen to me, to find a way to communicate with me, especially after traumatic incidents. To express regret, to make sure I was okay. It was as I didn't exist or that he didn't have space for me because he was always dealing with his own problems, his own wounds, his own cuts and bruises that he was trying to heal.

That's why I will definitely continue to be honest with my children, to sincerely express all my regrets even if little Lucija keeps grilling me.

∞

I turn sharply from the main road onto a dirt path and, after a bumpy ride of about a hundred metres, finally come to a stop. I don't know what's happening to me but I know that if I don't get out I will explode.

I step out of the car and the fresh air of the summer night washes over me. Here, in the middle of the countryside, there's less light pollution and the sky is filled with stars. Silence reigns, only the sound of one bird coming from the nearby forest. I breathe deeply and soak in the peace and freshness, here, alone in a meadow, beneath the stars.

In the evening, when the children had gone to sleep, and Mirjana had followed them not long after, I decided to go to a movie in nearby Kranj. The film Stigmata was not such an artistic success but still it touched me deeply, and catalysed a sort of chain reaction in me. It was the story of a young woman through whom something powerfully spiritual and mystical begins to enter the world, even though she resists it. This awakened the recognition in me of how I was also suppressing the deeper aspects of my being, as if I was living a sort of parallel life on some side track where I was just going through the motions, without spirit, without inspiration. Everything is okay, nothing bad or dramatic is happening, but all the same my soul is starting to suffocate.

The energy begins to surge uncontrollably inside me and I run down the dirt road and across the meadow, faster and faster, the moon and stars throwing plenty of light in front of my feet.

What am I doing with my life? A big part of my longings, my desires, the most precious of my strivings, I have simply ignored and tossed aside. I have somehow surrendered to fate. If I'm completely honest, I am really just waiting for the kids to grow up so I can honourably start a new life without anyone reproaching me. What a phony, that I don't have the balls to do it now, given what I feel. Maybe what I'm doing really is good for the children, or maybe I'm just trying to save my reputation, trying to make sure that everyone will still accept me. But maybe the fact that I'm not living authentically, not following my dreams, gives the children exactly the opposite pattern, the opposite role model from the one I would like to give them.

I suddenly stop and scream. And again. And again. To the sky. To the earth. To the forest which is now so close. And one more time to the moon.

I take a few deep breaths, look at the sky, and slowly turn back towards the car, waiting for me there in the darkness.

My heart is pounding in my chest. Maybe from running, maybe from fear. But now I know there is no way back. I am so awake now that I will never again be able to return to my sleeping life.

Once again the time has come to step away from what is known and safe, but stifling, into what is unknown, unpredictable, but also very much alive.

∞

*It's night and I'm driving my car along a winding unlit road.
Lidija is sitting in the passenger seat. All around us it's dark,
peaceful, not a living soul. We're discussing whether or not we
should make love. Lidija is not really for it, it doesn't seem right
to her, whereas I am all for it, and finally she agrees.*

*I park the car at the edge of the forest and suddenly we are
both naked, the roof of the car is open, and we can see the starry
sky above us. Lidija is somehow depressed, the whole thing is
upsetting her. She's not really into it but, because she has agreed,
she slowly straddles me in the seat where I'm sitting expectantly. I
slowly penetrate her as we sit embracing each other, gently
rocking. Lidija looks thoughtfully down over my shoulder. She
seems tired, burdened, while I am happy, ecstatic. I have a feeling
of completion as if, with this act, everything is in its right place,
the whole world.*

I wake up, write down my dream, and then lie back, awake,
staring at the darkness above me. Lidija has been a friend for
many years. Her son, Dev, is in between Filip and Lucija in age
and gets along well with both of them. Our two families go on
trips together and a certain inspirational connection has developed
between Lidija and me, even though, in my monogamous
condition, I have never really noticed her as a woman before. But
now, as I awaken from the relationship with Mirjana into a new
freedom, into a new life, I'm starting to feel a powerful attraction
to her. And she tells me that the attraction is mutual.

∞

Autumn 2000. I'm thirty-four years old and my world has
been turned upside down. I've moved out of the home I was
sharing with Mirjana and into the apartment in Ljubljana where I
first lived as a child and which I've now inherited from my
grandmother. I'm in a romantic relationship with Lidija – but for
the time being, we're not telling the children. I've lost some of
my friends who condemned my actions or who in some cases I
withdrew from, so that they would find it easier to be with

Mirjana and support her. To my great surprise, my parents have supported my decision and stood by me, even helping me practically and financially as well as morally. Although the break-up with Mirjana was extremely painful, we're still cooperating in raising the children and they're spending half the week with me and half with her.

I still don't know if I made a good decision. On the one hand, it seems that suppressing my deeper longings and persisting for twelve years in an unfulfilling relationship, mostly because of my fears and my inability to be truly authentic, cannot be good for anybody. On the other hand, I know that it was a big shock for the children and will have consequences of one kind or another for the rest of their lives. I felt an urgent pull to follow my inner calling, but was my action responsible? Was it in harmony with the love I feel for them?

I don't know. I really don't know. I see both sides of the picture. And some that are in the middle. Perhaps there are no simple or perfect decisions in such a situation, but rather each action carries the potential of a whole range of consequences, some beautiful and some painful. And the only reliable signposts for me are those that refer to the deepest questions of personal integrity, questions such as: What kind of person do I want to be? How do I want to travel through this life?

Wherever I turn, I will almost certainly celebrate the step I've taken and also regret it during the years to come. I worry about how things will turn out, above all because I love Filip and Lucija so very much.

∞

"Ach, Robert, to be honest I never had such a good feeling about you two even back when you started. I thought that you didn't really fit together, that you were too different. So I was really surprised that you stayed together for so long."

I'm having a drink with an old friend and we're talking about my divorce. It's the third friend who knows both of us well from the time we got together who has told me the same thing: that they had a bad feeling about it at the time, that they thought we didn't suit each other, and predicted it wouldn't last. I don't know if I should be angry or glad. I mean: they were my friends. Couldn't they have warned me or at least have communicated their uneasiness to me? But I also feel relief when I hear these things because they confirm my own understanding of the situation. At the same time I wonder how my life would have gone if, all those years ago, at least one of these friends would have grabbed me, looked deep in my eyes, and said:

"Listen, Robert, I'm worried about you, really worried. I know Mirjana, I know you, and I really have a bad feeling about your relationship. I don't think you fit together. So I'm asking you: do you really love her in the way you want to love the woman you're going to spend your whole life with? Is there really enough inspiration, enough flow in your connection? Is this really what your soul longs for? Does your heart really burn for her and for the two of you?"

Who knows if I would have been willing to listen, though?!

∞

"Then when you and Mummy live together again, when we all live together in the apartment in Ljubljana, will we still keep the old apartment in Šenčur?" Lucija asks, looking at me curiously, as we sit around the table painting on water glasses with special paint.

"Lucija, look, Mummy and I aren't going to live together anymore. We're going to live apart and each have our own life. But we love both of you more than you can imagine and we're going to take care of you."

I'm trying to answer their questions clearly and calmly but it isn't going very well. Filip stops colouring and lifts his gaze:

"But why? Why did you break up of all a sudden? Did you argue?"

"No, Filip, we didn't argue. We never argued very much. And I want to be clear, we didn't break up. I left. I am responsible.

Mirjana didn't change. It was me who changed. I realized that I wasn't really happy with her, that I didn't really love her. That I wasn't fulfilled by the relationship with her."

They look at me with wide open eyes, tears gathering in them. My heart is breaking.

"You used to love her and then you just suddenly stopped loving her?" Lucija asks. "Is that what happened?"

"Yes, something like that, or maybe I never really loved her as much as I thought…"

The children are disappointed, in pain, sad, confused. Their carefree lives have fallen apart and terrifying new dimensions have appeared, which they don't understand and are not ready for. If only I knew how to really be with them, to stand by their sides, to provide them with enough emotional support so that they could embrace the pain in their hearts and somehow process it. If only I knew how.

My heart breaks when I see the sparks in their eyes dim slightly.

Ten: A Successful Grown-up?

Time stops and I stare at Lidija in bewilderment. I somehow cannot believe what I've just heard her say. I stare at her numbly, silent, no words, and also no will to search for words...

We're sitting in a cafe and a moment ago we were talking about a difficulty we'd been experiencing in our relationship. The conversation became edgy. Suddenly I heard her say something which made my blood run cold. It really felt like she was intending to hurt me.

Everything inside me begins to collapse. All the love, the bliss, the magic that I've felt during the past six months: all of that crumbles in this moment of shock, in which I seem to be re-experiencing the coldness and isolation that I regularly felt during my childhood and adolescence with my father. And almost never in the years since then. I don't want to be in this kind of relationship. With this kind of communication, this way of treating each other. Never again.

There's only one thought in my mind: get up and leave forever. Forever. And don't ever look back. Because this is so far from me experiencing the care and tenderness and respect that I long for in a relationship, that I have absolutely no hope that we can ever be close again. In fact, one part of me has already left, gone, out into the cold rainy afternoon.

Another part of me is still sitting here: the frightened, powerless, dependent part of me which has no ability to fully face the situation. If it could, it would see that although I've been experiencing loads of beauty and that feeling of being in love which can carry me all across the sky, I am starting to notice elements of our relationship that worry me. This is the part of me that's scared to face the idea that perhaps merely love is not enough. This part of me wants to believe in love, regardless of the reality that I've been experiencing. This part of me just wants relationships to work out. This is the part of me that is determined to hold things together at all costs.

This part of me shrivels. And becomes numb. And just sits there.

∞

I'm standing staring at my bare feet sinking into the desert sand. I slowly look around and see sand dunes on all sides, nothing else. Well, here and there a solitary figure rises up on the dunes, moving slowly and thoughtfully on the soft sand. These are the other participants in this ten-day international retreat deep in the Sahara desert, led by a Frenchman, a former ballet dancer named Claude. We're learning to fully return to our bodies, to movement, to the here and now.

After a week filled with paying attention to being present in the body in the moment, in this desert environment with practically no visual input except the endless waves of ochre-coloured sand dunes, I begin to experience it all as a sort of calm and serene dream.

And now I'm just standing still because everything in me has stopped. The end of movement. My body won't move. My whole being won't work anymore. I slowly slide down into the sand and lie on my back. In the almost total absence of external sounds, my breathing and the beating of my heart are extra loud. I stare at the sky above me, all my muscles relaxed, the warm sand taking me in.

I'm infinitely tired. Infinitely. Of life. Well, maybe not of life itself, but of all of the striving in this life. Of the effort, of forcing myself, of constantly chasing goals. Of trying to do the right thing. And, as it struck me last night during one of the exercises we were doing, also of the exertion, of the energy it takes to care for everyone around me, the endless stretching beyond my own limits as I adjust and take responsibility for the feelings of anyone who happens to go past.

Suddenly I hear Claude's gentle voice right beside me, speaking in his strong French accent:

"Robert, how are you? What is going on with you, my friend?"

This guy is like some kind of cat. He comes up to me so silently and sits next to me in the sand.

"I'm fine, Claude, just fine. I am just so tired. My whole organism is so darn tired. Tired of moving through life."

I say the words slowly, without moving any muscle that's not absolutely necessary for speaking.

"I see, Robert, I see. Can you come with me now? We are completing the session here and slowly going back to the camp for lunch," he purrs in his velvety voice.

"Listen, dear Claude," I utter the words very slowly and barely audibly. "You go ahead and just leave me here. Just leave me here, please. I'll be fine, thank you."

I would like to lie for a hundred years right here in the warm sand. And then die, completely peacefully. I have no more energy to continue the struggle of life. Perhaps this is the most beautiful moment and the right place for me to die. To unplug myself. For my body just to dry up in this soft sand.

"Robert, please, I cannot leave you here. Please understand, I cannot leave you here. Please come with me, my friend."

Claude repeats the words sadly in his endlessly sweet French accent.

Of course he cannot leave me here. Unfortunately: because it would be such a beautiful and calm death.

"Okay, Claude, I'll come. For your eyes only," I quietly chuckle. "Just give me another five minutes, please. I will come. I promise."

"Très bien, mon ami. I will be waiting for you on the next dune, right over there."

Claude shifts his body with his cat moves about ten metres away.

I'm so weary, so infinitely and deeply weary. What will I do with this tiredness, this existential exhaustion?

∞

I sit down on the green wooden bench and sigh deeply. This is the same bench I was sitting on when I held that little grey rabbit in my lap and was melting in bliss. The same bench, the same apartment building, the same everything. Only the year is no longer 1970 but 2002. How time flies.

Evil omens surround me, weigh on me, press me down into the depths. Lidija and I are emptying this apartment, which I inherited from my grandmother and have recently sold. We've just bought a beautiful big top-floor apartment in a one-hundred-year-old house near the centre of Ljubljana, where we're going to move with our children. I just took out a big bag of rubbish and got overwhelmed with it all.

Something in my gut is screaming that this is not okay. That I'm somehow sleep-walking again, jumping onto a train that might be going in the wrong direction and which will be really hard to get off. Some devil keeps pushing me on and I can't stop despite the serious doubts gathering inside me.

Are Lidija and I really as connected and aligned as I want to believe? Or am I merely blindly in love with certain aspects of her, not wanting to see many other ones? Have I perhaps just thoughtlessly jumped into another relationship, without really honestly checking with myself? Have I really considered the whole picture, and above all the well-being of Filip and Lucija?

I sigh. I don't dare to think about it anymore. Things are already in motion: one apartment sold, the other bought and we're about to move in…

It will work out somehow, I tell myself, and slowly get up from the bench and go back up the stairs to the apartment.

∞

"Robert – I remembered your name right, didn't I? Can you please hold the yoke in front of you while I get something out of my backpack?"

I'm in a little single-engined propeller plane which has dual controls, sitting next to the pilot. I automatically nod and cautiously take hold of the yoke, which is like a steering wheel that controls the plane's movement.

"Okay, now I'm going to transfer control of the plane over to you. There: now you're controlling the plane. You're flying. Bravo!"

The pilot smiles, picks up his backpack from the floor beside him, and begins to rummage through it.

I hold the yoke, completely tense, and feel drops of sweat already starting to drip down my neck.

The pilot pulls a camera out of his backpack, screws an enormous telephoto lens onto it, and smiles at me.

"I'm a big fan of photography and it would be a sin not to take some photos on such a beautiful sunny day. You're doing fine. Just hold the course towards Lake Bled which you can see there in the distance. If you turn the yoke to the left, we go left, to the right, right, just like a car. If you pull it towards yourself, we go up. If you push it away, we go down. Then you have the rudder pedals at your feet. With them you can go ahead and slowly experiment a little, so I don't need to explain too much. You're doing great. It's just like driving a car, right?"

The pilot begins to look for motifs in the landscape below while I, completely rigid with anxiety, try to understand how all of the various controls and pedals affect the flight of the plane. Everything seems quite surprising, and not at all like driving a car. There are no reference points, no stability on any axis, the plane sways in every direction. The fact that Filip and Lucija are sitting in the two back seats doesn't make me feel any more relaxed. Although part of me is excited about flying a plane, another part of me is terrified with the responsibility.

The children had never been on a plane and often asked me how it was, what it felt like. I decided to surprise them on this sunny Saturday and booked a panoramic flight. When they realized at the airfield what was in store for them, they were speechless with excitement.

"Could you please take the controls? We're above the lake, there's a mountain in front of us, and I don't know if I can turn in time."

I try to speak calmly as my fingers grip the yoke, which is already wet from my perspiration.

"Robert, you go ahead and turn it. Slowly make a 180-degree turn. You'll see, it's not difficult, just give it a try…" the pilot responds casually, fully focused on taking photos with his gigantic camera.

"Listen, I tried already and there is no way I can make the turn in time. Seriously, please, take the controls."

"It's fine. It's fine. Just start the turn nice and slow, you'll see, it'll be fine…," the pilot murmurs.

My pulse begins to spike wildly.

"Look, really, let's stop joking. Please take the controls. I'm not going to pilot anymore."

I speak decisively and the pilot lets out a theatrical sigh and puts his camera back into his backpack and takes the yoke in front of him.

"Okay, okay, I'll do it. Fine, and now that I'm in control, let's do some serious flying."

The pilot smiles and goes into a nosedive, straight down towards the lake below. Chaos explodes in the little cabin. Filip, Lucija and I scream with one voice, waving our arms around trying to hold onto the ceiling or the windows. After pulling up above the lake, the pilot puts the plane into a steep banking climb with a 180-degree turn. The engine judders, the pilot laughs loudly, we scream some more, all of the unattached objects in the cabin are flying around us…

Finally the pilot levels off.

"OK, OK, I'm sorry. I was just having a little fun. We pilots need to enjoy ourselves too. Robert, you take the controls again, and fly the plane back towards the airfield. There it is. You see it? Right, kids? Your dad should fly the plane. He knows how to do it better than me, don't you agree?"

I instinctively grab the yoke because I don't want this lunatic to keep flying.

The flight back takes place in silence except for the clicking of the pilot's camera and the drip-dropping of my sweat. The children each stare out of their window. Not the type of experience I was hoping to bring to them.

When we approach the airfield, the pilots puts his camera away again and joyfully winks at me: "If it's alright with you, I'll do the landing, okay? I promise I'll be very gentle…"

As we slowly walk away from the plane, the pilot cheerfully waves at us: "Come again…"

I whisper to the children that we will now go for the biggest ice cream in the world just to relax our brains. Filip and Lucija both nod blankly.

"Oh, kids, I thought that crazy pilots like that only existed in the movies…" I grin at them as we lick our ice creams. I feel my whole organism finally calming down.

If I knew then that the children – who couldn't see from their positions in the back who had the controls and who didn't - would later remember the episode completely differently – that it was me who sent the plane into a nosedive and the pilot who saved the us at the last moment – I would have invested all my energy into repeating and clarifying the story, instead of just smiling with relief.

∞

We're sitting at the café and enjoying the warm spring sun like lizards. We've come to the Adriatic coast of Croatia for a Saturday outing. Filip, Lucija and Dev chatter on and on, reenacting scenes from the Back to the Future movies, which we've watched back to back over the last three nights. Lidija and I sip our cappuccinos and smile as we listen to them.

The five of us have got used to life in our patchwork family and it's all going quite well. All three of the children are with us most of the time and the apartment we've moved into is always full of life. My relationship with Lidija is less harsh, or maybe I have just got used to it and adapted. In any case, we're doing fine. There's a lot of love and cooperation, mutual support and good intentions, and that soothes me.

"Can we get ice cream?" the children ask, and point at the ice cream seller right next to the café where we're sitting.

"Of course," I say. "Here's some Croatian money. It's more than enough for three ice cream cones. Pick anything you want."

The children jump away happily. Lidija and I exchange smiling glances and then suddenly freeze when we hear the children speaking to the ice cream seller in English.

English! I never thought that people from the different republics of the former Yugoslavia would use English to communicate with each other. All of this was our homeland and all of its languages were our languages. But for our children, born in independent Slovenia, Serbian and Croatian are foreign languages that they hardly ever hear and certainly don't speak.

As we stroll along the coast and the children toss stones into the water, Lidija and I reflect on how that era is irrevocably over, notwithstanding all of our nostalgia. The children are growing up in a different world from us, and the world we knew with its great cultural diversity, full of joyfulness, love, good will – that world does not exist anymore.

∞

"It's all fine and wonderful, but is this what our life is going to be about from now on? All year we work like maniacs and then in the summer we go for a couple of weeks to Greece and in the

237

winter for a week's skiing in Italy. It doesn't make much sense, right?"

Lidija is thinking aloud as we slowly sip our iced coffees in the shade. We're on the Greek island of Kythira, watching the children busily digging their way through the sandy beach.

She's right, I think. We work far too hard. I have become a rather sought-after communications trainer and I'm leading workshops and trainings for various companies and organizations practically non-stop. I give lectures at conferences, I write articles, all the while still maintaining my private psychotherapy practice. Lidija is working during the day as a cultural assistant in the Dutch Embassy and in the evenings she helps me put together programmes for business trainings, reads the background literature for me, does the admin...

Is this all our life will be: work-work-work and the occasional holiday?

"Do you have an idea?" I ask thoughtfully.

"Yes, I do," Lidija looks at me conspiratorially. "What if we buy a van and go on a real hippy trip to India?"

Immediately everything inside me responds: "Wow, great idea! Yeah! Let's do it!"

I know straight away that this is not just a fantasy. While Lidija and I don't fully meet in many areas of life, we have a fantastic synergy in the area of manifestation. We actually manifest everything that we decide to, and so this trip will certainly happen.

∞

"Alright, this session has started. Tell me, please, what's been going on with you since our last session?"

I say the sentence that I've said a thousand times before, take a deep breath, and try to put my full attention on my client sitting across from me.

She's only spoken for a very short time when I realize that I'm already looking out of the corner of my eye at the clock on the wall. I mean: what time could it be if we've only just started the session? Only a few minutes have passed and yet I'm already looking to see how long it will be until the end of the session. And then there are two more therapy sessions to go before the end of my day.

My work as a therapist has become increasingly difficult. It's as if my whole system is in a panic, as if every cell in my body is screaming in dread whenever I'm sitting opposite someone who, consciously or subconsciously, expects some kind of salvation from me. The sessions don't bring me any fulfilment anymore, just fatigue, boredom, pressure and exhaustion.

An hour and a half until the end of the session.

Maybe it's because I automatically take responsibility for the lives of my clients and worry if they don't progress as quickly as I would like them to. If they don't experience some sort of deliverance immediately after the first session. If they suffer and struggle in their lives. Maybe it's because I don't even know how to take care of myself. To recharge my own batteries. Because I somehow keep giving and giving and have been exhausting myself. Maybe it's because I don't know how to ask for help and support from my mentors or friends or to find a space in which I could be heard, accepted and understood, in which I would be able to express myself, to let things out.

An hour until the end of the session.

It really is unbearable for me. Unbearable also on the meta-level because I know that many of my clients almost live from one session to the next, waiting to pour out their hearts to me in a way that they can't to anyone else in their lives, and that they trust me. And here I am looking at the clock and waiting for the session to end. The situation goes against my integrity. To work with only a quarter of my heart and yet collect money for it.

I'm going to stop working as a psychotherapist. I'll refer my existing clients to colleagues and bring this phase of my life to a close, even though it's become an almost inseparable part of my identity.

Just the thought of stopping gives me a sense of relief as if fresh air is beginning to flow through my entire system. Yes, I've decided, I'm going to stop giving individual therapy sessions.

Only half an hour until the end of the session.

∞

I park the car in front of the children's school and head towards the main entrance feeling very worried. Filip's teacher called me half an hour ago and asked me to come to the school urgently because Filip was in great distress. Fortunately I was in my home office and not at a workshop somewhere outside of Ljubljana and was able to come right away.

I spot the teacher and Filip by the entrance. Filip is looking at the floor and wiping tears from his face. The teacher smiles calmly and says: "In my opinion, it would be best if the two of you would take a little walk alone."

I thank her and put my hand around Filip's shoulders and we slowly walk into the sunny spring day.

"What's up, Filip?" I gently ask after a few minutes of silence.

"I don't want you to marry Lidija," he says with a trembling voice.

Oh, so that's what's going on. The preparations for our trip are gradually coming to completion. The plan is to set out by van in a few months' time for a six-month overland journey to India and back. Lidija and I had already been thinking about getting married and now we've decided to tie the knot before our departure so that we'll be less likely to have any problems in the relatively conservative countries we'll be driving through, where a family with three surnames and children from previous marriages might appear slightly suspicious. We had told our children about the wedding and now Filip is apparently upset because of it.

"Why don't you want us to get married, Filip?" I slowly ask.

"Because she's annoying. Because I don't like her. And because she doesn't like me. Because I don't like being with her. I don't feel good with her. She's constantly nagging. I like it much better when we're on our own: just you and me and Lucija."

His voice is shaking as he speaks through his tears. I know what my almost twelve-year old son is talking about. When I seem to adapt enough to Lidija's expectation's, it's all peace and love between us and I forget there was ever a problem. But when this is not the case, then there are explosions all over and a horrible atmosphere of tension and heaviness builds up, which is miserable for the kids and not at all what they were used to from before. And this heavy atmosphere seems to be finding its way into the very fabric of our family and becoming somewhat permanent. I really see the difference when it's just the three of us together and I witness how joyful and relaxed and happy the children are. Then it's painful to see how they lose much of this when all five of us are sharing the space. Despite everyone doing their absolute best to be kind to each other, the emotional safety, ease, warmth and cosiness that the children need and we're all longing for is just not really present. I see all of this, yet I keep postponing facing the issue. Especially now when everything is ready for our trip of a lifetime.

Perhaps going to India together will shift things. If not, I will deal with it all later, when we get back, I think to myself.

We eat ice cream and drink juice in the sun and I reassure him, telling him that everything will be fine, that they'll get used to each other, that Lidija doesn't mean anything bad, that it always takes time for people to get used to each other, that she loves him, that she's trying her best, that it's not easy for her either.

Filip stares sadly in front of him and slowly finishes his ice cream.

"You'll see, Filip. We're going to have a great time on our trip. We're going to be relaxed and rested and we'll have an easier time connecting to each other. Everything will be different. And if something bothers you, please tell me right away and we'll find a solution."

I'm speaking to Filip as we walk back to school. It dawns on me that he just told me exactly what bothered him and we didn't find any solution.

∞

August 2003. I park the van in a small parking lot beside the Throne of Solomon archaeological excavation site in western Iran. We've come to take a look at it before we find a place to sleep somewhere at the foot of the nearby volcano. I turn off the engine and Lidija and I look at each other. We burst into simultaneous laughter and say with one voice:

"We did it!"

And, wow, we really did do it. We really did set out on our great journey and now, two years after first getting the idea in Greece, here we are in Iran.

We bought a large second-hand van and refurbished it, fitting it out with five bed spaces, a kitchen, a 160-litre water tank, an outside shower and everything else we needed, and now we've been travelling for a month and a half already. We started at the Croatian Adriatic coast, witnessed the post-war pain in Bosnia, enjoyed the beaches of the Black Sea and the forests of Bulgaria. Then the children's eyes widened at the sight of the Istanbul bazaars. After a history lesson in Troy and an exploration of magnificent Cappadocia came our spectacular stay in the crater of a three-thousand-metre-high volcano in eastern Turkey, filled with little lakes. And now we're in Iran, this land with a noble history and an immense cultural legacy, which we've waited for so long to see.

Our children, Lucija being 8, Dev 10 and Filip 12 now, cannot stop marvelling at the endless hospitality and generosity of the people in these places. There was the time we were relaxing in the van and suddenly a hairy hand reached through the open window and placed a watermelon on the table. We only just managed to catch sight of our benefactor already walking away, as he turned towards us and winked and smiled:

"Welcome, welcome…"

Or the time when we stopped in the middle of some field in central Turkey and an old woman working the fields almost forced me to take half a bucket of peppers and tomatoes, running away grumbling when I tried to give her some money. Or the time when someone knocked on the door of our van, parked in the middle of nowhere, while we were already getting ready to go to sleep. It was a delegation from the nearest village offering us a glass of precious buffalo milk as a welcome gift.

"But why are they all so nice? Why do they all keep giving us stuff?" the children keep asking in amazement.

And I wonder why this is not something completely normal in this world of ours, for people to be kind and hospitable to each other. How come this is something that amazes us? What has the world come to that we are not astonished by war and violence but by kindness?

Mostly we camp in unsettled areas, in forests, deserts, beside lakes and rivers. We visit the places known from history and mythology, and we relax deeply. Into the moment. Into here. Wherever we are.

Yes, we really did it. I hope that the experience will be transformative for all of us, but especially for the children.

∞

"Didn't you see him?"

This is the first question the police officer asks me and all of a sudden the whole logic around which I was imagining this conversation falls apart.

243

We're in Bam, an ancient desert city in eastern Iran. We were waiting in the left-hand lane for a break in the oncoming traffic so I could turn, when something crashed into us from behind with such force that our three-tonne van jumped forward about a metre. When I stepped out of the van to check the situation, I saw a motorbike wedged under the van and a bleeding guy lying next to it, his thigh bone sticking out of his leg.

Lidija and I told the children to stay in the van and play, locked the door and waited outside for the police to come, surrounded by onlookers. I'd heard stories about how, if westerners got involved in a traffic accident in these countries, they automatically got the blame. As we waited for the police to arrive, I prepared all of my communication skills and my psychological strength. And now this police officer destroys me with his first question.

"Didn't you see him?"

I take a breath and slowly begin to explain:

"I'm actually curious how come he didn't see us. We were standing still, our indicator flashing, such a big red van, and he ran into the back of us. Isn't this more strange?"

"Hmm, yes, it is..." The police officer looks at the injured motorcyclist and then at our van. "It is strange, yes, but, all the same, you could have seen him if you were more attentive."

"I was looking ahead, so I would see when there was a break in the oncoming traffic, so I could safely turn left. But even if I had managed to see him coming towards me in my rear-view mirror, what could I have done?"

I speak slowly and patiently. I decide that I will not add any cynical remarks such as that I don't yet know how to make our van levitate instantly.

The police officer finds a taxi to take the wounded motorcyclist to hospital. Lidija is required to go with them in the presence of an armed officer. It's not clear why.

I remain with my police officer who appears to be the boss and we once again analyse the whole situation and finally come to the conclusion that I am really not guilty and am therefore allowed to go.

Later Lidija tells us that at the hospital the officer, after speaking to his commander on the phone, had told her that she could demand compensation for the damage to our van from the injured boy now lying on the hospital bed, his body broken. Which, of course, she happily declined to do.

In a couple of days, we continue our journey across the Baluchistan desert into Pakistan with a newly-fashioned wooden bumper.

We hope that the poor motorcyclist doesn't have lasting injuries.

∞

I'm standing in front of a fantastic cosmic scene. There are two enormous funnels of energy, one expanding to the right, the other to the left, within a sort of blue glow and barely audible thunder. The tops of both funnels seem to be touching right in front of me.

Then I notice that the tops of the funnels are not actually touching but that there is something between them, a sort of link that connects them. I go a little closer to the magnificent scene and I see that the link between the two funnels is a beautiful priestess with long thick dark hair. I realize that the two funnels are the past and the future and that the priestess connects them, holding the top of the future with her left hand and the top of the past with her right. The priestess is the non-existent and elusive instant of the present.

I notice that the priestess, while motionlessly holding the past and the future, is staring sternly at me. She is trying to tell me something. There is something I ought to figure out right now, something I ought to understand. I don't know what it is, no matter how hard I try. So I just keep staring at the scene in front of me.

As I am writing this into my dream diary I keep having a sense that this was not just a dream, but something more than that.

∞

"Take it, my friends, take it with you, take it back to Slovenia…"

The owner of the camp-site where we are the only guests smiles kindly. The children spotted his rabbit grazing in the grass and are now enthusiastically examining it up close, and he is immediately offering it to them as a gift. The generosity of these people has no limits, truly. Whatever we look at, whatever we like, they immediately offer it to us as a gift. Or they invite us into their modest homes to stay for at least a couple of weeks, if not several months.

We had many adventures on the road during our first crossing of Pakistan and the drive to Dharamshala in India, where our stay was spiced up with a small and intimate ceremony led by the Dalai Lama himself. We learned about this ceremony from locals, who fell in love with our kids and then told us this "secret".

After our return to Pakistan and getting caught up in wild political demonstrations in Islamabad, where we ended up having to replace the broken windows of the van with plastic ones, we headed northeast again on the famous Karakoram Highway for the climax of our travels.

We're in the Hunza valley now, deep among the mountains of northern Pakistan. To get there, we've driven past seven and eight-thousand-metre-high mountains such as Nanga Parbat and Rakaposhi, which seem to emerge from the edge of the narrow, uneven and rock-strewn road. Many say this is actually the legendary Shangri La valley. The people here are some of the healthiest and happiest in the world. The air is so clean and fresh that it feels like it cuts into your lungs. The mighty mountains all around are pouring their energy into us.

Legend has it that many soldiers of Alexander the Great's army stopped here during the invasion of Asia, refusing either to go further or return to Greece. They saw no point in going anywhere since they had found paradise on earth.

We too will be wondering for a very long time why we didn't stay in Hunza forever, why we turned back towards Europe, back into our crazy twenty-first century life.

∞

I'm standing in the apartment and staring around me at all the things that fill it. Things and more things. During our six months of travelling in the van, I had two small shelves inside a narrow cupboard, and it was enough to hold everything I needed. Here, in the city, we buy and buy, stuffing things into the apartment, and apparently it's still not enough.

When life was full, things were unnecessary. Not only because we didn't need them but also because if we would have had them, they would have drawn our attention away from the fullness of life. When life is empty, we try to fill it with things.

I remember that I had the same feeling when I was travelling through Africa. I felt truly free when I had nothing in my wallet. The moment I had some money, it attracted my attention, and I planned, speculated how I would spend it, made decisions. If I didn't have anything, I let myself go with the flow of life, in trust and surrender. And I immersed myself into the moment, in presence.

After returning from our magical travels, we were immediately pulled back into our 'normal' lives – the children going to school, the two of us to work. For some time we were sharing our memories and photographs with friends and family, and even gave public presentations about our trip in libraries around Slovenia, together as a family.

And then the impressions and inspirations slowly vanished, along with the rest of the past. What remains for me is the question of how to experience the fullness of life in the present moment.

∞

I'm staring at the computer screen and for the third time this week, I'm looking at an apartment in Ljubljana that seems ideal to me: big, bright and just across the street from Lucija and Filip's school. The three of us could have an ideal life there. The price is also right. I could buy it with little difficulty.

I've had enough of what I keep experiencing, in my relationship with Lidija, as being on a battlefield I never wanted to step onto. It's killing me, suffocating me. Not because I can't do it or because it would be too painful for me to bear, but because I simply don't want to live my life this way. I just don't want to fight about who is right and who is wrong anymore. I honestly don't care about this even a bit.

I long for ease, joy, lightness, an atmosphere of compassion, peace, safety and warmth. And I long for spiritual companionship, for deep resonance at the level of what we care for most in this existence.

But what actually pains me the most is that my children are not growing up in an emotional environment that would truly nourish them. An environment in which they could be relaxed, joyful, carefree, and in which they would not have to deal with all the tension in our household. For which I see myself as responsible, by choosing to stay in this situation.

It's also true that there is a great deal of beauty in my relationship with Lidija: above all, in co-creation, mutual support, collaboration. And, yes, as strange as it might seem, also mutual empowerment. Or am I just convincing myself of this, because I want so much for this relationship to work, for this whole constellation to work?

I don't know, I don't know, I don't know…

I feel completely torn.

∞

"In Tierra del Fuego, no one can hear you scream…"

I play with paraphrasing the tag-line from the film Alien. Well, at least I still have some humour in this hopeless situation. Hopeless in the sense that now, in December 2004, at the age of thirty-eight, the journey of my life is heading for an abrupt end. I know: it sounds dramatic and exaggerated, but somehow, from one step to another, this seems more and more likely.

I've been climbing across this glacier for hours and hours. My GPS indicates that I should keep going straight, but now I'm starting to think that there's something wrong with the GPS, or more likely with how I'm reading the information on the little screen. I'm now on such a steep incline that I'm on all fours most of the time. I keep losing my grip on the ice while just standing still, let alone when I try to take a step. Unwisely, I don't have crampons. I can't go up any more. Not down either because it's so icy I will slip. The fog is so thick that I can't see more than five metres around me. Anyway I see only frozen white snow. And white fog. My legs are shaking from exhaustion and my way too heavy backpack, in which I have a tent, sleeping bag, food, water, everything I need for a week of trekking in the wilderness, seems to be pulling me off the edge. I have no idea where I am. Each step seems risky, very risky, potentially fatal. Below me is a long steep icy drop and, below that, jagged rocks. At least that's what I remember from the beginning of the climb, before the fog came.

I came here to Tierra del Fuego, at the southernmost tip of South America, to be alone with myself for a month in the wilderness. I planned three long solo treks. And already on the first one, after only a few days, I find myself stuck like this.

I'm standing on a small shelf that I've kicked out of the ice so I can rest my sore ankles and my aching calves. I lean against the slope and breathe and think about what to do next. My backpack is cutting into my shoulders and pulling me down, but I don't dare to take it off because I'm afraid that I'll lose my balance and slide down the slope.

When I landed in the airport at Ushuaia, I had smiled when I saw the sign:

"Welcome to the End of the World."

That's what the locals call this wilderness.

And maybe it really is the end, I smile to myself now.

Considering that I tried to commit suicide twenty-two years ago, all this time since then has been a great bonus. And, in fact, I feel completely calm about the possibility that everything will end here.

Well, not completely calm. I would like to see my beloved children again. I would like to support them, love them, watch and accompany them through their lives. I've been thinking mostly about them during the long days of trekking.

I look around. The whole world is white. And I can still see only five metres in any direction. Total silence. It all seems more like a dream than reality.

I sigh and slowly and very cautiously straighten up. Well, I will slowly climb to the left and maybe I will come to the rocks at the edge of the glacier. There must be some rocks, somewhere.

∞

Mirjana is sitting in front of me, in tears, sobbing. She thanks me for always being so immensely good and fair to her in the past, and also for being so immensely good to her now, to her and to all people. I silently witness her tears and expressions of gratitude.

Suddenly things become chaotic. A hole opens up and from the depths beneath the earth a monster resembling a snake appears. It's actually a dragon with a feathered head. A crowd of people gathers and we join forces to chase the dragon back into the hole, back to the underworld. But the dragon won't comply and instead slithers entirely out of the hole. It's enormous and looks very dangerous. It soon becomes clear that the dragon is simply too powerful and there is no possibility of us pushing it back into its tunnel. So we attack it and try to kill it. But the more we attack it, the bigger and more terrifying it becomes. In fact our attacks seem to only strengthen it.

Suddenly I realize that the dragon doesn't want anything from us, that these are just our assumptions and fears, and that it's completely unnecessary to attack it. I try to tell the others but no one listens to me. They don't believe me. They're in a complete panic.

I can no longer watch these senseless attacks on the dragon who I know doesn't want to hurt us. It's simply confused and afraid, but we fear it because it's so powerful. I don't want to be a part of this violence. Making an enormous effort, I somehow succeed in taking off from the ground and I fly very far away.

∞

This Tierra del Fuego will chew me up and spit me out, I think, as I grip my knee in pain. I've stopped screaming my rage at the mountains and I am finally beginning to confront the situation. The other day I somehow managed to get myself off that glacier in one piece. Then I walked for a few days across the fantastic mountain ridges, slept beside emerald lakes under a million stars shining in the cold night sky, and fought the wind that tried to slap me to the ground. Today I descended beside a waterfall into a valley and stopped to rest in the forest. Afterwards, when I was swinging my enormous backpack onto my shoulders, something snapped inside my knee and I crumbled to the ground.

I've been having trouble with the ligaments around my knees for a few years now. Sometimes it's the right knee, sometimes the left. It usually lasts a couple of days before I can walk again without pain. And now I have at least a whole day, probably two, of difficult walking across hills and valleys and swamps in front of me, including clambering across hundreds of felled trees that the beavers in this place gnaw down everywhere as if obsessed. And there is still an icy river to be forged, and I must do all of this with my heavy backpack.

251

While I cannot even straighten my leg, let alone stand on it.

I drag myself to the bank of the river and lie down on the sun-warmed gravel. I'll put my tent up here and see what my condition is like in the morning. Until then I have much to think about.

Throughout these long days of walking, the realization has been growing in me of how much I love Filip and Lucija. There's a lot of pain when I realize that I'm neglecting their needs, sacrificing them for the sake of my relationship with Lidija. And for the sake of having a peaceful life, and for the sake of how other people see me... Crap!

I love them more than anything else in the world and yet I'm not really fully manifesting this love, despite knowing that the only thing that matters in life is love. To what extent I express it, to what extent I manifest it.

Will I be able to take the next step toward fuller integrity?

∞

Suddenly a portal opens inside me. In the middle of my head, or, more precisely, at the seat of my awareness. An entry point into a dimension that I didn't even know existed, yet it is now easily accessible to me. I don't even know how this happened.

I've been lying here for some time with my eyes covered and Ursula has been slowly guiding me through a process of visualization, relaxation and breathing. I was aware of everything the whole time, nothing strange was happening and then suddenly this portal opened. Or it was already open but I only realized it now, only identified it now. I don't know.

In any case, I now have total access to everything in a completely new way. In this infinite expanse and depth, I can remember absolutely everything...

...

all the way to the beginning of existence

in all of its vastness.

Everything is accessible

because everything is now.

Nothing is outside now

only that this now is infinitely multidimensional.

All of time is in this moment.

Cosmic peace.

I as a planet

and the peace, stability, gravitation I possess.

I as a cosmic entity balancing energies across the universe

and freedom, expanse, lightness.

Everything in this existence is my choice.

Expanse.

Pure awareness.

Everything is my choice.

Peace.

Silence.

...

A couple of months ago I came across the book Journey of Souls by hypnotherapist Michael Newton. Newton used hypnotic trance to regress his clients beyond this life into the state between incarnations. He records numerous examples of his subjects recalling their experiences between lives. The whole thing attracted me strongly and I immediately went on the internet to search for the nearest hypnotherapist using Newton's methodology. I found Ursula living in Salzburg, Austria, a few hours' drive away. I quickly arranged to go there for the weekend for a series of sessions...

My journey in the trance continues. I suddenly find myself in front of the apartment building where I lived in early childhood. I'm floating above that painted wooden bench, the same bench where I'd been so thrilled to hold the neighbour's rabbit in my lap. I see my mother beneath me. She is pregnant, sitting on the bench and smoking. She is nervous, very nervous. She's dissatisfied, and above all frightened. She's frightened of life, frightened of the future, frightened of everything. She has no trust in life, just worries and fears. The energy of that fear is the energy into which I will be born. This cloud of fear will mark me, shape me.

...

After the end of the sessions, while I'm driving on the highway through the Austrian Alps towards home, I integrate everything I have experienced during the weekend. One of my main realizations is that up until this point in my life, I have actually only been expressing about thirty percent of my power and potential because of a deep and somehow primal fear that I will be rejected, more than rejected, kicked off the planet, if I ever shine with my full power and beauty. That throughout my whole life I've been acting smaller and weaker than I am. In this way I've appeared less dangerous so that people around me wouldn't feel threatened and turn against me.

I drive through the Alpine valleys and realize that I am breathing deeper and deeper.

And at the same time, I realize that this portal at the centre of my awareness is still open. A little less open than it was during the session, as if the access to everything is beginning to fade slightly, but it's still there all the same. Like the contact between the peaks of the two energy funnels at the centre of my consciousness – one funnel leading into this reality, the other leading away from this reality into... into all realities. Into the ultimate knowingness.

I'm suddenly struck: didn't I dream about those two funnels a year ago, or two? With a priestess holding them and silently staring at me...

∞

The plaza in front of the UN headquarters in New York. I am a member of a spiritual group and today we have a meeting on the plaza with another group which is exploring the spiritual aspects of martial arts. At the meeting today, they will present their path and their discoveries.

A young dark-haired boy, the leader of this other group, explains to us that their practice also includes flying. Because he sees that we don't understand what he is saying, he tells us that he will show us so it will be clear. He sits in the lotus position, straightens his spine, lifts one hand up, and suddenly flies up vertically about thirty metres into the air. He motionlessly floats there for a few seconds then quickly comes down to the ground again and calmly says: "You see. That's what I was talking about."

We are all in shock. As if a path had opened to another dimension, a completely different reality. We begin to go a little crazy with the excitement of what we've just seen.

One after another, the other members of this other group begin to rise vertically into the air: some go ten metres high, some fifteen metres. The atmosphere becomes crazier and more ecstatic.

I'm suddenly seized by the desire to fly myself. I sit in the lotus position, straighten my spine, lift my left arm, and the next instant I fly up ten metres. I float there while trying to get even higher, but I cannot. I levitate for a while longer and then slowly let myself down to the plaza.

I'm completely ecstatic. I'm overwhelmed with an immense feeling of fulfilment and accomplishment. I have achieved the ultimate. I've arrived at the end of the voyage, at the finishing line. To fly with our physical bodies is the supreme achievement, the supreme ability.

I awaken with this feeling of fulfilment and accomplishment. I peer into the darkness above me and breathe deeply. The feeling of fulfilment expands my lungs and awakens every cell in my body. For the next several hours I feel carried around by this energy and there is no way I can go back to sleep.

∞

I'm in a room with about seventy people from all around the world. I raise my hand yet again and ask:

"Marshall, I do understand that you are here recommending deep connections, deep meetings, but what about all the times when I'm not in the mood to have a long conversation with every person I meet? And so if somebody asks me how I am and I'm not in the mood to provide a detailed description of all the dimensions of my inner world, all my feelings and needs, and so I just say that I'm okay and that's that…"

Marshall looks at me with his serious face, that furrowed brow, those bushy eyebrows, and offers a faint smile. There's a playful glimmer in his eyes.

"Well, whatever meets your needs."

We look at each other for a few seconds. I nod slightly as if to say okay, thanks, I get it. And it actually seems to me that I am slowly beginning to understand. I've already asked several different questions and I always get back a minimalistic but very clear response somehow based on the same point: ultimate freedom of choice and the question of what in a given moment nourishes the flow of life in me. I am always brought back to the field beyond rightdoing and wrongdoing that the Persian poet Rumi referred to.

This is the seventh day of a nine-day training in Switzerland with Marshall Rosenberg, the founder of the approach called Nonviolent Communication, and I am finally starting to get it. It was Lidija who persuaded me to sign up, convinced that it was the right thing for me. I arrived here feeling quite full of myself, proud of my twelve years as a practising psychotherapist and nineteen years of giving trainings and facilitating groups. I was pretty sure that Marshall would be able to learn something from me and not the other way around.

Ha-ha...

And although most of the concepts he uses are indeed familiar to me because of my previous experience, Marshall offers a kind of integration, a way for me to join together the three fields of my life's work that had previously always been separate from each other: deep spirituality, psychotherapy, and communication (including conflict resolution). All three of these very important areas in my life have begun to come together through an understanding of Marshall's concepts.

And they find a common denominator at the very centre of one of the key longings of my life: meeting other people, other conscious beings, at the level of our naked, innocent, vulnerable human hearts.

Lidija was so right, this is perfect for me.

∞

I'm reading Harville Hendrix's book Getting the Love you Want and all of a sudden my relationships with intimate partners have become clear, it all makes sense to me.

Hendrix says that we have a strong subconscious tendency to search for a partner with whom we can recreate the emotional situation in which we grew up. Therefore we look for a partner who will trigger the emotions that we experienced in childhood with our parents and caregivers. The combination of feelings and satisfied and unsatisfied needs alive at that time defines the precise atmosphere to which our personalities adapted as they were formed in those early years. This is the only environment for which we are truly prepared, in which we feel at home and to which we want to return in order to resolve what was unresolved and to finally grow up.

When I follow the author's instructions and explore my own internal reality, I have to smile because everything is so amazingly clear. My relationship with Mirjana was a perfect representation of my relationship with my mother. I constantly took care of her and felt powerful, manly, satisfied with myself, while at the time the life in me seemed to be slowly going out.

With Lidija, I'm re-experiencing my relationship with my father and, similarly to how I acted with him in my youth, I now walk on eggshells, taking care that I won't cause an eruption, that there won't be a reaction that will make everything explode and fall apart. I suffer in silence and just hold on, hoping for better times.

In both cases, it has to do with me taking responsibility for the feelings of others. I'm constantly trying to satisfy the people around me because I believe that only when their needs are satisfied will I have peace and freedom.

No wonder I walk around with such a heavy load. Instead of really living my life, I'm just forever re-experiencing my childhood. I am wondering how much of my current relationship is actually based on the free choice of my heart.

∞

"And the Slovenian Business Trainer of the Year 2007 is… Robert Kržišnik!"

My name shines on the screen and the audience bursts into loud applause.

I was invited to this big business conference as the last keynote speaker of the day and the organizers insisted that I should hang around after my lecture for the announcement. Now I know why.

I stand up, smile, accept the plaque and bouquet of flowers from the hands of the organizer, and step up to the microphone. The applause slowly stops and I see hundreds of faces in front of me waiting for the gracious words of the selected winner.

"Good evening once again. Believe it or not, this is a big surprise for me. I had no idea this was coming, the organizers were so skilful at keeping it secret..."

I smile towards the young women on my left and they beam happily.

Then I turn back to the public and it hits me. This is an enormous mistake. This is not me, standing like a penguin in this big conference hall, wearing a tailor-made designer suit, in front of hundreds of businessmen and directors and human resources professionals. I realize that I am a foreigner in a foreign land.

What happened? Since when has this been my life? What happened to the person who was interested in the passionate exploration of the nature of existence, who was interested in living close to nature, ideally in an eco-community with a powerful spiritual emphasis? How did I end up in the business world? Where did I go astray? When did I get lost?

I pull myself together and continue my thank-you speech:

"You know, this is a cosmic mistake."

The audience giggles.

"In my work, I am constantly striving to create a radically different situation. I'm trying to get all of us to sit in a circle as equal human beings and to connect on the level of our open and vulnerable hearts. To laugh together, cry together, to express our essential humanity. Yet now I'm standing in front of you and everyone is turned towards me, silently listening. It's precisely this kind of hidden hierarchy that I'm trying to transcend with my work. I use all of my efforts to try and make our social environment less like a pyramid and more like a circle. That's why, if I'm completely sincere, while being very grateful for the acknowledgement, I don't feel so good right now."

...

As I drive home that evening, I think about my life. We are a modern family. We live in a house in the centre of the city. We travel a lot. On the surface, everything is going very smoothly. And now I've won the award for the national business trainer of 2007. Of course all of this is great.

259

But at the same time, I'm knocked out twice a year by some sickness. Usually during the holidays, when my system knows that I can afford to get sick, as I don't have any workshops to do. If something does hit me at other times, I just carry on working all the same. Once I was so sick that I couldn't even drive a car and Lidija drove me to a workshop I was giving in the morning and came back in the afternoon to pick me up. Another time I fainted from exhaustion right before the beginning of a training and was taken by ambulance to the hospital emergency department.

How did I lose my way? How did I become some sort of successful business machine, mindlessly tearing along the highway of modern consumer life? Financial success, a beautiful and capable wife, foreign travel, fame. Everything looks wonderful on the outside, but underneath the glossy paintwork, my shiny car is rusting away from the inside and could break down at any time.

How did I get here?

Eleven: Endings

The squeal of brakes punctuated by the dull sound of a collision cuts sharply through the air. Everything stops in that instant, including the blood flowing through my veins.

Filip!

Half a minute ago, he'd got on his bike and raced towards the town centre, a route which would take him through the road junction a hundred metres from our house, a junction where minor traffic accidents often happen.

Did one of those young guys I often see revving their engines at the lights hit Filip?

The thought makes my head spin.

I throw aside the garden shears I'm using to cut the bushes, dash out of the garden, and run down the driveway and towards the junction.

A series of images flash through my brain: Filip motionless on the ground, a smashed bicycle next to him, a pool of blood collecting under his head.

This image makes the adrenaline in my body go wild. No one has ever run as fast as I'm running now.

If I find a scene like that, I'll, I'll… First I'll kill the driver who hit my son. My Filip. I'll smash his head on the tarmac. No words. Immediately. Without mercy.

Then I will tend to Filip.

But first I will kill the driver.

I'm at the junction. Two cars are stopped, their bumpers damaged and hanging off. It looks like one banged into the other one. The drivers are talking calmly, nodding to one another.

I take a deep breath and exhale.

Just in case, I step a little bit closer to check if Filip isn't lying around somewhere.

My heart is still pounding, my body shaking from adrenaline. I pull my phone out of my pocket and call Filip just to be completely sure.

"Hi" Filip responds, breathing heavily as he cycles.

"Hey, Filip. Is everything okay?"

"Yeah, sure, I'm just hurrying so I won't be late for training. Why? What's up with you?"

"Nothing, nothing. Everything's fine. Okay, great, have a good time. See you tonight."

I push my phone back into my pocket and walk back towards the house, still shaking. I could easily murder someone. Easily.

The distance between the spiritual, non-violent me and the deranged killer seems to only be about ten seconds apart.

∞

"Helloooo.." I hear Lucija's voice as she enters the house.

"Hey, Lucija, I'm in here," I answer from my home office.

I spin my chair away from my computer desk and turn to face the door as it opens.

"How's life?"

With a deep sigh, Lucija collapses on the couch and smiles broadly: "Very good…"

Then she looks into my eyes and says: "Actually I want to tell you something."

"What is it?" I stop the movement of my chair and look at her. "I'm all ears…"

"You know, the whole ride home from school on the bus, I was wondering if I could even imagine a better father than you. And I realized that I can't imagine how you could be a better father to me than you already are."

My fourteen-year-old daughter smiles and looks calmly at me, knowing that it can't be easy for me to take this in. I breathe deeply and my heart overflows with love and warmth.

"Wow, Lucija, that is so lovely to hear ... but still I can't quite accept it. You know that I see how I've been as a father quite differently, that there are many things I would do differently if I could turn back the clock."

"I know, I know," Lucija says lovingly. "But I just wanted to tell you how I feel."

"I know, and thanks so much. It warms my heart, it really does."

"And there's something else I want to tell you because I don't think you are getting it. I love being with you and I would like to be with you more, to spend more time hanging out with you. Can you understand that?" Lucija looks at me seriously.

Her words stun me. In the last few years, I've been withdrawing slightly to give my teenage daughter space to live, to grow, so she will have freedom, so that I won't be constantly looming over her. And now I hear that she would like to spend more time with me.

"I know," Lucija continues, "that you want to give me freedom and space, and thank you for that, but I also want to spend more time with you."

"Hmm, wow, thanks, Lucija, for telling me that. Of course. Gladly. Do you want to go for pizza?"

"Sure, but not now, I'm meeting friends in an hour." She stands up and slowly moves towards the door. "But we can do that tomorrow if you have time."

Lucija smiles, winks, and closes the door behind her.

I stare blankly at the door and think about all of this. How I carry in me this story that I'm a burden to people, that it's not fun to be with me, and how somewhere deep inside, in the most vulnerable part of myself, I long for people to find it enjoyable to be with me. And yet I see, for example, that my daughter wants to spend more time with me precisely because she enjoys it. It makes her happy.

∞

"Did you hit him?"

I hear these words through an unbearable pounding inside my head. And I slowly begin to regain consciousness. I'm lying on my side. On the road. I hear my breathing. Not far from me, the wheel of my mountain bike is still spinning. Ah, now I remember.

I've come with our camper van to the Croatian island of Krk to spend a week in the off-season calm, in solitude, cycling, reading books, playing the guitar. Today I went on a 60-kilometre ride on my bike and after a good ten kilometres a storm caught me. After only a few minutes, I was drenched and shivering from the cold so I turned back. I cycled as fast as I could in order to keep warm. During the last few kilometres, the sun began to shine and the road dried out, so I hurried down the hill towards my van, going fast on the familiar hairpin bends with no worries about skidding. Just before the last bend when I needed to brake, I saw to my horror that the road there was suddenly wet again. The branches of a large tree stretched across the road and water was dripping from them. I glanced down at my speedometer: 65 kilometres an hour. I knew I couldn't make the curve at such a high speed so, like it or not, I gently applied the brakes, despite the wet and obviously slippery surface. The bike instantly lurched beneath me and I flew high into the air. As my body slowly approached the tarmac again, the last thought I remember was:

"This is going to hurt."

And then there was darkness.

"Did you hit him?"

I slowly open my eyes. An older couple is standing not far from me, shocked expressions on their faces. I think they were in the VW van that I passed a little higher on the road. A younger man is standing next to them. He's stopped his car and he's the one nervously asking the question.

"No, no, they didn't hit me," I manage to croak, barely able to speak. "I fell on my own."

I slowly get up, with some help. I'm covered in blood. Practically all of my cycling clothes are shredded from sliding and rolling on the tarmac. My helmet is broken in two.

I slowly drag myself towards my van. No, no need to call an ambulance. Of course, everything is alright, I convince everyone around me, and above all myself, as I carefully rinse out the cuts and abrasions.

...

I wake up in the middle of the night with a terrible headache. I've never felt this kind of pain in my life. I feel like I'm going to pass out from the headache alone. Should I call the ambulance after all? I pick up my laptop and move slowly through the darkness outside to a little bench where I know I can get internet. I open the laptop and through the pain of this incredible headache begin to explore what this pain could mean and where to call for help...

...And I begin to come to my senses again. This time I'm lying on my side on the bench, holding my laptop to me. Hmm, it seems that I lost consciousness again.

I slowly stand up. The pain has completely disappeared. My head doesn't hurt in the slightest anymore. Maybe it was a swelling inside the skull that burst. By some logic, I think this is a good sign.

Relaxed, because there is no more pain, I go back to the van and lie back down in bed. Someone up there likes me very, very much.

...

The next few days I spend in caring for my wounds, cleaning them and thinking all the time about the fragility of this life. One second, one choice, one moment of not being attentive, and this fragile and tender body can die, just like that. Or get seriously damaged.

This life is such a precious gift.

And I am such a lucky guy.

∞

"Okay, what should I write in the minutes?"

It's Sunday. We're at our regular family meeting. Lucija asks the question, and the rest of us begin to formulate an amusing description for our resolution:

"Well, write that we came to the resolution that it would be desirable if the person who is to remind people of their tasks, the so-called slave driver, wakes up from hibernation and begins to fulfil this joyful mission lovingly and with gratitude in his heart."

Lucija smiles and types into her laptop. Dev, Filip, Lidija and I sip our tea, nibble on our biscuits, and wait for the next point on the agenda. This is one of the last family meetings where Filip will be present. He's about to move out on his own. Hmm, how quickly time passes. It wasn't long ago that we were playing Lego together.

"Shall I write that anyone who receives visitors is responsible for the condition of the house for the duration of the visit and after the visitors leave?"

Lucija asks this question when we come to discuss the impact that the increasing number of guests who come to visit our teenage children has on other members of the household.

I'm quite proud of this aspect of the cooperation between Lidija and me in our patchwork family with three teenagers: how we somehow succeed in using the practices from our training and facilitation work at home, finding ways of solving the problems of cohabiting under the same roof through dialogue. And we do truly cooperate under this roof, cooking, cleaning, tidying together, not from fear of being punished or in hope of reward, but from the understanding of the needs of everyone involved and the shared commitment to search for ways that will work for all of us.

"Okay, so I'll write the following resolution: If anyone is anticipating an especially difficult week, then they're invited to tell us at the meeting so we will know and will be more considerate and helpful throughout the week," Lucija says as she continues writing down the minutes, quite routinely.

About a year ago, Lidija and I wrote and published a book about establishing mutually respectful relationships in the family, based on our experience. I truly believe that the book is excellent and could be extremely useful to all parents and, indirectly, to their children. This book is yet another example of the extraordinary creative cooperation that I have with Lidija. When we work together, we explore, learn, and manifest with no difficulties or limitations.

"Okay, okay, yes, yes, yes, we understand. I'll write it down: the kids should buy alcohol with their own money and should not drink Robert's precious cognac of which they are not worthy."

I roll my eyes and smile: "Yes, a perfect summary ..."

But at the same time, it's also true that there is an undertone of seriousness, even coldness, at the meetings. As if we are happy on the surface, but actually quite cautious and slightly tense deep down. As Lucija often says, we function like well-mannered and respectful co-habitants, not like a family. No real warmth or emotional connection. This house has become a house of efficiency, a house of rationality and goal orientation.

"And then for the last resolution, shall I record that we unanimously agree that Robert is evil?"

"Yes, write down exactly that. It's the most important resolution of the meeting..."

I say as we all laugh and complete this meeting.

∞

I'm an archaeologist and I'm standing with my team in an extremely large and ancient subterranean hall. We've been exploring the hall for some time already, but still cannot figure out what its purpose was. We have enormous respect for the magnificent place and as we explore it we engage in occasional rituals.

I realize that we can understand the hall only if we entirely change the paradigm within which we are exploring it. With a sort of inner shift, I succeed in changing our perception in its essence and suddenly everything turns ninety degrees; the hall, the gravity, everything shifts.

Everything becomes clear in that instant; where the altar is, the place for rituals, what the purpose of this place is. Suddenly a fire on the altar ignites and everything comes to life. I weep from happiness and explain everything to my fellow archaeologists. We are completely beside ourselves.

Suddenly, from a corner of the hall, a kind of ancient creature emerges, an alien of sorts, and offers us two books. Then he wordlessly departs.

I flip through the books and find the description of an internal shamanic purification ritual intended for all people, not just the elite for whom spiritual rituals are usually intended. This internal shamanic purification begins with the drinking of a special thick fluid.

I'm ecstatic when I realize that this is now our, and therefore also my mission. To help humanity, and above all poor and simple people, to purify themselves and become free.

∞

This year, 2012, was not the end of the world as media outlets kept telling us that the Mayan calendar predicted, but it was the end, it appears, of my love affair with Zen which had lasted for decades. Well, perhaps not with Zen meditation, but at least with Zen sesshins, multi-day residential retreats during which there is total silence from morning until evening and which feature the practice of Soto Zen meditation, whose aim, put simply, is constant presence in the here and now, in this moment.

It's my third day at this Zen sesshin – recently I've been attending on average one each year – and I'm beginning to ask myself what the point of it is. After twenty-five years of meditation practice, my mind is relatively serene, not anywhere near as wild as it once was, and I no longer have any noticeable difficulties with presence in the moment. So I don't perceive much benefit anymore from sitting and meditating for several days at a time.

But more than anything else, I've been feeling uncomfortable about participating in these hierarchical and patriarchal structures, even if they do have a noble purpose and the pyramid is subtly constructed. It's not so much that these elements irritate me personally, but more that I think that just by participating in them I am passively supporting them. My values have for a long time been leading me in the opposite direction, towards a post-patriarchal world, where we all sit in a circle, bare and vulnerable, and together explore the unknown. Not back to a world where like obedient little school children we follow some sort of charismatic teacher, somewhere on high, above us.

It probably has a lot to do with my so-called 'sacred wound', the increased sensitivity to specific dynamics that develops in a person because of traumatic experiences from childhood. In my case of course the dynamics were created by my domineering, all-powerful, authoritarian father and the state of fearful submission to him which I and my mother found ourselves in.

At all the workshops, conferences, training sessions, and retreats that I've attended through the years, I've been acutely sensitive to the abuse of power on the part of the leaders. Often a facilitator would use their authority to shut down and override participants, or not take into account the interests of the less vocal individuals. I can't help myself from reacting when I see such things going on and I often find myself standing up for weaker participants in such workshops and trainings, even if it means I sometimes provoke the fury of the leaders. I'm only sorry that I don't manage to include my heart in these reactions. Because I

269

would love to be able to be empathic even when I do react, to feel compassion for the leaders and be aware that they are also vulnerable and wounded beings guided by their own pain and fear. I don't know how to do that yet in the moment.

Sesshin is coming to an end. My knees and lower back are already complaining loudly.

Yes, this is probably my last sesshin in this lifetime. Although this story is over, I feel enormous gratitude for everything that I've learned and experienced during my inner journeys with this practice.

∞

"Look, Dad, I want to tell you a few things. They're not so simple and I'll need some time to articulate them clearly. Can you give me five minutes so I can explain them in peace?"

I'm sitting with my father in the living room of the house in Kranj where we lived throughout my teenage years, so long ago now. We're alone. My mother, nervous and frightened of the confrontation she expects, has gone out for a long walk.

My father, half turned away from me, looking at the turned-off television set, quietly says: "Yeah, yeah, go ahead. I won't interrupt you. I'll listen…"

A few days earlier I'd received a letter from him in which he'd informed me that I hadn't returned some money to him that I'd borrowed fifteen years earlier. He threatened to sue me if I didn't pay him back the money immediately. Then he filled two additional pages with accusations that I had made up stories about his alcoholism, that I manipulated him, abused him, blamed him for things that never happened, that nothing I said was true, that he'd never done anything bad to me.

I'd transferred the money to him the same day and added twenty-five percent for late interest. And I sincerely apologized for having long since forgotten all about it. I asked him to in the future tell me about such things immediately so I could respond right away, because it was really too bad that years had passed with him still thinking about it, getting angrier and angrier, while I had simply forgotten about it. Finally I had requested a conversation in person.

"So, Dad, I'm forty-six years old and you are seventy, and I would like to clear up a few things or at least to clearly express myself. First of all, when you say that I manipulate you, that I accuse you, abuse you, make up stories, I would like you to tell me which words of mine are you specifically referring to, because I really don't know. For example, I don't remember reproaching you or accusing you or talking about the past at all during the last twenty years."

My father stares motionlessly at the blank TV screen and I continue:

"And I would also like to say this: you did drink during the years of my childhood and adolescence, a lot. On many occasions you were heavily under the influence of alcohol in my presence and this had a powerful impact on me. My childhood was to a great degree and in a very painful way marked by your alcoholism. If you wish to know specifically what I'm referring to, I can recount many memories for you. But I don't need to do this for myself."

My father looks at the floor. I see tears gathering in his eyes. I take a breath and continue:

"As far as I'm concerned, we don't have to talk about it. You don't need to apologize. I have no wish to accuse you, to blame you, or to address it with you in any way. I've mostly dealt with all of this on my own. To a certain degree I'm still dealing with it, but these are my own internal processes. However, I will no longer collaborate in denying that the past was how it was, because that would be to deny my life, my reality, my emotions, my pain."

My father pulls a handkerchief from his pocket, blows his nose, and wipes away his tears.

"That's really all I wanted to say. How is it for you to hear these things?"

After a minute of silence, my father speaks quietly: "Yes, I know. I really am sorry. A lot of things have been hard on me. I didn't know how to do it differently. I didn't have a father, as you know, and my stepfather treated me much worse than I treated you. I grew up in very difficult times and very difficult circumstances. I wouldn't be able to remember all the slaps, all the blows that I got whether I was guilty of something or not. I always loved you and I never wanted to hurt you. Now of course I would be a different kind of father, very different."

He takes out his handkerchief again, blows his nose and wipes away his tears.

"I know that you didn't want to hurt me. I know you had many problems and that you tried to handle them as well as you could. I know that you always loved me and you did the best you could in each moment." I slowly say.

My father lets out a sob, pulls out his handkerchief, blows his nose, wipes away his tears, and sighs deeply.

...

An hour later I get into the car to drive home and feel very calm. It seems that I've done something today that has been waiting for me for decades. Instead of passively cooperating in maintaining my father's world of denial, shame, secrecy, and pretending, I've begun to slowly create the world that I long for, a world of authenticity, truth and transparency.

Wow, what a relief.

∞

It is as if I'm sitting in a room full of some sort of extra-terrestrials. Or demigods. Fairy creatures... Forty people are in the room and no one really looks completely human. Their eyes shine like stars. Tears of bliss and from being deeply moved flow down their cheeks. Just their presence creates a kind of energetic gravity. The words they speak sound like the words of ancient saints. I want to just look at them, in love, and absorb all this beauty and let it fill my heart.

I turn to Robert Gonzales, my friend, my brother, who's sitting next to me. We look at each other and quietly say with one voice: "Wow!"

It's the third day of a seven-day retreat that we've called "Awakening to Life Intensive", which we're running together for the first time. We created and designed this retreat expecting the participants to achieve the greatest possible spiritual depth, but all the same, the place the group has come to already on the third day surprises us. We're not even half way through the retreat, yet already an astonishing liberation from life's shackles, an actualization of authentic selves, and, yes, an awakening to life, has occurred.

I'd met Robert a few years ago at a retreat that he was running in Germany. During a coffee break, we'd realized that we were connected by a shared history of spiritual exploration. We'd both started our journey with Enlightenment Intensives many decades before, he in California, me in Yugoslavia. We'd both learned directly from Charles Berner. And we'd both agreed that we were still missing the depth and intensity that Enlightenment Intensives offered, but that both of us were turned off by the undertone of hierarchy that seemed present.

Our conversations reawakened in me an almost intoxicated passion for the magical space that I'd experienced in the Enlightenment Intensives, which I'd stopped running nearly twenty years ago. I began to think of the concept of a retreat that would facilitate the direct experience of ultimate reality, deep awakening, bold exploration into the nature of existence, and at the same time would be based on the values of Nonviolent Communication.

When the concept was sufficiently developed, I'd tried to run the retreat once in France and once in Germany but I didn't attract enough participants. I regretted that such a good concept for a retreat would go unused and so I offered it to Robert, who was a better-known trainer and who, I was convinced, would immediately grasp the fundamental idea. Not only did he grasp it, but he wanted us to lead the retreat together. And so we'd begun a one-year process of refinement of all the details which culminated in this Awakening to Life Intensive, the first ever retreat of its specific kind.

It's already crystal clear that it won't be the last one, either, because the worlds opening up here are exceeding our expectations. We will have to fine-tune the schedule and the process, and above all be clearer about the intense nature of the retreat in the promotional material so people will know what to be prepared for. But already now it is obvious that this is, as the participants here have attested to and even written on the wall of the meeting hall, a retreat to live and to die for.

I was born in this world to do this. This is the very core of my mission. To create and hold the space for people to awaken to their ultimate nature, which can then begin to embody and actualize itself, yes, to get fully born. Where this nature can begin to free itself from multi-layered conditioning and confinement within limiting mental structures, and allow the stream of aliveness to flow in its fullness.

And to do this together with my dear spiritual brother, Robert, with whom I feel seen as never before, with whom I experience a deep spiritual companionship, and to whom I don't even need to say much because, well, because we both know.

∞

I open the door to the night. The cold winter air embraces me and I inhale the freshness into my lungs. Rok fastens his jacket, steps out of the house, and stands beside me.

"To tell you the truth, Robert, I don't feel like going home. I would rather just stay here with you."

Rok is my old friend, one of my closest. I've been regularly supporting him for years when he's been going through difficult periods in his life: from his divorce from his wife and a heavy tussle with her over their two daughters who he loves so much, to an existential crisis regarding the meaning of his work and his life in general. He's been in a very expansive period for the last half year but now he has slid into depression again. He's spent the last few hours with me.

"Hmm, yes, I can imagine. Not exciting to go back to your flat, to be alone."

I smile at him. One part of me would like to invite him to stay, to stay for several days even, but the other part of me is exhausted: exhausted from the non-stop leading of workshops and interaction with people who need support, answers, guidance. I'm exhausted from supporting everyone around me. I need silence terribly, to be alone, to have no one expect anything from me.

"Do you want me to drive you home?" I ask him with an encouraging smile. "I'd be happy to give you a ride."

"No thanks. I'll walk," Rok says with a melancholic smile. "The cold air suits me, airs out my system."

We hug and he whispers into my neck: "Really, thank you for all you have done for me."

"Of course, Rok, it's a pleasure. Hang in there." I smile, wink at him, and close the door.

Something inside me has become very tired of supporting others. It seems like I've been doing it my whole life: from my childhood when I listened to my mother talking about her pain for hours and hours, to the thousands of hours of sitting in therapy sessions and the workshops that I've constantly been leading, and on and on. Even many of my friends have got used to coming to me for help and support: apparently I listen to them so well that it's easier for them to hear themselves. Also, so they tell me, they get good ideas from me. Or they simply feel safe and accepted and deeply understood. I'm like a computer programmer to whom friends come for a visit with their laptops under their arms, just to quickly fix something while having a beer.

It's not at all unusual that friends will come around on a two-hour 'social visit' and will spend an hour and fifty-five minutes talking about their problems and then look at their watches and say: "Uh-oh, I better go. But how are you? I'm sure you're okay.

You're always doing great, aren't you? You're amazing, always doing well." And off they go.

No, I'm not. I'm not always great. Sometimes I am, sometimes I'm not. I have issues, dilemmas, problems, and I also need support, to be seen in my humanity.

And right now I need to be alone and not see anyone for the next twelve hours and then I have another workshop.

Rok has made a lot of new friends in the past couple of years, mostly from the practice group for Nonviolent Communication here in Ljubljana. They all like him a lot and socialize with him, so I know he'll find the support he needs. I am no longer the only one. Not everything rests on my shoulders.

∞

Some powerful, unstoppable force is annihilating everything in one great wave: everything, absolutely everything. Time, space, mass, matter, energy, the entire universe and myself with it, and my self-awareness. Everything is disappearing into nothingness, into complete nothingness…

…and I find myself in front of a fountain, the fountain of the universes, the fountain of the multiverse. This is where all universes are born, each with its own time, its own space, its own laws of physics. Like an enormous mass of sand that rolls and pours into itself. Each individual grain of sand is a single universe, a space of manifesting possibilities…

…

…the foundation of which is a constantly undulating chaos.

Creation in eternal emergence.

Amorphous in its nature, without any trace of stability.

Spatial infinity, temporal infinity.

One hand in infinity, the other in the present moment.

The large is decanted into the small, the micro feeds the macro.

Space consumes itself, linearity does not exist.

I am within everything, everything is within me.

From the present moment to the next moment there is eternity,

an infinite field of the possibilities of creation

in which this momentary manifestation is also born.

The emergence of common time and space

is an extraordinary event,

the birth of this universe;

that is why life is so precious.

It allows us to reside within the infinitely undulating chaos,

but to try and capture all of this with our mind

is endless torment.

There is no point in trying to capture the incomprehensible,

still less in worrying, in any kind of worrying.

The only sensible response is to be amazed,

to enjoy the marvel of creation and all its combinations.

As an illusory individual I have no other meaning;

as a whole we create meaning along the way,

through the infinite flow of creation.

...

Woooow! Only a second or two has passed in this-worldly time but my journey has actually lasted millions of years. Salvia Divinorum, the ancient Mexican herb, used for radical shamanic mystical journeys. Whoooo...

My role in this life is connected with the experience of primal chaos. Somewhere deep inside me, I know that.

And that is also all that I know.

∞

The fire crackles and I slowly close the door of the wood-stove. I sit down, watching through the glass as the flames slowly rise over the burning wood and feeling the warmth beginning to penetrate into the room. Evening has fallen outside and total silence reigns.

This is my perfect haven.

A few years ago Lidija and I bought a hundred-year-old stone ruin overgrown by brambles, in a remote part of the Slovenian coastal area with a mild Mediterranean climate. We threw ourselves into renovating it, sparing nothing either in money or creativity, and now it's a perfect little house in which there is nothing but stone, wood, and clay. And the best solar technology. Everything is made to measure. Everything is softly rounded, warm, gentle. There are only four little houses in this peaceful settlement, all occupied by people with alternative life styles, and there are many days when I see no one at all.

I put down my guitar and put on some water for tea.

Spending time in this paradise nourishes me on all levels. Especially when I'm here alone, which I usually am. When I'm here with Lidija, it's perfectly okay but somehow a certain tension and anxiety is present in the background, and consequently my tendency to be careful and ready to adapt is awakened, which means I am never really fully relaxed. So I mostly prefer to be here on my own. Sometimes I come for only one night, but in most cases for an extended weekend, and occasionally for several weeks at a time. I endlessly enjoy following my inner peace, which the environment here nurtures so well.

It's midnight now, time for my encounter with the stars. Around this time I usually walk through the orchard I've planted, and along the little path in the woods, to the meadow where the view opens to the valley below. All around me: woods, silence, darkness. And above me: stars, millions of stars. They smile at me and somehow enter me. Or I enter them. I don't know which.

In the past year I've been travelling around the world much more than before. I'm invited to lead or co-lead workshops and retreats on practically all continents, and consequently I have the sense that my world is becoming wider and deeper than before. Some new life is opening.

It's not just new inspiration and learning that I get; what is most precious are the new friends I've made around the world as a result of my work as a trainer in Nonviolent Communication. Contact with them has deepened my insight into what's possible beyond current social norms and frameworks. How we can follow the call of the heart and the soul in full authenticity and aliveness...

What moves me more than anything else with these new friends and acquaintances is the unimagined openness, sincerity, and also intimacy, that is being created among us on very deep levels. All of a sudden most of the relationships that I have had until now in my life seem like a sort of nursery school. Yes, really, a new life, a new frequency of being, is opening and inviting me into it.

I suddenly hear in the silence the barely audible rustling of leaves and the cracking of branches. Something is slowly and cautiously approaching me through the woods on my left side. Maybe a deer or a fox, probably not a wild boar, which would make more noise. I sit there without moving so as not to frighten the creature, whatever it is. The steps approach me. Now it's already out of the forest and in the clearing where I'm sitting.

I turn my head to the left very slowly but can make out almost nothing in the darkness. The moon has not risen yet and the night is pitch black.

Suddenly a deer is right next to me. It reaches its head curiously towards me and for a few seconds we look into each other's eyes, maybe a metre apart. Then it slowly turns away, looks around, and peacefully walks into the night.

Feeling enchanted and deeply moved, I remain seated. What a blessing.

∞

Although it was not conceived in this way, everything in the enormous hall appears as a sort of mystical ritual, something very ancient. There are more than two hundred of us. We're moving, dancing, rolling over each other, falling on the floor, either alone or in pairs, in little groups of three or four, whatever happens. And all in total silence. Well, the hall is not entirely silent because two musicians are sensitively performing minimalistic music. They're improvising, inspired by what they are witnessing. They are playing a whole range of traditional instruments: flutes of different types and sizes, drums, a didgeridoo... We dance in a state of ecstasy, without verbal interactions or comments.

Contact Improvisation. How grateful I am to have found it. Of course it would have been better if I had started doing it thirty years ago when my body was stronger and more mobile. But why complain? I'm grateful for every moment on the dance floor. I'm exploring the same qualities through Contact Improvisation that I've been exploring my whole life: freedom, authenticity, connection with myself, connection with others, acceptance, surrender. Only here it's embodied, manifested. There's no way to bluff, to pretend, to pull the wool over my own eyes...

As I ecstatically move through the space, I feel a palm on the nape of my neck. The pressure increases and my body adapts by bending forward, the other body leans into me and then, feeling the firm support I'm offering, gives its weight to my lower back and immediately rolls upwards, supported by my backwards-reaching arms, as I stand up, to end up lying across my shoulder. It's Julie, a young Scandinavian professional dancer who I've already met a couple of times at different Contact Improvisation festivals. I recognize her energy right away. The trust we have in each other is tangible in our dance.

We roll across each other, turning in the space, falling to the floor, rising up again. Everything is spontaneous: free bodies playing with each other like little puppies. I never know where and in what position my body will be in the next moment. I just follow the flow and surrender into it.

Sexuality and physical intimacy were always indivisibly connected in the social structure where I grew up and was formed.

Now for the first time, they are separate. I can be completely free in my physical proximity without feeling any kind of sexuality in myself or in others. Just freedom, playfulness, joy in life, and trust, warm human trust. I feel a particular joy in dancing with men – maybe because up till now I have had much less physical intimacy with men, because of the stigma attached to it.

Julie gets pulled into another group of three dancers and winks farewell to me from the shoulder of one of them. All the better, actually. Julie is as agile and powerful as a cat and dancing with her has always been a wild and physically exhausting experience. I could use a little break.

I sit on the floor next to the wall at the edge of the dance floor and drink water from a bottle. Enchanted, I observe the shamanic scene in front of me. Everyone looks somehow stoned from the beauty of what they are experiencing. Their eyes glow with a sort of sacred rapture. Their bodies calmly and easily spin and roll. A tender, warm, loving aliveness is all around, spontaneously and softly flowing.

And I suddenly realize: our bodies are three-dimensional portals into this world.

Just as black holes are three-dimensional portals into some other universe, our bodies are three-dimensional portals into this world. This is how our consciousness enters this lifetime. Truly.

Three-dimensional portals into this manifestation, into this moment.

The whole universe suddenly makes so much sense.

With this realization, my perception changes, deepens, clarifies. And there's nothing for me to do but close the water bottle, place it in the corner, stand up and allow my body to pull me back into the flow of life.

∞

Autumn 2014. A Sunday morning. I'm slowly sipping my morning tea, reading a book, and enjoying the solitude and silence in our fairy house where I've come for another long weekend when the phone rings. It's Maša, a good friend for many years.

"Oh, Maša, good morning! What an honour to hear from you on this Sunday morning. I'm so happy. What's up?"

"I'm afraid I'm not calling with good news," Maša says slowly. "Where are you?"

"In my dream house, sipping tea and reading."

"Ah, okay, then I'll just tell you: Rok committed suicide."

I say nothing. I'm in shock. There's a drumming sound in my head.

"What... oh no... whoa..."

"Yes, Robert, I'm sorry. He was found this morning."

It can't be true.

Rok.

Is.

Dead.

Everything inside me resets. Everything is erased and is slowly composing itself into a new reality.

Maša tenderly tells me the details.

Dear Maša.

Then I hear her say as if from a distance:

"Robert, we'll talk later. Is that okay?"

"It's okay. Thank you for telling me. We'll talk later."

The silence in the little house is deeper than usual.

One part of me cannot completely accept this reality: that my dear friend, Rok, is no longer with us. Just like that, so suddenly, he left our world. How can this be true? All of a sudden, just like that?

Abruptly I am overcome with anger. I cannot fucking believe it! He always called me when he needed help, when he was under pressure. He always turned to me. He even called to consult me when he was buying a new car and was vacillating between two colours. I was always the first one and very often the only one he consulted. Only now, when he was clearly in a terrible situation and thinking about suicide, he didn't call.

I'm flooded by memories. How we went on a bike trip together and pretended to be a gay couple so that we could get the only private room at a hostel. And how happy he was when we went out 'for a beer' but always ended up drinking tea. And how happy he was in his new relationship with Ceri. How fulfilled, inspired, reborn, glowing, and emotional he felt. And how at the end of the first Awakening to Life Intensive, he had cried and sobbed and thanked me for pulling him out of the hole he had fallen into.

Tears are flowing down my cheeks in the silence and solitude.

And the last time I saw him, two months ago: I surely didn't pull him out of any hole then! How I regret not inviting him to stay with me. Why wasn't I with him the whole night and day, the whole week, the whole month? Maybe we could have figured something out. Maybe something would have shifted. Maybe he would have told me he was considering suicide. Maybe, maybe…

I call Lidija to tell her the sad news.

…

Rok is always with me during the following days, always in me. I cannot sleep in a closed space so I sleep out on the balcony. I feel his presence the whole night. He visits me, speaks to me, calms me. Then he bids me farewell.

Rok, my dear, dear friend, travel well.

Everything inside me is wounded. Everything is ruptured. My whole network of friends, the whole community is wounded. Nothing will ever be as it was.

∞

"I'm going to take a month to think about whether I still want to be in this relationship where I feel no connection."

I hear Lidija's voice. She is standing in the middle of the room and looking at me.

My immediate inner reaction is: okay then, let's split up for good and be done with it. I've already heard the suggestion that we should separate three or four times this year: that it makes no sense, that we no longer have any real connection with each other, that I should go ahead and find myself a lover in order to not waste my life. And so on and so forth.

But that is not what I say. Instead I come out with:

"Well, that's not quite okay with me. What am I to do for this month while you're thinking about things? Pretend that everything is normal?"

My question is more rhetorical than anything else. I'm tired of this relationship, maybe not of the relationship itself, but of adapting to it. If I didn't keep adapting to her, then we would have split up very many times in the past years.

All this time, I've been trying so hard to see the beauty in her, the love, to focus on the positive and avoid facing the deeper reality, the pain, the disappointment, the fact that I no longer even know what I really feel and what I don't, no longer know which part of me is authentic and which is merely adapting to the situation.

But recently the pressure to hold things together feels less strong. It seems to me that our field is beginning to dissolve.

...

In the end, we decide that she will not have her month, but that we will keep working on our relationship instead and try to re-establish our connection. I don't know if this makes sense or if we are just putting off the inevitable. Because we've already been trying for a long time. Including regular evening conversations in which we try to connect deeply, but after which more and more often we end up going to bed separately, and with a sense of disconnection.

Maybe we've given to each other all we have to give. Maybe we've created everything that we have to create. And that was a lot. Love, friendship, mutual support, synergy, trust, beauty, exploring the unknown, learning the new. There has been loads of beauty.

There is gratitude in my heart. And dark clouds hovering over me.

∞

"Hellooo, hellooooo, hellooooooo…"

I hear a whispered, yet clear and faintly echoing voice… somewhere inside myself, somewhere inside my being.

Surprised, I open my eyes. I am lying in the darkness on my own narrow mat in a circle of around forty people. Others, young and old, from all around the world, are sitting or lying on mats. A shaman from Brazil is leading the all-night ayahuasca ceremony. He is small, very gentle, loving, well-meaning. About an hour earlier, we each drank a glass of the thick dark liquid that had a surprisingly familiar taste. But how could I possibly know this very strong and specific taste?

"Helloooooo, helloooooooooo, my name is Ayahuasca, Ayaaaahuuuaaascaaaa…"

A voice inside me keeps repeating this and suddenly I realize that a silver snake is streaking through my whole being, through my energetic body, as if it wants to touch each curve, each corner, fast, precise, gentle…

This is definitely not my imagination. The experience is so clear, so real. Once again, I direct my attention toward my inner being, my inner space, and it suddenly opens into…

...

the centre of the galaxy,

the red, pulsing, enormously wide centre of the galaxy.

Vastness, enormity, eternity, peace.

And lying across the centre of the galaxy

is the cosmic dragon.

Magnificent, calm, ecstatically awakening,

with an extra-dimensional magnificence

that the mind cannot grasp,

though it tries with all its might.

The cosmic dragon

that is in the cosmos and the cosmos in it,

that is also in me and I in it.

The inside is a metaphor of the outside and vice versa.

Oneness with the cosmos.

The cosmos that finds physical form in this body,

in this manifestation.

The cosmic dragon, this living force,

that awakens through me

into this world,

in its innocent majesty,

blessed,

joyful,

serene.

Inhaling into this world,

exhaling into the cosmos.

...

∞

March 2016, Palestine. EcoMe is a centre founded by a group of young Israelis with the help of activists and pacifists from around the world, with the intention of connecting Palestinians and Israelis. It's located at the edge of the desert, not far from the Dead Sea. Because the centre has chosen Nonviolent Communication as their approach to communication and conflict resolution, I have been invited to lead a training for conflict mediators and a couple of other workshops as part of a ten-day festival.

And now after the end of the day's programme I'm sitting on a little bench opposite Noa, under the infinite starry desert sky. We've been talking for nearly an hour: about life, our childhoods, the patterns that we've carried from childhood into our adult years, the barriers that prevent us of from fully shining in life, about exploration and discovery, yes, about the miracle of life…

I first met Noa about a year and a half ago when I was in Palestine as a trainer at a ten-day international training in Nonviolent Communication. She was one of the many participants from Israel. She struck me the moment I laid eyes on her and I felt a strong sense of recognition, a connection that I very rarely feel so quickly with people. If ever at all. Aware of the structural power that I had as a trainer and the possibility of transfers and projections, I held myself back as I always do in such contexts, and we did not speak very much during the training. We had almost no contact after the training either, but she somehow remained present in me. I was unable to forget her.

And now, a year and a half later, we meet here at EcoMe, and our conversation is acquiring broad and deep dimensions. It flows like a river that's been dammed for a long time. Now the floodgates have been lifted and a powerful flow is freed. Our conversation is like a joyful dance in a space of freedom, warmth, ease. I feel so incredibly relaxed and deeply met.

Our energies pull each other towards an encounter in raw authenticity, without expectations, without trying to make an impression. An encounter between two open, trusting, fully conscious beings under the desert stars. Yes, everything is full of trust.

When the conversation comes to our present relationships, I clearly state that I am happily married. It seems funny that I emphasize it, as if I need some sort of safety belt.

Because the intensity and beauty of this meeting is shaking me to my very foundations.

∞

My boots are rubbing more and more, making blisters on my feet. Which surprises me because I've already walked many trails and climbed many hills in these hiking boots and never had any problems. Now, the second day into this three-day hike with Lidija in the Slovenian forests, the soles of my feet have become pretty raw.

It's as if blisters are also forming inside me. I don't like to lie or hide in general and even less in partnerships. Yet now I am doing exactly that.

In a few days' time, Lidija will travel to the US for a one-month learning programme that means a lot to her. Soon after she leaves, I will drive off to co-lead a ten-day training in the south of France. And then I'll be going on a one-week road trip with Noa through Spain and to Portugal.

After our meeting at EcoMe, Noa and I noticed this field of friendship, companionship, and trust deepening between us. A soul recognition that has opened up an incredible flow of connection. We've spoken over Skype a couple of times since, have acknowledged that something magical is opening up, and have agreed to spend a week together to allow this connection to reveal itself. To see what wants to emerge. We've been very clear that we have no desire to go in the direction of a romantic or even sexual encounter, but rather to simply meet in innocence and friendship, with curiosity and openness.

I haven't said anything to Lidija about all of this.

And now it's eating into me, like my boots eating into my feet. We have to rest often so I can take them off. Lidija is chatting. She's happy, in a good mood, while I'm gloomy because

I don't feel any connection between us, and above all it's as if my insides are being eaten away.

I don't like to hide things. I hate it. It's suffocating me inside.

I didn't tell her about my travel plans with Noa, as it would surely ruin her stay in the US and the valuable learning experience she hopes to have there.

Moreover, facing the vanishing eros in our connection, Lidija and I recently agreed to shift into an open relationship and to be free to tell or not tell each other about other intimate encounters we might have. So I also have a sense that I am very well within this agreement, as this is not even going to be a sexual adventure, as I am really not interested in that, but in the exploration of the magic of spiritual intimacy such as I have been experiencing with other new friends in my life.

So it all seems OK. Rationally.

But still I don't have a good feeling about it. It's not a good decision, but I don't know what would be better in this situation.

I will tell her when we both return from our trips.

...

"This is by far the most romantic thing we've done together for a while," Lidija says joyfully, while I clench my teeth because of the painful blisters. I shudder. It's not the least bit romantic for me. Everything seems dry and empty.

And on top of it all, I am hiding and lying.

∞

Noa and I stop for a picnic somewhere in western Spain, by the banks of a river in the middle of a forest. We've been travelling for a couple of days now, heading west from Barcelona, where I picked her up, towards Portugal. We drive through the wide-open landscapes, going on walks, having picnics in the countryside, swimming in lakes, playing the guitar and ukulele, singing, dancing, laughing. Joy, ease, openness, friendship. A sincere and open encounter in beauty, authenticity and gentleness. It's the innocent meeting of two hearts for which I have longed my whole life.

And there is love. So much love.

Lying on my back, I gaze up at the trees above me and listen to the murmuring of the river, and suddenly right in front of me, for an instant, a vision opens up of a sort of honeycomb with an infinite number of portals. Each portal leads to a different life, a different life path. Through one, I am with Lidija in the same way I have been until now. Through a second, I am with Lidija in a somewhat different way. Through a third, I am with Noa. Through a fourth, I am alone. And so on and so forth. There are hundreds of them, maybe thousands.

For an instant, I disappear beneath a powerful wave of awareness...

...

...that there is no right or wrong choice.

There is no more right or less right way to live life.

All life's possibilities are absolutely equivalent.

They all exist at the same time.

They all exist.

All these possibilities express the fullness of life.

Each possible life

is in essence full of the experience

of aliveness.

The full experience of manifestation.

The full experience of existence.

It doesn't matter,

it's all one.

...

...

I don't know how my life will unfold. I only know that I want to walk it in integrity. In full responsibility both to my own heart and to the stars above me.

The first thing I will do when I return to Slovenia is to have a conversation with Lidija, to sit down with her, look her sincerely in the eyes, say to each other what we have to say, and to explore how we want to continue our life. Together or each on our own.

∞

Rays of sun fall onto my face through the crown of the plum tree and I slowly awaken. Hmm, how fantastically deep and calm was my sleep in the silence and gentle energy of our little stone house. I slowly turn on my side and open my eyes.

And I'm shaken by a sudden realization that takes my breath away: Lidija and I are splitting up!

Wow, it's really true: Lidija and I are separating.

For the last few days I've been waking up in the mornings like this, shocked into this new reality. I haven't even grasped it rationally, let alone emotionally.

A few days ago, we had a conversation on Skype – me in Slovenia, she still in the U.S. I started by honestly telling her that I hadn't felt a real connection with her for a long time, that I don't sense her at this new frequency at which I have been making new connections, new friendships in recent years. And that I don't have much hope for our relationship. And I heard her answer that we should separate right away. And I said to her that I wanted to wait for her to return, so we could take more time, discuss things together, and decide how to proceed. And I heard from her that it made no sense to draw it out and prolong the agony, that it would be best to make a sharp cut if that's how I see things. And I said that I would like to take at least twenty-four hours before we made such a dramatic decision.

And I then spent all that time thinking about it all, connecting with myself with all the honesty I could muster. And again and again, I arrived at an internal clarity that it would be best to split up. Although, looked at rationally, it doesn't make much sense: nothing bad has happened between us recently, we live peacefully together, we have two houses, one of which is my own personal paradise, life flows calmly and easily onwards.

During these 24 hours I had several conversations with my closest friends, the ones who know both of us, and all of them supported me in the decision for us to split up. This came as a real surprise. I almost counted on them rejecting the idea. Some of them even said that they were amazed that we had stayed together for so long. The same old story.

It was a very difficult decision, very close. I could have decided either way. Staying together would be the rational decision, with the focus on predictability, calm, and stability. To separate was a decision of the heart, the soul, and a step into the unknown.

In the end, I decided for my heart.

And in that very moment an abyss opened between us, as if we had suddenly become strangers. Perhaps it's because I'd been holding things together all of these years. Now, when I properly let go for the first time, it is as if an elastic band were released and our relationship has snapped into a state of diametrical opposition.

And this is how I wake up now, day after day, in a sort of post-apocalyptic shock. Then I slide through the day on a wave of diverse and sometimes even panicky thoughts, only to glide, towards the evening, into a sense of peace, serenity, and deep realization that everything is alright.

And when I lie down in the meadow under the stars I feel incredibly free and peaceful.

∞

It's a warm sunny Saturday in September and I'm sitting across from Lidija in a circle of friends, on the grass in the orchard next to our beautiful house. I've experienced so many enchanting things right here in this orchard, right here on this meadow, under this sky. And today we're having a separation ceremony here, witnessed and supported by our friends.

We start by expressing our gratitude to each other. There is enormous gratitude in me: for all the support that I've received from Lidija, for her trust and faith in me, for the beauty that I've experienced through her, for the shared creativity, the learning, the discovery, for the exploration of life, and for the love.

Yes, there is a lot of gratitude in my heart.

I take my guitar and play and sing Fragile by Sting. It somehow suits the moment. Yes, truly …*lest we forget how fragile we are…*

There is also a lot of regret in my heart. Most of all because I wasn't clearer in the relationship, more direct, more authentic, more decisive. If I had been, things would have been resolved much more quickly, to the benefit of all involved, and with much less pain. So, I cannot really blame Lidija for any of the wounds and scars that I collected on my heart during these 16 years; they were all a consequence of my choice to follow my inner patterns to adapt, to keep on believing, to push aside my own pain and need for self-care. Nobody was forcing me into anything.

After Lidija returned from the US it all became like a roller-coaster. We had many beautiful, mutually supportive and honest conversations, and we had many painful and rough ones. There was gratitude and pain, appreciation and rage, new hopes and many regrets. There were invitations to reconsider our decision. And I knew there was no way back for me.

Now we bow to each other and begin to untie our hiking boots, the laces of which we have symbolically tied together for this ceremony. A couple of years ago, we bought the same model of hiking boots and walked many paths together wearing them. Now we will each walk in these boots in our own directions.

We speak our well-intentioned blessings to each other for our future separate journeys. There is nothing other than affection in my heart and the desire for Lidija's life to be beautiful and full. I have no resentment in me, just openness and affection. I know that in each moment we both tried to give of our full selves, as much as we knew how to give.

At the end of the ceremony, we stand in thoughtful silence around the fire that I'd lit before we started. There is a desire in me to preserve the holiness of the connection we once established. Although we have created a beautiful closing, our voyage together did not turn out the way I would have wanted. I only hope that we will know how to preserve the best that we succeeded in creating together and remain open, supportive, and friendly to each other.

∞

"How are you? How is it going?"

I'm sitting beside my mother's hospital bed. She was diagnosed with lung cancer a month ago and they've just done a second procedure to withdraw fluid from her lungs. She's lying in bed, fragile but smiling.

"I'm alright, quite alright," she responds with a weak voice. "It doesn't hurt too much and they are so wonderful here, taking such good care of me, so attentive and kind. I am so grateful."

"Oh, that's good to hear."

"And how are you? How is it with your new friend? Her name is Noa, if I remember correctly."

"It is so incredibly beautiful. You know, nobody has ever loved me so much as I feel loved by her. Our relationship is a real blessing. I've never experienced so much love in my life. Well, you know what I mean. I don't want to compare with the way a mother loves..."

"I know, I know, and I'm very happy for you," she smiles.

"How is it for you, Mum? You have an endlessly dynamic life with a son like me, don't you? There's never any peace, always some sort of dramatic change going on. It's not boring, is it?"

"Oh, that's for sure," she laughs. "Ow, I shouldn't laugh. It hurts when I laugh." She takes a deep breath and continues. "But you know, I completely understand you, really. I do understand you, whether you believe it or not, and I completely accept your decision. Please believe that".

"And there's something else that I perhaps haven't told you before. Many years ago, when you came back from military service and you started to go to those Enlightenment Intensives and were getting ready to travel to India, I was completely out of my mind with fear. You see, I had hoped that you would settle down after the military and that you would – how can I say it? – begin to live a more normal life. I don't know how to say it any other way."

"It's okay," I smile at her, "I understand…"

"Well, I used to complain about my fears to my boss at the hospital, a very respected doctor. She was also very much into astrology. That was her hobby, and she approached it with all her studious and scientific seriousness. She made charts and horoscopes for all of us, her colleagues and also for the members of our families.

Back then, she looked deep into my eyes and said something I will never forget: 'Look, Helena, in the Chinese zodiac, your son has the sign of the fire horse. In the old days, women in China would often go for an abortion if they knew their child would be a fire horse. People born under that sign are driven by such a powerful energy, such forcefulness, that it's not easy to live with them. They're wonderful people and they only want to do good, but the people around them tend to get burned by their hot flame. And on top of this, in the Western zodiac your son has Aquarius sun with Sagittarius in the ascendant, for good measure. So, Helena, just give up on the idea that your son will be an average man. He will never settle down. Never! He will always be drawn forwards, always drawn somewhere up, somewhere among the stars!'

And you know, my dear son, at that moment I just accepted it and got used to it, and I love you just the way you are."

I hold her hand in mine. I squeeze it and we look at each other and smile and wipe away our tears.

Twelve: And New Beginnings

"…When you asked me a couple of weeks ago to prepare a speech for your funeral, I said of course I would, but on condition that you would be here, listening, and not flying around somewhere else. You promised me that you would and so I trust that you are now here, listening attentively…"

January 2017. A sunny but very cold morning, the snow squeaking underfoot. I'm standing on a small podium in front of the other mourners, surrounded by the neoclassical colonnades at the entrance to Ljubljana's main cemetery. I'm reading the eulogy at my mother's funeral.

"…Supposedly we don't remember people by what they said, but by how we felt around them. I dare to say that we're going to remember you as a person with whom we felt safe, welcome, and loved. As a person around whom we all had a sense that you only wanted the best for us, that you were trying to support and contribute to us in the best way you could. That you cared for us. Even more than you cared for yourself, actually."

The funeral takes place with only the close family members present, in accordance with my mother's wishes. We're all in shock somehow because we had considered my mother relatively healthy and tough for her age. Then she was suddenly diagnosed with lung cancer and now, only three months later, we are burying her.

"…There are many of us who love you very much. Who are grateful for your love and goodness. Who realize that you touched us and enriched our lives. And what can give more meaning to a human life than the awareness that someone contributed to the lives of others, enriched them?

During my last visit, you, as usual, touched on the theme of death and as we were talking about it, it seemed to me that you were tranquil, at peace with it. Which gives me hope that you have embarked on your next voyage with a sense of inner peace.

Dear mother, dear grandmother, travel well, wherever you are heading."

As I speak the last words, I start to sob and the tears begin to flow. I wipe my nose and take a step back. It's time for the funeral procession to the graveside. I take in the cold air and the silence of the moment and nod to the funeral assistants. Our chosen music starts playing on the sound system, mother's favourite singer-songwriter from her homeland in Prekmurje.

We slowly follow the cart carrying her ashes, making our way among the sea of graves, accompanied all the way by the music, which carries far on the still morning air.

I have a powerful sense of regret as I slowly walk with Lucija, Filip, and my father. I regret that I wasn't with her to hold her hand during her last moments of life. I'd gone with Noa on a two-week road trip, asking the doctors beforehand how things looked for my mother. They told me that they could offer no guarantees but she would probably live for many more months. My mother also said we should go, that it was no problem, that she felt better. I arranged with my father to contact me if her condition worsened, so we could come back right away.

Of course her condition worsened immediately after our departure and of course my father kept it a secret for a couple of days, even though I had constantly been asking him for information. He said later that he didn't want to ruin our holiday. By the time I got him to tell me that her condition was much worse, Noa and I were already in central France. We turned around immediately and rushed back to Slovenia but I was too late.

She died on the last day of 2016 and my father and I brought in the new year together in the silence of the family house.

The procession slowly approaches the family grave. From the distance, across the silence of the great city cemetery, my mother's song can still be heard: *In whose place this flower blooms…*

∞

"My love, thank you for trusting me. Hmm, I love you so much..."

Noa is sitting across from me, looking at me with loving eyes, gently smiling.

I stare at her and somehow energetically experience as if my brain has seized. My mind got all confused and came to a halt. My internal system is just not used to this and it floats helplessly in the air.

For a couple of hours I had pondered about how to tell her something quite vulnerable, and rather frightening. I was convinced that my sharing would trigger a reaction in her, some judgements. That she would become upset, sad, hurt, that she would not be able to understand what I was actually trying to say, that she would react strongly. And then we would have a conflict, followed by a long period of trying to clear it up.

But instead I got only acceptance and love.

How unknown this is to me! How accustomed I have been all my life to receive judgements and reactions. How these have somehow been a normal part of intimate relationships. This was probably even the reason that I got involved in relationships where there was a lot of criticism: because it felt familiar to me, known.

And now, in shock, I am realizing not only that I can be loved the way I am but that there is actually more love outside than I am capable of receiving. That the amount of love that I experience is not conditional on how much love is outside, but by the amount I am capable of receiving.

Wow. I have longed for this my whole life and I am only just beginning, at the age of fifty, to learn how to live within this field of love and acceptance.

∞

I'm sitting in the vast and peaceful city cemetery in the awakening spring. Kržišnik Helena, 1944 – 2016 is written on the gravestone. Above her names are those of my father's mother and stepfather. How time passes.

I sigh and slowly stand up. I straighten the burning candles on the stone grave cover, smile sadly, say farewell in my thoughts and slowly set off on the little path towards the distant exit.

After I've walked about ten metres, an invisible force stops me. So powerfully that my whole being shivers for a moment. I stand still.

"Stay awhile. Don't go. Stay. Wait. Don't go."

I clearly hear the words in my being, echoing somewhere inside me. Not really as words but as a hardly recognizable yet still very evident vibration.

With the hair standing up on the back of my neck, I turn and go back to the grave. I stand there and close my eyes.

The breeze starts blowing.

Somewhere inside me I hear the words:

"Everything is alright. Everything is alright. I love you. Don't worry. Everything is alright. I love you. Everything is alright."

My heart opens with warmth, with love. The river of life flows. I smile.

Later, as I walk towards my bike that I'd left by the entrance to the cemetery, I feel peace, joy, and gratitude in my heart.

∞

"Gamble everything for love,

if you are a true human being..."

For the first time, I think I really understand this verse by Rumi.

The night is full of stars and I sit on a deck chair in the meadow not far from my soul's haven, the perfect little house which will soon be sold because of the divorce.

And once again the starry expanse enters into me and floods me with immeasurable gratitude. Gratitude for whatever brought me together with Noa. Gratitude to the whole of life.

I don't know how long this blessed love will last, maybe a few years, maybe until the end of my life, but already I am grateful for every moment.

I wake in love. I go to sleep in love. How much of the beauty of true love is it even possible to experience in this life?

I'm grateful that I have returned to my true path and it has once again begun to breathe under my feet, widening, deepening.

I am returning to miraculous life.

I breathe more fully than I have for a long time.

∞

Noa and I are walking through a little wood near her home in the hills above Jerusalem. It's evening. We walk quietly along the path between the trees and talk. There's a lot of love between us, a lot of tenderness. We step through an opening in a fence that divides the wood in two, and stop on the other side to continue our conversation.

Suddenly Noa becomes silent and takes two steps backwards, away from me. She stands there, looking at me without expression, all her energy pulled back into herself. I stand completely alone. Abandoned, rejected, not only by Noa, but by all the women in the world. Deeply shaken, in shock even, I begin to move backwards towards the fence. I know that my best friend, Jaka, is on the other side of the fence. I will go to him.

I approach Jaka on the other side of the fence and for a few seconds we are connected in friendship, closeness, but then he also suddenly backs away from me, taking all of his energy with him. I realize in that moment that I am not only rejected by him, but by all the men in the world.

Anger and rage begin to accumulate inside me. I start screaming at Jaka and also at Noa on the other side of the fence:

301

"But what have I done to you? Why are you rejecting me? What have I done to you?"

I begin to grow in my rage and become a sort of gigantic Hulk, with the energy of my rage lifting me into the air. I float above the little wood. I look at Jaka and Noa below me and continue screaming – no, roaring – at them:

"But what have I done to you? Why have you rejected me? What have I done to you?"

My rage becomes stronger and stronger. I rise into the stratosphere above the earth and scream louder, with more and more pain…

… and I wake up in bed, screaming so powerfully that it lifts me into a sitting position. Noa is beside me, startled awake and terrified.

Much later, when we've calmed down and Noa is sleeping in my arms, I continue to process the emotional energy flowing through my body. Ultimately it's all about a deeply held belief that there is no place for me in this world. I have had that sense throughout my whole life. My father, from the depths of his own personal swamp, never had the capacity to really see me, to be with me. My mother, with her fears, was completely dependent on my father and also didn't have the inner space to really see me, to really be with me.

Neither of my parents, nor any of my other relatives who witnessed what was happening in our home, ever asked me how I was, how I managed to deal with all of it. No one expressed any concern. The whole space was occupied with the problems of other people.

So I just stayed in my little room, looking out of the window at the crane on the building site across the street. Alone and without any place of my own in the family.

I fall asleep with a sense of sadness and tenderness for that forgotten little boy.

∞

Noa and I make love, gently, joyfully. In the cloud of the flow of love, in the naked meeting, in the smile of our hearts.

And once again I am overwhelmed by the powerful feeling that I've already experienced three or four times during our lovemaking; my energy wakes up and wants to create life with Noa's energy. It is as if our two energies, our two beings somehow recognize each other, and demand creation.

It is as if something ancient and powerful has suddenly awakened with a very clear purpose. This has never happened before in my life, and yet with Noa it has already happened several times.

For many years, I was pretty certain that I would not have any more children. I even enjoyed the feeling of freedom and internal space when my children grew up and left home. Now, all of a sudden, this internal impulse, which is definitely not coming from my mind, has emerged. It's something larger than myself and my own choosing. In a way, it's terrifying how it has appeared so forcefully. On the other hand, it's also calming because it has so much clarity and magnificence. There's no need to decide what is right, what isn't, what I want, what I don't, because it's completely clear that life wants this. That the life flow I have with Noa wants to create a new life and is inviting a new human being into existence.

Whooa! I'm 51 years old and it looks like my life is not slowing down at all.

∞

I'm driving slowly along the winding roads of the Portuguese countryside. Noa is by my side. We're talking calmly about relationships, about life, comparing the patterns that we carry with us from childhood. And suddenly it's as if a veil has fallen from my mind. As if someone has opened a curtain and a shining light has poured over me.

I'm overwhelmed with a deep realization, a deep insight, and with it such a stream of emotions, mostly shock, sadness and

303

disorientation, that I can no longer drive. I stop the car on a parking area by the road and run about fifty metres down a little path to a place where the view opens out onto the valley.

I shout out into the valley. Once, twice, three times. The echo disperses and it's quiet again.

Something slowly crystallizes in my mind. The introversion, which I had always been convinced was just a part of my nature – that it was just the way I was, always seeking solitude, being stressed by fast conversations in bigger groups, being almost unable to approach people and start conversations – was not a natural part of me but a survival strategy that I had developed during childhood.

To be alone in my world brings me the most safety and predictability. Interaction with others, especially with many people together, is dangerous, creating the possibility of pain, defeat, disappointment, the fall from paradise. To be in contact with people is extremely exhausting because I have to pay attention to so many things: to harmony between us, to their satisfaction... To be alone in my world is a relief, which is why I always return by the shortest path to my little, safe, and predictable personal paradise.

At the same time, this is really not how I want to live my life: hiding from full engagement somewhere in my little cave.

I stand and breathe deeply above the valley and slowly integrate this experience. Rationally, it is not such a big deal, but in terms of energy, I feel as if I have just experienced a powerful concussion.

After a while, I take a few steps and look around me. Noa is sitting on a rock five metres behind me, watching me patiently and lovingly.

Where did this amazing creature come from, she who so patiently accompanies me and supports me in these encounters with all of my shadows? How did I ever deserve to be with this queen of love and beauty?

We slowly make our way back to the car. I am deeply grateful that during these weeks of exploring Portugal, she has remained lovingly by my side, with me, as this mass of things repressed in my past has been continuously oozing out of me. I can imagine that our trip must feel to her like an emotional roller-coaster.

We continue our trip. Sometimes with friends, wandering around Portugal to look at properties and at existing communities, in pursuit of our desire for a piece of land where we could create an eco-settlement with our friends, with relationships based on compassion, support, authenticity, and the shared exploration of the miracle of life.

∞

This is probably one of my last weekends in this sanctuary of mine, this most beautiful house in the world. Because neither of us wanted to live in a place in which every corner had been co-created, we decided to sell it, and a buyer has already paid a deposit. In a few weeks' time I will move the last of my boxes out and hand them the keys.

I go out in the middle of the night, into the meadow in the middle of the orchard. I want to fully connect with this place as I begin bidding farewell, with gratitude. I say goodbye to the nature here, the trees, all the beautiful and calm energy that has brought me so much happiness and support during the past years.

Because dance has become a very important part of my life, I decide to include movement in my farewell. I connect the Bluetooth speaker, take off my flip-flops, and put on one of my all-time favourite pieces of music: My Song by Keith Jarrett. I stand in the meadow and close my eyes.

Already the first notes awaken my body, which begins to spontaneously respond with movement, with the improvised dance of this moment, a dance with the stars and the moon above me, a dance with the damp grass under my bare feet, with the trees and the bushes in the orchard, with the forest beyond the orchard…

After the dance, I sit on the deck chair, out of breath but full of life. Suddenly, a familiar energy speaks to me, touches me deep inside my being, entering through some sort of an inner portal. It addresses me respectfully and gently, but also powerfully. By now I recognize this energy, which first spoke to me during my first ayahuasca ceremony, and I have no other name for it but the cosmic dragon.

This dragon energy greets me, thanks me for the dance, and tells me that it will now dance for me. I sit on the deck chair and stare into the darkness around me. A strong wind suddenly arises and spins around the orchard, rustling the leaves, moving the bushes. My heart pounds wildly.

After a few minutes the wind suddenly calms down and I hear the voice inside me:

"Now you dance for me again."

I have nothing to think about. I get up, spontaneously take off all my clothes, and put on the next of my most favourite songs: Ano Zero by Egberto Gismonti.

I dance naked around the orchard, more joyful and alive than I have been in a long time.

After that it's the dragon's turn again. The wind rushes eagerly through the trees, rustling leaves and bending branches.

And so we take turns several times and then in the end we dance together: I with the wind and the wind with me.

When I sit down later, I wonder what I just experienced. I certainly didn't imagine all of this, since the wind kept rising in a very obvious and sudden way, and then also calming down in the same manner. Just a coincidence?

What is certain is that after that first ayahuasca ceremony, this energy of the 'cosmic dragon' entered me, entered my life. And it keeps appearing to me everywhere, always reminding me of its presence. After my separation from Lidija, for example, I temporarily took an apartment in Ljubljana that had a balcony looking out onto an enormous dragon painted beautifully on the facade of the neighbouring building.

While I think about these things, I'm gazing at my beloved stars above as they smile down from the heavenly vault through the crystal-clear night. And I notice my attention attracted by one of them, to the extent that I cannot tear my eyes away anymore. It isn't any of the few stars that I'm familiar with. As it keeps calling me, I take my phone and open an app for identifying heavenly bodies. I point my phone towards the star and it identifies it as Eltanin. I google the name and discover that this derives from the Arabic al-Tinnin, the great serpent, while its other name is Gamma Draconis. It's the right eye and brightest star in the constellation of Draco, the dragon!

You've got to be kidding me, I smile at the sky.

∞

It's seven in the morning and I slowly and ceremonially light a large candle. I'm in the middle of a group of 35 participants in the second Awakening to Life Intensive retreat in the US, the sixth in a row that I've run together with Robert Gonzales. Our collaboration and co-leadership are continuing effortlessly.

The flame of the candle, which symbolizes group focus, burns and will continue burning until ten in the evening when we end our day of work. We sit in the circle, starting and ending each day in silence. Absolute silence reigns in this beautiful octagonal wooden building in the middle of a forest in Virginia. Outside, to the east, the sunrise slowly takes shape amidst the singing of the forest birds.

I love to sit in silence with a group of people, with our collective intent, our collective attention. Silence is much better at connecting me with the life in me and the life in people around me than any words could possibly be.

I perceive in myself so much that is new, so much that is fresh…

And I realize that perhaps the common denominator of all of this newness is that I am beginning to love life. Ever since Noa and I have been together, this gentle, yet deep feeling has been rising in me of being in love with life as I never have been before. During the last ten years I have often felt tired of life, of struggling, even though my life has apparently been relatively easy and fulfilled. Now I feel reborn, and, yes, I have begun to love life. And maybe for the first time, I begin to sincerely hope that I will live for a long time.

I am overwhelmed by gratitude. That life brought me to Noa, this miracle on earth. That she was waiting for me for so long. And that she invited me back into the magic, back into the bold exploration of the mystery of existence.

I love this life and our exploration of embodying love.

∞

I'm sitting with Lucija on the thick carpet in my apartment in Ljubljana, sipping tea, and both of us are wiping tears from our eyes. She's talking to me about the anxieties she had in childhood, about her pain, fears, disappointments, loneliness... She's describing to me the times when she didn't receive the acceptance, support, and love for which she longed.

I feel deeply sad to hear how some of my actions, but above all my inaction, painfully affected her childhood and adolescence. Especially the times when I didn't stand up for her and the moments when I failed in my search for balance between my relationship with Lidija and my love and care for my children. It hurts so much.

Lucija looks at me and says:

"But, look, I'm only telling you this because you asked me to. Because there were not that many things that hurt me and that I would want to tell you. There was much, much more of what was beautiful in my childhood and adolescence, and I have only gratitude in my heart for you and for all the support and love and care that I always got from you. And that I still get."

"I know, Lucija, I know, and thank you. It is very sweet to hear that. Yet now it's really important to me that I hear about all of the things that hurt you, wounded and disappointed you, that you remember as unpleasant and even painful experiences. I want to hear it, I want to face it all. I want all that pain to receive space, to be expressed, and to be held by love. So please, do continue!"

"Yes, I know, I know. Okay. Let me try and remember more."

Lucija smiles and closes her eyes. And we continue crying and laughing together.

As I had done with Dev, when a week ago he responded to the same request of mine, to tell me what had accumulated in him during all the years that we had spent together. And we'd sat on the same carpet, spending a similar evening together in tears and laughter.

Filip on the other hand had assured me that he had nothing to tell me, that he was living a happy and successful life and that it therefore seemed pretty clear that there had been no traumatic events in his childhood. I was not fully convinced by this explanation, but I accepted it.

When Lucija leaves later that evening, we embrace for a long time at the door. My heart melts from all the love and trust that we share.

Deeply moved and grateful, I close the door behind her and remain sitting on a kitchen chair for a long time.

∞

I set off in the middle of the night on the narrow path that leads from our little house down into the valley. I hear the packs of jackals singing their laments in the darkness and laughing to each other across the valley. We're temporarily living at the very edge of an alternative village in the north of Israel, right next to a nature reserve. We're surrounded by peace, silence and the Mediterranean forest filled with wild boars and foxes, and with wonderful people as neighbours.

But tonight I am tense, very tense, and I need to be alone. I cautiously step along the narrow path into the complete darkness and silence of the nature reserve.

I feel confused. I love us, Noa and me. There is so much beauty in the space we have created and so much more beauty opening to us all the time. In the last year and a half of my relationship with Noa, I have received enough love for my whole life and I've walked along the paths of internal healing and liberation. I am in deep gratitude for it all.

Yet at the same time, I feel tired of living in a relationship. One part of me wants to be alone, in peace, just to rest in solitude. In ease, freedom, silence. Do I really want to fully enter into a new relationship and everything that entails? I'm 52 years old. Do I have enough energy for a new round?

All of sudden, from behind the silhouette of a bush about two metres in front of me, the deep grumbling voice of a wild boar. I also hear the nervous steps of a number of large bodies on the dry leaves.

I stand still on the path and the hair on the back of my neck bristles. Wild boars range freely around the valley during the night, and hide during the day, giving space to the people. That has been the agreement for decades and I'm breaking it. Everyone has warned me that it's not a good idea to meet a group of wild boars in the middle of the night.

I breathe deeply, realizing my fragility.

I don't know what else I can do except to loudly and calmly project my voice in the direction of the growling animals:

"Good evening, my friends. I am just on a walk because I'm a little tense and I need to cool my head. I will walk a little in the canyon and then turn back and walk past you again on my way home. I won't go off the path. I don't want anything from you. So please, just ignore me."

I don't know if this helps but maybe they will understand that my energy isn't dangerous.

I slowly continue in the darkness.

I realize that my tiredness is not the result of relationships themselves, because it can be very beautiful to be in a relationship, and relationships can nurture life in me very much.

What I'm tired of is adapting in relationships, of overextending myself, of trying to satisfy the expectations of others, of taking responsibility for the feelings of my partners, of saving everyone around me...

My desire for solitude is not so much a need in itself but more an attempt to escape from all this weight, all this pressure.

To escape from captivity. To be free.

To be free.

Actually I already am free, totally free. Especially in this relationship with Noa. And even regardless of that, in each moment of my life, I'm entirely free. Entirely free to make space for everything that's truly important to me. To take care of myself and all my needs. To throw off all the pressures and the responsibility.

I am entirely free.

I stand still with this deep awareness of freedom expanding inside me. I breathe deeply and try to capture this freedom with my breathing, to feel it inside me and through me, but I cannot. Freedom is too large to be captured. Freedom is complete and boundless.

I stare into the almost full moon and smile spontaneously.

The jackals are singing again and I slowly turn back.

In this perfect freedom, I suddenly realize that I have arrived. That I have found my home. My home is the field of love that Noa and I have been opening and nourishing.

I have found a home in which I can unite this manifestation here with the beyond.

Feeling a deep sense of peace within myself, I walk back through the dark valley, under the moon and the stars, past the wild boars, and, I slide into bed next to Noa.

∞

"…and then I had another dream where I…"

Noa is speaking to me during a video call and I have to interrupt her:

"My love, wait a minute please. It looks like we have a bad internet connection and every time you start to speak, I miss the first sentence or two, and then it's okay again. Only the first two sentences are always problematic…"

It's the lunch break in the middle of this big 10-day international training in Nonviolent Communication in the Netherlands, where I'm one of the five trainers. Noa is in Israel in our little wooden house on the hill and we are having our regular video conversation.

And then an idea hits me:

"So I suggest that each time you start to speak, you first say I love you, I love you, I love you three times, and then continue normally. I think that will work just fine, then," I laugh. "Deal?"

Noa's face shines with joy. Her eyes glow:

"Alright. Agreed. So: I love you, I love you, I love you. I'm pregnant."

I smilingly stare into the screen for a few seconds before I understand.

Wow, she's pregnant. We're going to have a child.

I look into her face shining with the light of love. What a supreme honour it is to be with her. As I've told her many times already, it's the cosmic jackpot for me. And now we're going to have a child. Albeit a little sooner than we thought.

This soul must have a good reason to be in such a hurry, I smile to myself.

∞

Another ayahuasca ceremony. I drank the brew a good hour ago and now I'm sitting on my mat and looking at all the beautiful people around me. How much beauty, love, and

312

tenderness is gathered in this room. Some people are lying down, some sitting, two playing a song from the Brazilian jungle, many others singing along.

Suddenly an energy awakens inside me. The one I know already: cosmic, powerful, the dragon energy. My body starts to slither toward the centre of the room on its own. My breathing becomes deeper and after a few minutes of lying in the middle of the room, the energy lifts my body into a dance. The wild, flowing, powerful dance of life, joy, and creation. The dance of breadth, vastness, possibilities. The dance of existence.

And then I collapse onto the floor. Into darkness. Into nothingness…

…

Breathe in.

Breathe out.

Slowly, very slowly,

awakening to life.

Breathe in.

Breathe out.

Awakening into the world

that celebrates life,

the manifestation of which

is what I call myself.

Breathe in.

Breathe out.

Cosmic smile.

All that the life in me needs

is the loving smile of a fearless heart

that comes from myself, not from elsewhere.

I express my welcome to the life in me,

my welcome to my being.

Fear and worry fall away.

Bliss.

The cosmic smile.

Breathe in.

Breathe out.

I am welcome in this world,

where I can experience the unique

and extraordinary phenomenon

that we call love.

I am welcome in this world

where I can rest from the chaos of eternal creation.

Breathe in.

Breathe out.

And the cosmic smile.

...

∞

"Good morning, my love…"

I hear Noa's voice, when I play her video message which just arrived as I was getting out of bed. In the very first second of seeing her face on the screen and hearing the tone of her voice, the cells in my body relax, my heart opens, my whole being responds with an internal smile of joy. I experience the frequency of our mutual activation, the vibration of our perfect contact, a sort of bathing in love and tenderness.

And when I think about it after our conversation, regret floods through me. Regret that I entered into my two longest intimate relationships in the past despite not experiencing this kind of connection and flow. That I stayed in relationships which were not the kind my heart longed for. I gave everything I had to give, but in the end things came to the point that both of my last two partners were left in pain.

Pain that was also created by my choices.

And I strongly regret that. I don't want to go through life giving pain to others, especially not to those who are closest to me.

This regret will be in my heart forever.

∞

I'm sitting on the balcony of my Ljubljana apartment in the late evening and looking at the large dragon drawn on the façade of the neighbouring building. I slowly bid him farewell. This is the last time I'll be in Europe this year. I'm here to lead several workshops and then I'm going to empty my apartment in Ljubljana and temporarily move to Israel. Into our little wooden house on the hill, where we will dedicate ourselves to the arrival of our son.

After the last ayahuasca ceremony, something shifted in me quite radically and the old structures have been sliding away. Something new is awakening. Something both new and ancient.

Suddenly I am overwhelmed by an internal impulse and I speak out loud:

"Dear Fear. My dear Fear which has accompanied me throughout my whole life. I am grateful to you for protecting me from pain during the vulnerable years of my childhood. I am grateful to you for using all your strength to shield me from disappointment, loneliness, and defeat in my later years. You tried to enfold me in an atmosphere of safety, predictability, and stability. You were trying to help me the best way you could.

And now I no longer need your services. Now I would like to enter life more directly. To encounter life in its fullness, its rawness. To face all of its many forms.

Therefore, in gratitude, I bid you farewell. Thank you once again."

I take a deep breath and smile up to the sky, to the stars. For an instant, it seems that they smile back at me.

∞

The phone pings. It's a message from Lucija, who's in Barcelona where she's gone to study art. She's sending me her latest artistic photos along with a message about how she is. I'm completely enthusiastic about this daughter of mine. She paints, takes photographs, initiates humanitarian projects from Palestine to Guatemala, attends my training for conflict mediators, is preparing a documentary film about the decline of the baobab tree in Madagascar and other parts of south-east Africa, works in refugee camps... And much, much more. All of this and she's only 23 years old.

And then there is Filip: on the move every day. A professional acrobat, manager, stunt performer, acrobatics teacher, organizer... He lives an extraordinarily dynamic and successful life, full of laughter and joy. It seems to me that at the age of 27 he already understands what this human experience is all about, how to manifest, how to transform. He wastes no time dealing with the projections of others, but follows his own heart, and it looks like he can easily overcome any obstacle that stands in his way.

Both of my children have an enormous amount of knowledge, understanding, capability, and maturity for their years. There is hardly anything I can tell them anymore. I can only sit in the audience and applaud.

And I can also embrace the joy, pride, and satisfaction in my heart. Despite my many regrets, I can all the same pat myself on the shoulder that I did in fact support them to shine fully in their lives.

∞

I'm visiting my father for the last time before I travel to Israel for five months. We're talking about what he wants to talk about. I mostly listen as he talks about Trump, neighbours, the past, how he's arranged the furniture in the house, about some acquaintances who I hardly know... I have long since abandoned any hope that we might talk about personal matters, feelings, life.

I feel how the tension that I've carried with me my whole life has finally dissipated. The idea that I had to care for this relationship, hold it together, constantly adapt, be full of understanding. I think I always tried to behave like his parent, not like his child. And this concrete pillar of my personality has finally started to crumble.

I now sit and look at this old man in front of me. I see a man who had a very difficult childhood. He was born in the midst of the Second World War, when Ljubljana was under Italian occupation. He never knew who his father was. His mother fed him with various and ever-changing stories about that. He grew up in the post-war poverty, with an alcoholic and aggressive stepfather. He had to work to support himself even while he was studying at the same time.

I see a person with many scars and wounds. I can only imagine the amount of pain, fear, loneliness and confusion he has gone through in his life and that he's probably still carrying somewhere deep within himself.

Who am I to reproach him?

He did the best he could at each moment in his life. As I did. And everyone else.

When I forgive him, I am actually doing a favour to myself.

∞

It's the middle of the night and I'm lying on a big wooden platform that I built with a young guy from the neighbourhood on the rocks next to our little house so we would have a flat place in the sun. For exercising, for dancing, and for connecting with the stars.

I look at those dear friends above me, my sisters, the stars, and as they slowly enter me, my breathing deepens and expands. A smile spreads across my face.

Mmmmmmmmmmmmmmmmmmmm.

It's been enough. Enough difficulties, obstacles, strain. I've done my share for this life.

I'm not broken or ruined and don't need to repair anything in myself. I don't need to fulfil anyone's expectations. I am entirely free. I am welcome in this world, in this life, just the way I am.

Mmmmmmmmmmmmmmmmmmmm.

My inner being is widening and expanding through time and space. Wholeness, calm, serenity.

I can finally enjoy the fullness of this manifestation, this life. This mystery of existence. And I am still amazed at the possibilities, the combinations, the evolutionary flow of life. Yes, I can enjoy the marvelling too.

I am entirely free to create whatever it is that I want to experience in this miraculous universe. Free to fully manifest the cosmic presence in my earthly life.

Free to finally answer the call that is rising somewhere in the depths. Free to continue on the path that I started on decades ago. The path of merging worlds into wholeness. The path of empowering life.

There is no need for worries or fears, because everything is already perfect in its wholeness. All is one.

Peace, gratitude, and the cosmic smile across the serene starry sky and through the entirety of my being.

Welcome, Robert, welcome to this miraculous life.

∞

January 2019. The setting sun paints fantastic colours across the sky and the clouds scattered across it. The birds are singing. There is peace all around, deep peace. I look at Noa, how she glides across the terrace in grace and serenity. An embodied goddess of love and beauty. Her belly is already very big. Our son will be born in a few weeks' time.

I am ready now. In peace and love, I await this being who has decided to incarnate to us and to explore this life together with us.

I am prepared to welcome him.

∞

Beep-beep…..beep-beep….. beep-beep

Beep-beep…..beep-beep….. beep-beep

The machines that monitor life functions beep in perfect rhythm. I sit beside the sophisticated plexiglass incubator and insert my hands through the two openings in it. My right hand rests on the chest of the tiny body inside, my left softly strokes the head which is turned toward me. Motionless, we look at each other. I don't know if his eyes can really see, but I feel that I see the whole universe in them. And it seems to me that this being, this soul is looking through the little baby's eyes from some other dimension.

I speak quietly to him:

"My dear son. You are very welcome in this world, very welcome. Your mother and I are very happy about you and are joyfully welcoming you. And outside this room, there are many people who are also looking forward to meeting you. Soon we will go home, to our little house in the countryside where there is peace, silence, and beauty. Now you are in this incubator because, for reasons that are unclear, the level of sodium in your little body fell to dangerous levels and the cells in your little body are having difficulty communicating with each other. Now you are getting sodium slowly and carefully delivered to your body through this little tube so the balance will be restored and your little body will return to full vitality."

My voice trembles and tears flow down my cheeks.

How unpredictable this life is. How quickly everything can change.

Less than a week ago, Noa's waters broke in the evening and her contractions slowly became more frequent. The doula and

319

midwife came and we spent the next 48 hours in intimacy, calm, and beauty, occasionally singing and dancing, and also roaring with Noa when she had really strong contractions. It was not only the three of us supporting Noa but a wide circle of friends who were also with her, breathing with us, sending support, love, prayers, and meditation. I only wish that every woman who brings forth a new life on this Earth would receive this kind of support.

And then the birth did not progress. Noa was getting more and more exhausted. An obstetrician, who the midwife and the doula knew and liked to work with, came and spent a few hours with us. Then he advised us to go with him to the maternity hospital since so much time had passed since Noa's waters had broken.

And that's when everything changed so dramatically.

Beep-beep…..beep-beep….. beep-beep

Beep-beep…..beep-beep….. beep-beep

The little boy in the plexiglass incubator slowly turns his head upward and closes his eyes. I pull my hands out of the incubator, wipe my tears, and then put them back in the incubator and lay them on the tiny body again.

After our arrival at the maternity hospital, it was discovered that the baby's pulse was weak and Noa needed an emergency Caesarean section. Noa was taken to the operating room, and I was left to pace up and down the hallway, overwhelmed with a powerful flood of emotions. And then very soon this little creature was placed in my arms. Noa herself had to remain in intensive care because of the low level of sodium in her blood. I was taken with the baby to another ward where we spent a long night together. The little creature cried all night on my bare chest, my head bobbing up and down, because it was the third night in a row that I hadn't really slept.

And then Lucija, dear Lucija, in faraway Madagascar, heard the desperation in my voice on a message that I'd sent her and immediately activated a circle of our friends to come and help, because she knew that I would not ask for help myself. Three dear friends appeared like Amazonian angels, arriving in the hospital the next morning aglow with endless love and energy. They fed me, took the baby for a while so I could sleep for an hour on the armchair, went to discuss matters with the hospital staff. My heart melted from the love and support they gave us.

Finally Noa was brought to us and the little creature was able to latch onto her breasts. Peace and relief returned.

Beep-beep.....beep-beep..... beep-beep

Beep-beep.....beep-beep..... beep-beep

And then, not even three days after the birth, just when we were supposed to go home, the baby's own sodium levels have fallen to dangerously low levels and he has to go into intensive care. Noa and I take turns being with him.

The more I look at how peacefully he is sleeping, the calmer I feel.

Presence sharpens, space bends, the illusion of time disappears...

...

Only existence

outside the illusion of time and space.

Only existence

in which everything is alright.

Maybe not always in line with expectations and images,

but all the same everything that unfurls

is the miracle of life,

in which nothing can go wrong.

Wrong does not exist in this universe.

Everything is the manifestation of infinite potential.

Everything is the miracle of life.

There is no reason to worry.

Peace.

Serenity.

...

Beep-beep.....beep-beep..... beep-beep

Beep-beep.....beep-beep..... beep-beep

...

Almost as suddenly as the balance in this little body was disturbed for no clear reason, it was restored back to normal.

And now we are home.

Peace, silence, love.

The moon shines outside. The wind gently murmurs in the tops of the trees. A fox calls to her cubs from somewhere behind our little house.

The flames crackle in the fireplace.

Dorian sleeps peacefully on Noa's breast.

I look at him and I am aware of the eternal being that is entering, through this little body, into this dimension of life.

A new life is beginning.

For him. For me. For all of us.

In each moment a new life begins for all of us.

Welcome, Dorian, welcome to this miraculous life.

Made in the USA
Coppell, TX
18 March 2020

16961751R00187